THE PEOPLES OF THE BIBLE

THE PEOPLES OF THE BIBLE

by

Wilson W. Crook, III

February, 2017

CreateSpace, a DBA of On-Demand Publishing, LLC
(an Amazon Company)
Charleston, South Carolina

Front Cover Photo (center, top): The Temple Mount (Jerusalem) today as seen from the Mount of Olives. (Photo by Ginny Crook).
Front Cover Photo (center, bottom): Remains of an Israelite Four Room House, City of David, Jerusalem.
Front Cover Photo (left, top): Small Canaanite Jar with Bull Motif.
Front Cover Photo (left, bottom): Babylonian Winged Deities.
Front Cover Photo (right, top): Edomite Cup of God Qos.
Front Cover Photo (right, bottom): Judean Pillar Figurine.
Back Cover Photo: Ruins of First Century A.D. Capernaum - the home of Jesus during much of his ministry.

INTRODUCTION

Over the last 30 years, I have been involved in the study and teaching of the Bible in Adult Sunday School within the Presbyterian Church – first with the "Bible Discovery" class and now in its new format known as "Present Word". I originally became involved in teaching Adult Sunday School primarily for two reasons: first, in my business travels I have always been disturbed when I opened a nightstand drawer in my hotel room and found "the Bible", which consisted solely of the New Testament; secondly, I have seen the glazed look of both young people and adults alike as they read certain passages in the Bible which mention large groups of people that seemingly have no modern day counterpart (*"When the Lord your God brings you into the land where you are entering to possess it, and clears away many nations before you, the Hittites, the Girgashites and the Amorites and the Canaanites and the Perizites and the Hivites and the Jebusites, seven nations greater and stronger than you"* Deuteronomy 7:1). All of the peoples mentioned in the Bible were real and played various roles in the development of Israel as a nation and the establishment of God's Kingdom on earth. As a result, I have always tried to insert into each of my classes a "Historical Background" section which includes relevant archeological and/or historical facts that support or enrich the specific scripture lesson of the class. This has resulted in the creation of over 550 class paper handouts as well as the acquisition of hundreds of authentic archeological artifacts from the Levant and Mesopotamia.

Over the years, a number of people have asked me either to record my classes or to write a book on Biblical archeology. Having been involved in the recording of teaching lessons while employed by ExxonMobil, I know how complex and difficult it is to effectively capture a lesson because many classes include both visual handouts and artifacts in addition to the spoken word. As a result, I have chosen the latter route and thus the creation of this book.

So what is this book about? What it is NOT is a comprehensive, scientific treatise on the archeology and historicity of the Bible. I have purposefully chosen not to include specific references throughout the text in order to make the material more readable. However, I have included an Appendix at the back of this book listing a number of excellent texts covering various Biblical archeological subjects in more detail should the reader be moved to learn more about a particular subject. What this book is meant to be is a relatively brief, companion reader to a Bible study class that provides some useful material about the Peoples of the Bible and their cultures. In this regard, I have started with the Sumerians, the people of Abraham, and then proceeded chronologically through the Old and New Testaments. Chapter 2 deals with the Egyptians with a specific focus on the time period during the Israelite captivity and subsequent Exodus. Chapter 3 covers the land of Canaan, the so-called "Promised Land", and the various groups that made up the Canaanite city-states. The most extensive chapter is Chapter 4 which covers the Israelites, beginning with the archeological evidence of their presence in Egypt, continuing through the Exodus, the Conquest of Canaan, the period of the United Monarchy (Saul, David and Solomon), the Divided Kingdoms of Israel and Judah, the Babylonian Exile, the Persian Province of Judah after the Babylonian Exile, and ending with life in Judea under the Romans in the First Century A.D.

Chapter 5 covers the peoples who surrounded Israel throughout the Old and New Testaments, beginning with the Edomites, Moabites and Ammonites to the east, the Aramean Kingdom of Syria to the north, and the Phoenicians and the Philistines to the west. The remaining chapters deal with those peoples who periodically influenced or physically controlled the land of Israel including the Assyrians (Chapter 6), the Babylonians (Chapter 7), the Persians (Chapter 8), the Greeks (Chapter 9) and finally the Romans (Chapter 10). In each of these chapters, I have tried to include as many photos of actual artifacts as possible in order to augment the text.

I am frequently asked the question, "Is the Bible true?" My consistent reply has always been that at the end of the day, a person's belief in the Bible will always be a matter of personal faith; science cannot "prove" every detail provided in every book of the Old and New Testaments. However, what can be said is that an amazing number of new discoveries are being made almost daily and many tend to strongly support the narrative of the Bible.

It is sincerely hoped that this book will, in some small part, bring to life the ancient Peoples of the Bible. If, after reading this book, the information included causes you to think differently about these ancient peoples when you read or hear the scripture, then I have accomplished my primary objective. I hope you enjoy it and to God be the Glory!

CONTENTS

FIGURES

FIGURES

FIGURES

FIGURES

TABLES

1. SUMERIANS

Sumeria is generally regarded by most historians as being "the cradle of modern civilization." That does not mean Sumeria has the world's oldest cities, but it does appear to have one of, if not the oldest formalized civilization. The Sumerians are generally credited with the invention of or the formal adoption of the following traits inherent to modern civilization:

- Cities and formalized city-states
- Government, notably a monarchy
- Organization and division of a labor force
- Wheels / Carts / Chariots
- An organized military force (army) with uniforms
- Organized trade and commerce
- Agriculture and irrigation
- Metallurgy (refining ore to metal)
- Use of fossil fuels (bitumen and asphalt)
- Firing of clay; mass production of ceramics (kiln, potter's wheel)
- Writing (cuneiform) and literature
- Formalized schools and education
- Mathematics
- Science
- History
- Law

The Bible tells us that Abram (later Abraham), his father Terah, his wife Sarai (later Sarah) and the rest of his family came from "Ur of the Chaldees" (Genesis 11:28; 11:31; 15:7). The term "Chaldees" is a much later name for the people living in the delta of the Tigris-Euphrates River which we now know was originally inhabited by the Sumerians. Abraham is the father of Judeo-Christianity (and Islam as well); thus if Sumeria is the cradle of civilization, it is also the cradle of Biblical history as well.

Sumeria was originally settled by Indo-European peoples (non-Semitic) who, by their own records, "came from the north and the east" into the land between the Tigris and Euphrates

Rivers (Mesopotamia) sometime before 5300 B.C. The Sumerians called themselves "*sag-giga*" or the "black haired people" and are believed to have originated either in the area in and around the Black Sea or possibly even the Indus River Valley in India. They initially settled in the fertile delta between the Tigris and Euphrates Rivers in what today is southern Iraq and Kuwait. Soon thereafter, a number of loosely-allied city-states sprang up including the cities of Ur, Eridu, Uruk (Biblical Erech), Lagish, Nippur, Kish, Nina, Girsu, Umma, Issin and Larsa (Figure 1). The Sumerians called the land that they settled "*Shumeru*" (*Shinar* in Hebrew and *Sumer* in English).

While credited with a number of "new" inventions, the Sumerian people brought with them agriculture, specifically the cultivation of barley, as well as irrigation and sophisticated, well-developed ceramic (pottery) manufacture. Archeologists see many of these traits present

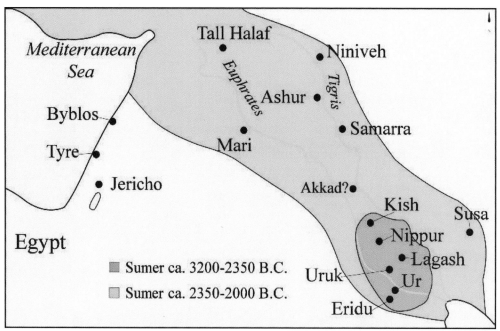

Figure 1. Initial civilization of Sumeria (tan) in the Tigris-Euphrates River Delta and its later expansion to the northwest (blue) by King Sargon the Great (ca. 2334-2279 B.C.). (Map illustrated by Lance K. Trask)

in remnant civilizations that line the southern part of the Black Sea. Subsurface unmanned rovers are discovering additional evidence of possible settlements that are now covered by the Black Sea. While the connection between these early settlements and the Sumerians has yet to be completely worked out, their discovery does lend some credence to the idea that the Black Sea area may indeed be where the Sumerian peoples originated.

By 3300 B.C., a number of large cities (greater than 10,000 inhabitants) had formed in the Tigris-Euphrates River Delta. Each of these cities appears to have been largely independent, governed by a local ruler who took the title of "King." The city-states were allied into a loose confederation primarily based on trade and commerce but also for mutual defense. As the population in the Tigris-Euphrates Delta began to expand, the Sumerian civilization needed to grow so the lands to the north and northwest, again "between the rivers" or in Mesopotamia, became incorporated into the growing empire. As the civilization spread, the Sumerians found they could not control or protect the more remote outposts and colonies without a permanent protection force. Therefore, a formalized military, including standardized uniforms and weaponry, was established (Figure 2). With expansion of the culture, the once independent Sumerian city-states more frequently began to come under the overall control of a single ruler. The expansion of Sumeria reached its zenith during the so-called Akkadian Period, led by King Sargon II (ca. 2334-2279 B.C.).

Around 3100 B.C., the Sumerians invented a form of writing known as "cuneiform", named for the triangular-shaped reed stylus used to make marks on tablets constructed from clay. Cuneiform writing was originally merely a form of picturing an item with a symbol that often resembled the object being described. With time, cuneiform became more phonogrammic, or word oriented, and ultimately evolved into a series of complex triangular shapes and

Figure 2. The so-called Royal Standard of Ur which depicts Sumerian soldiers, cart-like chariots, uniforms and weapons. Excavated by Sir Leonard Woolley in 1927-28 in the city of Ur, it is currently on exhibit in the British Museum, London. (Photographed by the author in the British Museum)

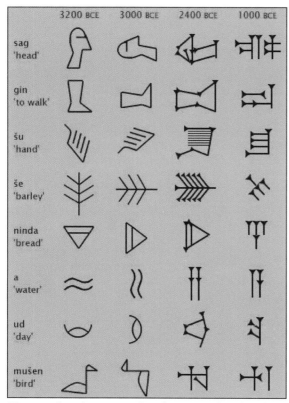

	3200 BCE	3000 BCE	2400 BCE	1000 BCE
sag 'head'				
gin 'to walk'				
šu 'hand'				
še 'barley'				
ninda 'bread'				
a 'water'				
ud 'day'				
mušen 'bird'				

Figure 3. An example showing the development of cuneiform writing over time. (From www.ancientscripts.com)

lines which represented phonetic sounds (Figure 3). Writing soon became a dominant fixture of Sumerian society, recording such varied events as royal decrees, legal agreements, business transactions, marriage contracts, literature (poems and sagas), mathematics, history and science. Cuneiform lists and definitions, forerunners of modern dictionaries, have been recovered. Cuneiform tablets have even been found contained within clay "envelopes," the envelope having a summary of the document contained within.

With the development of writing, some form of institution to teach both the reading and writing of cuneiform was needed. Special schools were formalized in which young boys were formally trained to be "scribes". Teachers, usually elder scribes, would create "practice tablets". They would inscribe a simple name or phrase on one side of the tablet and then the students would memorize the inscription and try to replicate it on the reverse side. These "school practice tablets" are very distinctive as they are typically large and circular in shape, as opposed to the more typically rectangular shape of the majority of cuneiform tablets. As most of these practice tablets were destroyed at the end of the school day, few have survived and those that have are highly prized artifacts.

Archeologists have now uncovered somewhere between 500,000 and 2,000,000 cuneiform tablets from Sumeria, Assyria, Babylon, Persia and elsewhere. Only about 100,000 of these have been officially translated and even fewer published, primarily because there are so few people in the word capable of reading and transcribing cuneiform. We owe our ability to read cuneiform documents to a number of researchers over the years from both the University of Pennsylvania and the British Museum, foremost among which is Sir Henry Rawlinson. The largest collection of cuneiform documents lies in the British Museum (approximately 130,000 tablets), followed by the Voderasiatisches Museum in Berlin, the Louvre, the Archeology Museum in Istanbul, the Yale Babylonian Collection (40,000 tablets), and the University of Pennsylvania. To the archeologist, the presence of writing opens an entire realm of insight into an ancient civilization because rather than having to guess the function of objects, cuneiform tablets actually "speak" from the past and reveal many facets about Sumerian life that otherwise would have remained hidden. Examples of several Sumerian cuneiform tablets can be seen in Figures 4-7.

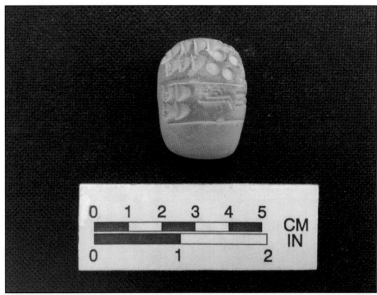

Figure 4. Early Sumerian cuneiform tablet dealing with measures of barley. The dots represent 10 and the half-moon shapes represent 5. (Wilson W. Crook, III Collection)

Like all Ancient Middle East cultures, the Sumerians worshiped a pantheon of gods which represented many earthly and heavenly features. Some of the more prominent included An (Heaven), Enlil (Air / Wind), Utu or Shamash

Figure 5. Sumerian cuneiform administrative document dealing with wages (Ur III, ca. 2050 B.C.). (Wilson W. Crook, III Collection)

(Sun), Nanna or Sin (Moon), Enki (wisdom and cunning), and Innana (goddess of fertility, thunderstorms, love and war). It appears that many of the Sumerian cities had a special protector god or goddess. For example, Ur was a city that was under the protection of the Moon

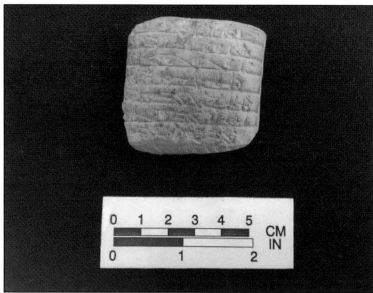

Figure 6. Sumerian cuneiform tablet dealing with measures of palm oil (ca. 1900 B.C.). (Wilson W. Crook, III Collection)

Figure 7. Sumerian school boy practice tablet from the Ur III Period (ca. 2,000 B.C.). The three lines are common personal names: Ur-zi, Ur-Shara, Ir-Igi-Kur. (Wilson W. Crook, III Collection)

god, Nanna or Sin. An was the protector god of Uruk; Enlil had his home at Nippur; Utu at Larsa and Inanna at Uruk. People were free to worship any or all of the deities as they so chose. However, unlike most of the other ancient cultures of the region, the Sumerians also had one god which they retained as their "personal god". This was usually one deity that they felt "spoke" to them, which they retained for their particular protection. This personal god could be passed down from father to son ("the god of my fathers") or it could be one unique to that individual. Frequently people would carry a cylindrical bead with carvings of his or her personal god on it around their necks as a protective medallion. These "cylinder seals" as they are called today by archeologists, cannot be read directly but must be rolled across a wet piece of clay in order to reveal the entire inscription (Figure 8).

A key driving force in Sumerian life was to become eternal, not in terms of eternal life but to have as many descendants as possible who would remember your name and who you were. Thus, large families with many descendants would be the means by which an individual could "live forever".

A center point of religious life in Sumerian cities was the main temple or "Ziggurat". These structures were built of mud bricks in a layer-cake style and often reached heights in excess of 100 feet (Figure 9). The actual height of these structures has to be estimated as none have remained intact. The Great Ziggurat of Ur measured 210 feet by 148 feet, with three or four levels and was composed of

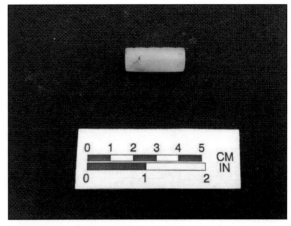

Figure 8. Sumerian cylinder seal made of chalcedony depicting a worshiper before the moon god Nanna (Sin).
(Wilson W. Crook, III Collection)

tens of thousands of sun-baked mud bricks. Many of the bricks used to construct a ziggurat were stamped with the name of the ruler who ordered their construction (Figure 10). Ziggurats, which roughly translates to "the temple between Heaven and Earth," are believed to have had a shrine or temple structure on their apex.

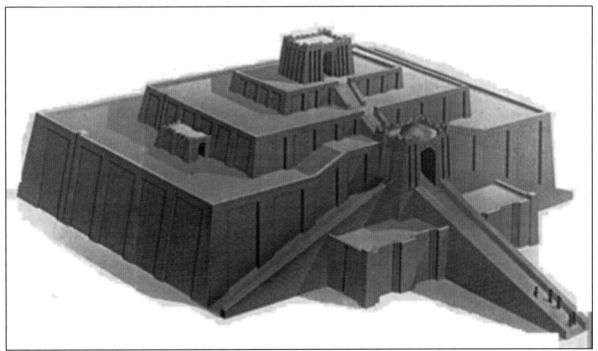

Figure 9. Reconstruction of the Great Ziggurat of Ur.
(From ancient-origins.net)

One of the more unusual religious features found in ancient Sumeria is the "Eye Temple" at Tell Brak in northeastern Syria. There, a large temple has been excavated which is

Figure 10. Brick from the Great Ziggurat of Ur dating to 2039-2047 B.C. The cuneiform inscription reads: "Amar-Sin, called by the god Enlil to Nippur, the one who raised the height of the temple of Enlil, mighty male, King of Ur, King of Four Quarters". (Wilson W. Crook, III Collection)

dedicated to an unknown goddess, possibly to Belet-Nagar, a local fertility deity. The intense dedication to this goddess is evident in the thousands of "eye idols" that have been found in and around the city (Figure 11).

After thriving for over 3,000 years, the Sumerian Empire gradually began to decline after ca. 2050 B.C. as the salt content in the Tigris-Euphrates Delta steadily increased. Sumeria was overrun by the Elamites (from Persia) about 1940 B.C. and the political control of the region moved north out of the Tigris-Euphrates Delta to Babylon by about 1900 B.C. Shortly thereafter, Sumeria ceased to exist as a recognizable entity.

Most of what we know about Sumeria today is due to the efforts of the British archeologist, Sir Leonard Woolley, who is recognized by many archeologists today as the first true modern archeologist with excellent excavation techniques. Between 1922 and 1936,

Woolley led a series of joint excavations between the British Museum and the University of Pennsylvania at Ur and other Sumerian cities. His incredible discoveries, many of which can be seen in the British Museum and the Museum of Archeology on the campus of the University of Pennsylvania, reveal a civilization where wealth and art had reached new highs. Of note, Leonard Woolley also had two interesting side lights to his archeological career. First, one of his students during the excavations of the Hittite city of Carchemish before the First World War was Thomas Edward Lawrence, later to become world famous as "Lawrence of Arabia". It is often asserted that both Woolley and Lawrence were actually mapping the area and spying on the Ottoman Empire for the British Government under the guise of an archeological dig.

Second, a young female British writer frequently visited Woolley's excavations at Ur and fell in love with and later married his primary assistant, Max Mallowan. The writer was so intrigued by the Sumerian excavations and discoveries that she later used it in her novel, *A Murder in Mesopotamia*; her name, of course, was Agatha Christie.

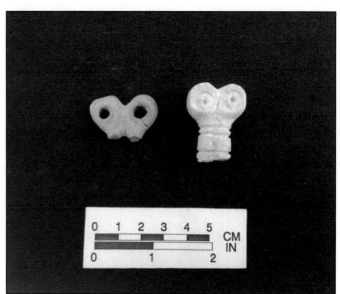

Figure 11. Eye Idols from Tell Brak, Syria. (Wilson W. Crook, III Collection)

One intriguing feature of the Sumerians is how they relate to the Bible. While every other group of ancient peoples described in this book are mentioned in the Bible, there is no mention of "Sumeria" or the "Sumerians" *per se*. However, if one looks at the seemingly enigmatic first nine verses in the beginning of the 11th Chapter of Genesis, perhaps there is a hidden meaning that may indeed relate to Sumeria:

1. *Now the whole earth had one language, and one speech.*

2. *And it came to pass, as they journeyed from the east, that they found a plain in the land of Shinar, and they dwelt there.*

3. *Then they said to one another, "Come, let us make brick, and bake them thoroughly". And they had brick for stone, and they had asphalt for mortar.*

4. *And they said, "Come, let us* build ourselves a city, *and a* tower whose top is in the heavens; *let us make a name for ourselves, lest we be scattered abroad over the face of the whole earth."*

5. *But the Lord came down to see the city and the tower which the sons of men had built.*

6. *And the Lord said, "Indeed the people are one, and they all have one language, and this is what they begin to do; now nothing that they propose to do will be withheld from them.*

7. *"Come, let us go down and there confuse their language, that they may not understand one another's speech."*

8. *So the Lord* scattered them abroad from there over the face of all the earth, *and they* ceased building the city.

9. *Therefore its name is called Babel, because the Lord confused the language of all the earth; and from there the Lord scattered them abroad over the face of the earth.*

Everyone is familiar with the story of the Tower of Babel; but does this story tell us more? Does Genesis 11:1-9 actually contain a concise history of Sumeria? By the Sumerians' own history, they came to the Tigris-Euphrates Valley from the "north and the east", just as it says in Genesis 11:2. They indeed settled in the plain between the two rivers near its delta, which they called "Shumeru" or "Shinar" in Hebrew. We know from the abundance of cuneiform tablets recovered from the various Sumerian cities that all the people at the time spoke the same Sumerian language (Genesis 11:1). Moreover, as the Sumerian Empire began to expand northward through the Tigris-Euphrates Valley, this one language became the *lingua franca* for the entire Mesopotamian region. We also know from an almost complete lack of stone outcrops in the region that the Sumerians built virtually everything out of sun-baked mud bricks, which they cemented in place using naturally-occurring asphaltum (tar) from seeps that still can be seen in the region today (Genesis 11:3). The Sumerians constructed large cities, some holding more than 10,000 inhabitants, and great temples (ziggurats) – all out of tens of millions of mud bricks. Ziggurats, or the temple between Heaven and Earth (Genesis 11:4), were the tallest man-made structures the earth had seen to date. Like so many civilizations throughout history, the Sumerians lauded their superiority in trade, commerce and military might over all of their neighbors. As the culture began to weaken toward the end of the third millennium B.C., they were eventually overrun by their neighbors, the Elamites and the Babylonians, and the Sumerian Empire ceased to exist by roughly 1900 B.C. Not only was the empire destroyed, but almost all vestiges of their former greatness were erased as the center of civilization in the region moved north to Babylon and the language and writing of the region changed to Akkadian or Old Babylonian ("Akkadian" is a cover term that includes a number of Semitic languages and dialects of Mesopotamia including Akkadian, Assyrian, Babylonian, and others). The remnants of the once great Sumerian Empire were scattered all across Mesopotamia (Genesis 11:8). However, in one sense, the "conquered" became the "conquerors" as the Akkadians and the Babylonians adopted virtually all of the Sumerian customs and civilization. Even today, a few Sumerian words and terminology survive in our own culture. For example, the Sumerians called the main political leader the "*lugal*" or "the big man", and the *lugal's* dwelling was known as the "*e-gal*" or "the big house".

One of the greatest pieces of Sumerian literature is the *Epic of Gilgamesh*, the story of a great hero-king from the First Dynasty of Uruk. Numerous versions of the 11 tablet epic have been found throughout Mesopotamia but of special interest to Biblical scholars is the story related on tablet 9 because of its similarity to the account given in Genesis 6-9. The text tells of the creation of humankind and the animal kingdom, the institution of kingship in five antediluvian (pre-flood) cities each under the care of a deity, the decision of a divine counsel to send a flood to destroy the wickedness of mankind, the communication of the coming flood to a righteous man named Ziusudra, the coming of the flood, the survival of Ziusudra in a boat (with his family and certain animals), his offering of sacrifices after the flood, and his endowment with eternal life and settlement in the paradise land of "Dilmun" – usually identified with the island of Bahrain in the Persian Gulf. Because of the similarities to the story of Noah and the Ark, Biblical scholars for years have debated which civilization may have borrowed the story from the other for its own purposes.

We are told in Genesis 11:31 that Terah took his son Abram and his daughter Sarai, Abram's wife, along with his grandson Lot, and left Ur and moved to Haran, a city in northern Syria in the farthest reaches of the Sumerian Empire. Why move to from Ur to Haran? Perhaps Ur was being overrun by the Elamites and was no longer a safe place to live. In Joshua 24:2 it states that Terah "worshiped idols". The protective deity of Ur was the Moon god, Sin. The only other city in the Sumerian Empire that also was dedicated to Sin was the city of Haran. So did Terah move the family to the only refuge left that was protected by his personal god?

The last great mystery that the Bible presents to us about the Sumerians is the story of Abraham and his conversion to monotheism. Why did God choose, of all the people on the face of the earth, a Sumerian named Abraham (Abram) and why would Abraham have listened to and responded to God's call? Remember, of all the ancient peoples of the Middle East, the only ones that had this belief in a "personal god", in addition to the pantheon of other deities, were the Sumerians. Thus, when God spoke to Abraham, perhaps he readily accepted that the entity speaking to him was his "personal god". In addition, God's promise to Abraham that he would make his descendants as numerous as "the sands of the beach" (Genesis 22:17) or "the stars in the sky" (Genesis 26:4) would have been the most seductive appeal that could have been made to a Sumerian whose core belief was that this was his pathway to immortality. Sumerian personal gods could also be passed down to the members of your family and thus become "the god of your fathers" as is so often mentioned in the Bible.

2. EGYPTIANS

Egypt, known as the "Gift of the Nile" is strategically located at the northeast corner of Africa, bordering on the Sinai Peninsula and Palestine. Bounded by vast deserts to the west and to the east, and naturally defended by the Mediterranean Sea to the north and a series of major cataracts on the Nile River to the south, Egypt is an oasis sustained by the Nile and largely cut off from the rest of the world. It is a part of Africa but doesn't really belong culturally to Africa; it is a part of the Levant (Palestine and the Ancient Middle East) but is not physically located in Asia. Even the Egyptians themselves did not historically have a name for their country; it was known as the "Two Lands" referring to Upper and Lower Egypt. Lower Egypt is the land of the Nile River Delta while southern Egypt, moving up the Nile River, is Upper Egypt. Egyptian Pharaohs frequently did not refer to themselves as "King" but "Lord of the Two Lands" and wore a double crown for both Upper and Lower Egypt.

Egyptian history is very complex and it is not the purpose of this book to delve into all the details of the various Pharaonic dynasties and controversies surrounding their dates (there are at least three somewhat accepted chronologies for Egyptian history). Therefore, I have included here a brief background of the beginnings of Egyptian civilization and then a more detailed focus on the period that directly impacts Biblical history: the New Kingdom and specifically the 18th Dynasty.

At the end of the Pleistocene (the last "Ice Age"), the Nile River Valley was one of the only habitable areas on the eastern margins of the Sahara Desert. Then starting around 10,500 years ago, monsoon rains began sweeping the Sahara region transforming it into a lush oasis full of lakes and wildlife. Human settlement from the Nile River soon followed and vast networks of settlements spread across the Sahara including the domestication of wildlife such as sheep and goats. However, starting around 7,500 years ago and culminating about 5,500 years ago (ca. 3500 B.C.), retreating monsoon rains led to the re-desiccation of the Sahara Desert. The end of the rains coincided with the repopulation of the Nile River Valley and the beginnings of modern Egypt.

As mentioned above, Egypt was traditionally separated into two cultures, Upper and Lower Egypt. The leader of Upper Egypt wore a white crown while the leader's crown of

Lower Egypt was red. Sometime during the period before about 3100 B.C., the cultural differences between Upper and Lower Egypt may have taken on a hostile dimension, potentially in a dispute over water (irrigation) rights. Some Egyptologists have argued that the emergence of a main chieftain, later to be called "Pharaoh", was due to the culture's need to build, maintain and control agricultural canals and irrigation projects. Around 3100 B.C., a legendary figure from southern Egypt known as "Menes" conquered the northern chieftain and united Upper and Lower Egypt, resulting in the founding of the city of Memphis. The political unification of Egypt thus marked the beginning of "Dynastic" or "Pharaonic" Egypt. The ruler of the two lands was given the name "Pharaoh", which literally means "great house" or palace.

Like all the people of the Ancient Middle East, the Egyptians worshiped a large pantheon of gods and goddesses. Chief among these was Amun (Amon), god of the world and king of the gods. Later he was merged with the sun god, Ra, to become the even more powerful (Amun-Ra). Other major Egyptian deities included Anubis (jackal-headed god of funerals and embalming), Anuket (goddess of the Nile), Bast (cat goddess), Hathor (goddess of love), Horus (falcon-headed god of war and the sky), Isis (goddess of magic and marriage), Ma'at (goddess of truth and justice), Nut (goddess of the skies), Osiris (god of the underworld and the afterlife), Ptah (god of creation), Tawaret (goddess of childbirth and fertility), and Thoth (god of scribes and wisdom). These are but a small fraction of the total Egyptian pantheon. Even by the standards of the Greeks, who themselves had an extensive pantheon of gods and goddesses, the Egyptians pantheon appeared huge. The Greek historian Herodotus observed, "They are beyond measure religious, more than any nation . . . their religious observances are, one might say, numerous". The Egyptians seemed to have had a god, not only for every earthly and celestial entity, but also ones for a great number of animals (cat, jackal, lion, baboon, hippopotamus, goose, vulture, crocodile, snake, frog and scorpion). Religion affected every area of Egyptian life: ethics, piety, politics and death. If all of the archeological artifacts that are somehow connected to religion (temples, funerary structures, cultic statues, monuments, mummies, etc.) were removed, little of Egyptian culture would remain.

Egyptian history is described in terms of "dynasties", each dynasty representing a series of rulers who shared a common origin, usually from one family. Beginning about 3100 B.C., a total of 31 dynasties are recorded ending with the introduction of the Greco-Roman Period in 303 B.C. The dynasties are lumped together into periods of relative stability ("Kingdoms") separated by periods of instability, weakness or even invasion ("Intermediate Periods"). The great periods of Egyptian history are as follows:

- Archaic Period (Dynasties 1 and 2) – ca. 3100-2700 B.C.
- Old Kingdom (Dynasties 3-6) – ca. 2700-2200 B.C.
- First Intermediate Period (Dynasties 7-10) – ca. 2200-2000 B.C.
- Middle Kingdom (Dynasties 11-13) – ca. 2000-1700 B.C.
- Second Intermediate Period (Dynasties 14-17) – ca. 1700-1550 B.C.
- New Kingdom (Dynasties 18-20) – ca. 1550-1100 B.C.
- Third Intermediate Period (Dynasties 21-25) – ca. 1100-656 B.C.
- Late Period (Dynasties 26-31) – ca. 656-303 B.C.
- Greco-Roman Period – ca. 303 B.C. – 641 A.D.

Of particular note, the Old Kingdom, especially during the Fourth Dynasty, is the period when the great pyramids were built. Pharaoh Khufu (the Hellenized "Cheops" as described by Herodotus) moved the royal burial site to the Giza Plateau (near modern day Cairo) where Egyptian pyramid construction reached its zenith. This included not only the Great Pyramids but also the associated burial boats, causeways and temples.

At the end of the Old Kingdom, a period of political uncertainty and weakness ushered in a dark age for Egypt. Egyptian historical texts record "Seventy Kings of Memphis who reigned for 70 days". The texts describe wars, civil strife, and tombs being desecrated. There also appears to have been an incursion in this period by raiders from the east who separated Upper and Lower Egypt preventing trade. During the waning years of the 6th Dynasty, a significant "Asiatic" population appears to have infiltrated into the Nile Delta region. The Egyptian term "Asiatic" refers to any of the Semitic peoples from the area east of Egypt including both the Levant and Mesopotamia. It is unknown if this settlement by foreigners included any Hebrews but it is thought to pre-date the migration by Joseph and Jacob's family as recorded in Genesis.

The beginning of the Middle Kingdom restored a period of stability to Egypt, primarily due to the re-conquest of the central portion of Egypt and the reunification of the two kingdoms. The reunification of Upper and Lower Egypt ushered in a rebirth in Egyptian power making the 12th Dynasty one of the most stable, prosperous and peaceful periods in Egyptian history.

Thanks to vigorous international trade, the Middle Kingdom was also a period of great wealth and Egypt began to wield considerable influence in the region of the Levant.

The halcyon days of the 12th Dynasty were soon replaced by a gradual decline back into uncertain times during the 13th Dynasty. Numerous Pharaohs ruled in this period, each for a relatively short time and without leaving many monuments behind. The decline in prestige of the Pharaoh may be linked to uncertain climatic conditions during this period. The Nile apparently went through a period of late floods which failed to recede causing crop planting to be delayed too long for sufficient grain to grow before the summer heat. Droughts were also present during this period further exacerbating the food supply. As Pharaohs were seen as living gods who were able to control the life-giving waters of the Nile, their failure to do so led to a decline in Egyptian authority. This led to the end of the Middle Kingdom and the beginning of a second great period of instability known as the Second Intermediate Period.

The Second Intermediate Period is also known as the "Hyksos Period", so-named for the rulers from ca. 1700-1550 B.C. The word "Hyksos" has traditionally been translated to mean "Shepherd Kings", but this may be a mistranslation and the word may be more properly interpreted as "Foreign Rulers". There is also some disagreement amongst scholars whether the Hyksos gradually migrated into Egypt or entered through a full-scale invasion. The Roman historian Josephus, quoting the 3rd Century B.C. Egyptian historian Manetho says:

"I know not why, a blast of God's displeasure broke upon us. A people of ignoble origin from the east, whose coming was unforeseen, had the audacity to invade the country, which they mastered without difficulty or even a battle"

While Egyptologists may argue over how the Hyksos came to dominate Egypt, there is a growing consensus that their place of origin was Syria-Palestine. The Canaanite peoples (see Chapter 3) were renowned throughout the Ancient Middle East for their expertise and prowess with the small, two-wheel chariot. Thus, a fast-moving, mobile invasion led by chariots could have provided the mechanism for the Hyksos takeover of Egypt. These foreign invaders ruled Egypt for the next century and a half.

The Bible is unfortunately fairly vague about the precise time period when the Hebrew people migrated into Egypt as none of the rulers during this time are named except by the title of "Pharaoh". However, the Hyksos Period when foreigners controlled the Nile Delta region and northern (Lower) Egypt provides a likely time period for Joseph to have come to prominence and for his family to have settled in Goshen on the eastern side of the delta (Genesis 39-50). Joseph's rise to power from an unknown servant to a high ranking official is not without precedent in Egyptian history. Bay, a non-Egyptian, rose by royal favor to the rank of "Chancellor of the Entire Land" during the 20th Dynasty (ca. 1200 B.C.).

In the years following Joseph's death, the Hebrew population grew to the point that the Pharaoh began to see their presence as a potential threat. In Exodus 1:8 we are told that "a new King, who did not know Joseph, came to power in Egypt". This "new King" may in fact refer to a new dynasty and not just a different ruler than the one mentioned in Genesis. While we do not know the exact date of the Hyksos' arrival in Egypt, their expulsion is well documented. Pharaoh Ahmose I succeeded to the throne in Thebes around 1576 B.C. Egyptian accounts tell of how Ahmose I in exile in the south, amassed a great force of new chariots, comparable to those of the Hyksos, and trained his army to fight in the same mobile manner as his enemy. In the fifteenth year of his reign, he finally drove the Hyksos out of Egypt for good and firmly established both the 18th Dynasty and the New Kingdom.

The All Important 18th Dynasty

Again, while the Bible is silent on the identity of the Pharaoh "who did not know Joseph" and who was also the Pharaoh of the oppression recorded in the Book of Exodus, the 18th Dynasty provides the likely period for Israel's oppression, bondage and Exodus from Egypt. But since the 18th Dynasty lasted for over 250 years, we are left to puzzle over the exact timing of the Exodus and who was the specific Pharaoh of the oppression as well as the Pharaoh of the Exodus.

The absence of direct archeological evidence or mention of the Exodus by Egyptian rulers has caused some scholars to question the historicity of the entire Exodus narrative. These scholars, known in the archeological world of the Ancient Middle East as "Minimalists", have argued that the Israelites were just another Canaanite tribe and their "Conquest" of the Promised Land was the result of an agrarian revolt of the country farmers against their city-dwelling overlords. However, the Exodus tradition is too deeply entrenched in Hebrew heritage throughout the entire Bible for it to be dismissed as a complete invention of later Biblical writers. In recent decades, an opposing position has formed (known as the "Maximalists") whose proponents generally agree that an Exodus of some sort did take place, but there is disagreement on exactly when it occurred. This disagreement on the date for the Exodus has led to two positions – the so-called "Late" Exodus theory and the "Early" Exodus theory.

Supporters of the Late Exodus cite Exodus 1:11 which states "so they built for Pharaoh treasure cities, Pithom and Ramesses". The city of Ramesses, or more properly Pi-Ramesses, was built by the great Pharaoh Ramesses II (1279-1213 B.C.), inferring that Ramesses II must be the Pharaoh of the Exodus. This has been "confirmed" as fact by Hollywood in the epic film, the *Ten Commandments*, where Ramesses II is seen as the autocratic ruler who would not let the Israelites go ("So let it be written, so let it be done"). Supporters of the Late Exodus date further cite that there are major destruction layers at the Canaanite cities of Hazor and Lachish, cities known to have been destroyed by Joshua, dating to approximately 1230 B.C. Add 40 years for wandering in the wilderness and the date for the Exodus is approximately 1270 B.C. – during the reign of Ramesses II.

However, there are a number of problems associated with this line of reasoning. First, the city of Pi-Ramesses was known by a number of different names throughout Egyptian history, only the last of which was Ramesses. Initially the city was called Rowaty, the "door of the two roads" during the 12th and 13th Dynasties. Then the name was changed to Avaris ("the royal foundation of the district") during the Hyksos Period. The name was changed yet again by the rulers of the 18th Dynasty to Perunefer ("happy journey"), and finally to Pi-Ramesses during the 19th Dynasty. Therefore, calling the city by its most recent name does not precisely confirm when it may have been built by Hebrew slaves.

Second, we are told in Exodus 1:12 that following the building of Pithom and Ramesses, the Hebrews multiplied greatly ("the more they were oppressed, the more they multiplied and spread"). This was followed by an escalation of oppression by the Egyptians (Exodus 1:13-14) and then the Pharaoh's decree that all male Hebrew babies should be put to death (Exodus 1:15-19). The Israelite midwives ignored this order and the Hebrew population continued to expand. Moses was then born, raised in the Egyptian court and exiled to Midian at age 40 (Exodus 2) where he "stayed for a long time", during which "the King of Egypt died" (Exodus

2:23). All of these events imply that a significant amount of time passed between Moses' exile and his return from Midian, which is difficult to squeeze into the first nine years of Ramesses' reign plus the modest 15 year rule of his father, Seti I.

So, if the Exodus did not occur during the reign of Ramesses II, when could it have occurred? Supporters of the "Early" Exodus theory point to I Kings 6:1 which states that "in the four hundred and eightieth year after the Israelites had come out of Egypt, in the fourth year of Solomon's reign over Israel, in the month of Ziv, the second month, he began to build the Temple of the Lord". Solomon is generally believed to have taken the throne around 970 B.C., so the fourth year of his reign would have been ca. 966 B.C. Add 480 years to this and the date for the Exodus of approximately 1446 B.C. would fall directly in the middle of the 18th Dynasty. Supporters of the "Late" Exodus date say that the 480 years referred to in I Kings 6:1 is not meant to be a literal number, but instead represents 12 idealized generations of 40 years apiece. However, when one looks at the original Hebrew in the Book of Kings, verse 6:1 is written as "eighty and four hundred years". When Hebrew numbers are written in ascending order, as in I Kings 6:1, they are meant to be literal and not an idealized representation. Further support for the "Early" Exodus date comes from the Hebrew Talmud which states that the 17th and last Jubilee year occurred during the Babylonian captivity in 573 B.C. Jubilee years were celebrated at the end of seven, seven-year cycles, or every 49 years. Seventeen cycles of 49 years equals 833 years; when added to 573 B.C. the date for the first Jubilee year is determined to be 1406 B.C. The first Jubilee year was celebrated when the Israelites came into the Promised Land after spending 40 years in the wilderness. So add 40 years to 1406 and once again a date of 1446 B.C. can be determined for the Exodus.

If Ramesses II was not the Pharaoh of the Exodus, then who was? To answer that question, the 18th Dynasty needs to be examined in more detail. The New Kingdom, and the 18th Dynasty in particular, contained some of the most famous Pharaohs in Egyptian history. Pharaohs from the 18th Dynasty are listed in Table 1 below:

Table 1. Pharaohs of the 18ᵗʰ Dynasty, ca. 1576-1295 B.C.

Pharaoh	Years of Reign
Ahmose I	ca. 1576-1551 B.C.
Amenhotep I	ca. 1551-1530
Thutmosis I	ca. 1530-1517
Thutmosis II	ca. 1517-1506
Hatshepsut	ca. 1506-1483
Thutmosis III	ca. 1506-1452
Amenhotep II	ca. 1452-1418
Thutmosis IV	ca. 1418-1408
Amenhotep III	ca. 1408-1352
Akhenaton	ca. 1352-1336
Smekhare	ca. 1338-1336
Tutankhamun	ca. 1336-1327
Aye	ca. 1327-1323
Horemheb	ca. 1323-1295

Note that the dates for each Pharaoh's reign are listed as "circa." This is due to the fact that there are at least three major competing Egyptian chronologies (and several more have been proposed) which can differ by as much as 25-30 years depending upon which one is used. You will also note that many of the dates of the Pharaohs' reigns overlap. This is due to the customary procedure of making the designated heir co-regent during the last few years of a Pharaoh's life. Moreover, Egyptologists use different anglicized spellings for the Pharaohs' names. For example, you will see the more familiar "Thutmosis" but also "Thutmose" or "Tuthmosis" or even "Thothmes." I have selected one convention for the names and dates to use here but they are by no means the only ones in the literature.

Using the "Early" Exodus date of 1446 B.C., Thutmosis III (and not Seti I) becomes the Pharaoh of the oppression and Amenhotep II (and not Ramesses II) the Pharaoh of the Exodus. So what do we know of these two Pharaohs?

Thutmosis III was the eldest son of Thutmosis II and a minor wife. His father died when Thutmosis III was a very young child. Hatshepsut, his step-mother (and primary wife of Thutmosis II and the daughter of Thutmosis I) assumed the role of co-regent and actually ruled as Pharaoh for her step-son. In fact, Hatshepsut attempted to rule as a conventional male

Figure 12. Hatshepsut as Pharaoh including the wearing of a false beard.
(On exhibit in the Cairo Antiquities Museum).

Pharaoh, frequently depicting herself with the traditional false beard (Figure 12). When she died in ca. 1483 B.C., Thutmosis III became one of the greatest Pharaohs in Egyptian history (Figure 13). He led a total of 17 military campaigns into Palestine, eventually extending Egyptian control to Syria and the border of modern day Turkey. He is considered by most historians as the greatest warrior and general in Egyptian history and is frequently depicted on monuments and temples as a giant of a man "smiting" his puny enemies. All the accounts of his reign of 54 years, 23 under Hatshepsut and 31 as sole ruler, portray him as being extremely bombastic and arrogant. Moreover, Thutmosis III was the first Pharaoh to have depictions made of slaves making bricks and building monuments (Fig-

ure 14). All of this fits well with the description of the Pharaoh of the oppression as depicted in the Book of Exodus.

Interestingly, some indeterminate time after the death of Hatshepsut in ca. 1483 B.C., there was an intentional effort to erase her memory from Egyptian history. Many of her inscriptions were erased by chisel marks and her monuments, including great obelisks, were either knocked down or walled up in order to hide her name. It is unknown who the author of this erasure from history was or why it was done. However, the Book of Exodus could offer an explanation. In Exodus 2:5-10

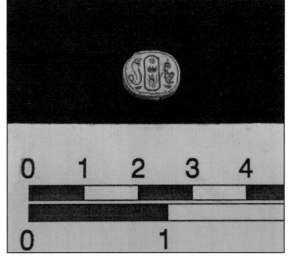

Figure 13. Scarab bearing the cartouche (name) of Pharaoh Thutmosis III.
(Wilson W. Crook, III Collection)

Figure 14. Depiction of slaves making bricks during the reign of Thutmosis III. Tomb of Rekhmire, Vizier to Thutmosis III – Luxor tomb TT-100
(Biblical Archeology Review, March/April 2014)

we are told that the daughter of Pharaoh rescued the baby Moses from the Nile and raised him as her own son. If Thutmosis III is indeed the Pharaoh of the oppression, then he is also the Pharaoh that banished Moses to Midian. If his step-mother and co-regent was the daughter of Pharaoh mentioned in Exodus, he could easily have harbored a great hatred of Hatshepsut. That, coupled with his probable resentment of her usurpation of the throne for 23 years, could have provided ample reason for Thutmosis III to order her removal from Egyptian history.

When the Pharaoh who banished Moses died (Exodus 2:23), Moses returned under God's instructions to set the Hebrew people free from their bondage. The new Pharaoh encountered by Moses would have been the eldest son of Thutmosis III, Amenhotep II. According to most Egyptologists, Amenhotep II took the throne when he was between 18-21 years of age and ruled Egypt for much of the latter half of the 15th Century B.C. However, Egyptian records present a bit of a conundrum regarding his life. In the early years of his reign, he is described as the greatest warrior and athlete in all of Egypt. An inscription found near the Sphinx on the Giza Plateau attests to the young Pharaoh's prowess:

"He was one who knew horses; there was not one like him in this numerous army. There was not one therein who could draw his bow. He could not be approached in running. Strong of arms, one who did not weary when he took the oar; he rowed at the stern of his falcon boat as the stroke for 200 men."

In the fifth year of his reign (ca. 1447 B.C.), he led his first military campaign into Palestine and Syria. Accounts of his triumphs are very similar to those of his father, full of arrogance and bombast. The arrogance of these early descriptions matches the Pharaoh of the Exodus ("Who is the Lord that I should obey him and let Israel go. I do not know the Lord and I will not let Israel go." Exodus 5:2). Then in the 7th and 9th years of his reign (ca. 1445-44 B.C., 1443-42 B.C.) he led two further campaigns into Palestine. However, these raids were noticeably different from both his first foreign invasion as well as those of his father. In fact, the entire focus of the campaigns dramatically changed from one of conquest and expansion of territorial influence to one centered on acquiring military weaponry, notably chariots and horses. Moreover, these later campaigns of Amenhotep II also focused on gathering large numbers of slaves. A total of 730 plain chariots, 1,032 painted chariots, 60 chariots of gold and silver, and 13,050 weapons of war were captured along with 820 prime chariot horses. In addition, the accounts record that a total of 101,128 slaves were brought back to Egypt. Even if the numbers are exaggerated, the focus of the expeditions remains clear – replacement of military equipment and the slave labor force. The focus on capturing slaves in large numbers is most notable. During the 17 great military expeditions of Amenhotep II's father Thutmosis III, only about one-third that number of slaves was captured. Moreover, the accounts of these latter two campaigns of Amenhotep II in Egyptian records are very subdued and contain none of the braggadocio of his first expedition. Interestingly, after the end of the third campaign in 1442 B.C., Amenhotep II led no more foreign ventures for the remaining 24 years of his reign.

So what happened between 1447 B.C. (the first great campaign of Amenhotep II) and 1445-42 B.C. that would affect such a dramatic change? Clearly one distinct possibility would be the mass Exodus of the Hebrews in 1446 B.C. The loss of the chariot arm of the army in the Red Sea coupled with the loss of the slave labor force would have necessitated the restocking of both inventories in the aftermath of the Exodus.

But what about the fate of Pharaoh Amenhotep II? Both the books of Exodus and Psalms strongly suggest that the Pharaoh was killed in the returning waters of the Red Sea along with his men ("and He saved them from the hand of the hater and redeemed them from the hand of the enemy, and the water covered their adversaries; not one of them remained" Psalm 106:10-11). Moreover, if Amenhotep II was the son of Thutmosis III who succeeded his father upon his death, why wasn't he killed by the 10th Plague as first-born of Pharaoh? It turns out that Amenhotep II was not the eldest son of Thutmosis III. Egyptian records speak of an elder son, Amenembet (Amenemhat), who was listed as "Overseer of Cattle" – a typical title for a Royal Prince. Evidently he died before his father and thus his half-brother Amenhotep II became Pharaoh.

Statues of Amenhotep II early in his reign depict a man with a round face, large ears and a square chin. Statues of reportedly the same man later in his life show a man who looks physically very different, with a more elongate face with prominent cheekbones, smaller ears, and a rounded chin (Figure 15). While stone statues can be idealized, the appearances of the two Amenhoteps are very dissimilar with completely different facial skeletal features. Are we looking at the same man or are we looking at the possibility of two Amenhotep II's – one a great athlete and warrior/king who was killed while chasing the Hebrews (Amenhotep IIa), and a replacement (possibly a relative of some sort) who filled in and took the Pharaoh's name to

Figure 15. Side-by-side comparison of statues of Amenhotep II from early in his reign (left) and later in life (right). Is this the same man?

preserve the outward appearance to Egypt's neighbors that all was well (Amenhotep IIb)? In 1898, the mummy of Amenhotep II was found in the famous Valley of the Kings by Victor Loret, head of the Egyptian Antiquities Department. This mummy has recently undergone a complete examination using a CAT-scan which showed the man buried as Amenhotep II was no more than 40-45 years old at the time of his death. Amenhotep II was known to have been between 18 and 21 years old when he assumed the throne and he reigned for a total of 37 years. Thus, he would have been in his mid- to late 50's when he died. So who is in Amenhotep II's tomb?

While much of this remains highly speculative, there is a growing consensus among scholars that Amenhotep II was certainly an enigmatic figure and there is much more to his reign and life than we currently know.

Lastly, one of the major arguments used by the Minimalists to deny the historicity of the Exodus is the complete lack of evidence that the Hebrews were ever in Egypt. In this regard, supporters of the Minimalist theory cite that in all the copious texts of Egyptian records that have survived, there is no mention of the Exodus and any of the events surrounding it (Hebrew slaves, Moses, the ten plagues, etc.). In rebuttal, any event that demeaned the power or status of the Pharaoh or Egypt would NEVER have been recorded. Writing was considered sacred in Egypt, giving reality to whatever was being recorded. This is one reason we have so many records of Egyptian events and history today. However, by deliberately NOT recording an event, it was as though it never happened. Why then did Moses not mention the name of the Pharaoh when he recorded the events of the Exodus and placed them in the Ark of the Covenant? Egyptians seldom recorded the names of the foreign (enemy) kings they conquered so as not to give power to their name. Moses, who was raised in the Royal Court as a Prince of Egypt, was possibly just following the writing style that he knew.

For years the exact location of Pi-Ramesses (Rowaty, Avaris, and Perunefer) was lost to history. Recently, a group of Austrian archeologists have rediscovered the city in and around the modern Egyptian town of Qantir (Tell el-Daba). Years of Nile flood events have deposited layers of fine silt over the site such that a large city now lies completely covered by agricultural fields. Sub-surface scans using Ground Penetrating Radar and magnetometer surveys have revealed the extent of the city including its great palaces and temples. Sub-surface mapping also shows the residential district of the inhabitants of the city and its builders. Among these scans is potential evidence for some very distinctive house structures known archeologically as "Four Room Houses". These structures are known from only one place in the Ancient Middle East - in the typical houses constructed by the Israelites once they entered the land of Canaan.

Finally, archeologists have been studying the basal part of a granite statue that has been in the Egyptian Museum of Berlin since 1913. The statue base was purchased from an Egyptian merchant by the German archeologist, Ludwig Borchardt, discoverer of the famous bust of Queen Nefertiti which also resides in the Berlin Museum. The inscription on the base of the statue has three name rings (cartouches) superimposed on the figures of "Asiatic" prisoners. The first two inscriptions can easily be translated as meaning "Ashkelon" and "Canaan". The third name is partially obscured because the base is broken, but scholars now believe it spells "I-S(h)R-IL" or Israel. The style of the inscription is believed to date from the reign of Amenhotep III (ca. 1408-1352 B.C.) and if so, would provide strong evidence for both the Exodus narrative and an "Early" date of ca. 1446 B.C.

After the Exodus, Egypt continued to have periodic interaction with Israel, notably in the Biblical events of Solomon's marriage to Pharaoh's daughter, Pharaoh Shoshenq's (Biblical Shishak) invasion of Israel following Solomon's death, Pharaoh Necho II's battle with King Josiah at Megiddo in 609 B.C., and Joseph, Mary and Jesus' sojourn to Egypt to avoid King Herod's slaughter of the innocents. However, after the Exodus, the Egyptians played only a tangential role in the history of the Israelites and the Bible.

3. CANAANITES

One of the Peoples of the Bible that figured very prominently in the early history of Israel were the Canaanites. The Bible is replete with references to the land of Canaan and its inhabitants, the word Canaan or Canaanite occurring some 160 times in the Bible. The Canaanites were a Semitic people that occupied the area of Palestine sometime before 3000 B.C. Their exact origin is unclear as it is uncertain if the Chalcolithic (Copper Age) inhabitants of some Palestine cities, such as Jericho, later became the Canaanites or if they were a people that migrated into the region and settled in areas that had previously been occupied. If the latter, scholars believe they most likely originated from the nomadic tribes of northern Arabia and modern day Jordan. What is clear is that there are significant material differences between Chalcolithic Canaan and the subsequent Early Bronze Age culture, which many archeologists mark as the beginning of the Canaanite period. The Canaanites occupied virtually all of modern day Israel and the Palestinian State as well as parts of southern Lebanon and western Jordan. The origin of the name "Canaan" remains obscure. Many scholars believe it derives from an Akkadian word that meant the "land of purple", referring to the murex shell-dyed cloth that the region became famous for. "Canaanite" also combines the Sumerian root for "to sink below" with a common suffix to mean something like the "Westerners" or the "Sundowners". Later in the history of Israel, the word Canaanite became almost synonymous with "merchant".

Actually the term Canaanite only truly applies to a single group of peoples but has been used to describe all the nations (peoples) who made up a loosely-knit political confederation in Palestine prior to the settlement of the region by the Israelites. In the Bible, the Canaanites are more accurately referred to as "the seven nations of Canaan" and include from south to north, the Hittites (southern Canaan south of Beer-Sheba), the Perizzites (southwestern Canaan all the way to the "brook of Egypt"), the Jebusites (in and around Jerusalem), the Amorites (both sides of the Jordan River Valley), the Canaanites (Mediterranean coast from Ashkelon to Mount Carmel), the Girgashites (west of the Sea of Galilee and in the Jezreel Valley), and the Hivites (north of the Sea of Galilee) (Figure 16). The Bible also occasionally used the term "Amorite" as synonymous with Canaanite.

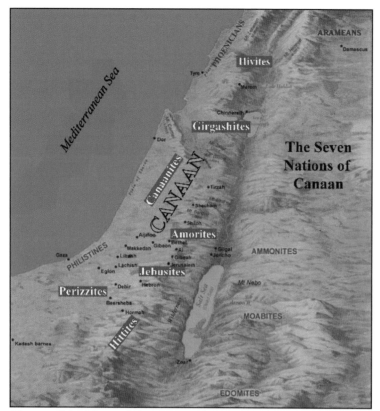

Figure 16. Map of Canaan with approximate locations for the seven Canaanite nations. (Map illustrated by Lance K. Trask after www.bible-history.com)

The Canaanites adopted a Greek city-state like organizational structure with each major city being governed by its own "King". Groups of cities were then loosely knit into regional confederations, each under one of the city Kings who then acted as the Paramount Chief for the region. For example, when Joshua began his northern campaign, King Jabin of the city of Hazor organized all of the other "Kings" in his region in a confederacy to oppose him (Joshua 11:1-3). There was a strong division of labor and power in Canaanite society between the cities and the surrounding rural areas. While the cities were clearly dependent on the rural areas for food production (barley, wheat, olives, olive oil, dates, figs, grapes and pomegranates), the power in the social structure was retained in the cities.

Throughout Canaanite history there was a strong relationship, wanted or unwanted, with Egypt. The Egyptians always believed that the land of Canaan belonged to them and they carried out numerous military campaigns to reinforce this idea. Attesting to the long-standing Egyptian influence / control over the region, there have been a number of documents found both in Egypt and in Canaanite cities that speak of tax levies, treaties, and the like. Egyptian artifacts, notably scarabs, have been found throughout Palestine in Canaanite cities.

The Canaanite language is one of two main branches of the Northwest Semitic family of languages, the other being Aramaic. These languages are related to but separated from the Semitic languages of Mesopotamia – Akkadian, Assyrian and Babylonian. Based on clay tablets found at the Canaanite site of Ras Sharma, the specific Canaanite language appears to have been in use in Syria and Palestine as early as the third millennium B.C. By the end of the Late Bronze Age (ca. 1200 B.C.), the Canaanite language had evolved into several distinct regional dialects including Phoenician, Hebrew, Edomite, Moabite and Ammonite. In addition to their language, the Canaanites also developed their own writing. Located geographically between the cumbersome writing systems of Mesopotamia (cuneiform) and Egypt (hieroglyphics), the Canaanites developed a simplified written language that was destined to become the predominant means of writing around the world – the alphabet. Our ability to read and write by means of alphabetic symbols is traceable back to the Canaanite alphabet.

The Canaanites had a sophisticated culture characterized by internal production and manufacture (ceramics, bronze implements) as well as external trade and commerce. The latter was centered on surplus agricultural products (olive oil in particular) as well as dyed cloth and clothing. As purple was the traditional color symbolizing royalty, wealth and status, Canaanite dyed cloth commanded a premium throughout the Ancient Middle East and the eastern Mediterranean region. One of the best examples of the wealth generated by this regional trade is the presence of prestige goods in most Canaanite sites, especially in the latter part of the Bronze Age (ca. 1550-1200 B.C.). Of particular note,

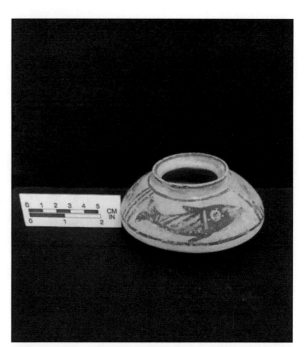

Figure 17. Imported Cypriot pottery bowl from Megiddo (Late Bronze Age). (Wilson W. Crook, III Collection)

thin highly decorated ceramics from Cyprus and elsewhere in the Greek Aegean were noted status symbols in Canaanite society (Figure 17), so much so, that they have become distinctive archeological markers for determining Late Bronze Age Canaanite occupations.

The Canaanites were exceptional engineers, constructing large walled cities that contained massive palace structures, temples, and grain storage areas. Many Canaanite cities were built with an outer and inner wall design, with the area between the walls developed as a sloped "glacis" (defensive sloped ground in front of a wall), making an attack of the inhabitants within the inner wall more difficult.

The Canaanites were truly master potters. Pottery production was extensive, largely using local clays found throughout Palestine. Both decorated and non-decorated (plain utilitarian ware) were common. As pottery styles frequently changed through time, the presence of certain decoration, the angle of the rim to the body of the pottery vessel, the thickness of the vessel walls, etc., can all be used to define specific time periods throughout the Early Bronze Age (ca. 3300-2200 B.C.), the Intermediate Bronze Age (ca. 2200-2000 B.C.), the Middle Bronze Age (2000-1550 B.C.), and the Late Bronze Age (1550-1200 B.C.). While the Canaanites continued to exist into the Iron Age (ca. 1200-539 B.C.), the persistent intermixing with the Israelites makes a pure Canaanite Iron Age ceramic difficult to identify. Typical pottery items found in Bronze Age Canaanite sites include storage jars, cooking pots, simple bowls (Figure 18), carinated bowls (Figure 19), jars (Figure 20) drinking cups (Figure 21), jugs and juglets (Figure 22), and chalices.

Figure 19.   Carinated bowl from south of Jerusalem (Late Bronze Age).
(Wilson W. Crook, III Collection)

The Canaanites also excelled in creative artistry, especially in jewelry and stone work. Canaanite craftsmen produced exceptional pieces of jewelry – earrings, pendants, armlets and rings – made from thin sheets of

Figure 18. Small ceramic bowl from Megiddo (Middle Bronze Age).
(Wilson W. Crook, III Collection)

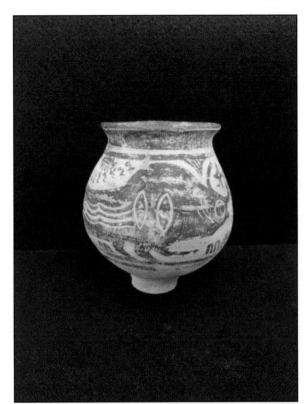

Figure 20. Small jar from the Jordan Valley with detailed bull motif. The bull frequently was identified with the god Baal (Late Bronze Age).
(Wilson W. Crook, III Collection)

Figure 21. Drinking cup from Hazor (Late Bronze Age).
(Wilson W. Crook, III Collection)

Figure 22. Black juglet from Beth She'an (Early Bronze Age).
(Wilson W. Crook, III Collection)

gold and silver. Many of these were made with sophisticated techniques including engraving, fine filigree, inlay and the like. Canaanite metallurgists cast bronze mirrors, daggers, swords, tools and religious figurines. Molds have been discovered at Canaanite sites indicating standardized production of some bronze forms.

Even though the Canaanites were never unified as a single political entity, they seemed to have enjoyed a superior reputation throughout the region as skilled warriors, especially in their use of small, highly mobile two-wheeled chariots. There are numerous records of other regional powers, notably Egypt, using Canaanite chariot forces as hired mercenaries to augment their armies. Chariots were more of a flat land weapon, well suited for the coastal plain or the

Jezreel and Jordan valleys but not suitable in the central highlands that run north-south through the land of Canaan. The Israelites would later exploit the terrain of Canaan by conquering the highlands first and then capturing the lowland plains and valleys over time.

Numerous bronze weapons have been recovered from Canaanite sites including swords (Figure 23), arrow points (Figure 24) and spears (Figure 25). The latter were cast as single, socketed points – a unique feature amongst Bronze Age weapons of the time. Perhaps the most identifiable Canaanite weapon was the so-called "duckbill axe" (Figure 26). This weapon earns its name from the twin holes cast near its base through which lashings were strung to hold it firmly to a wooden handle. Paintings from Egyptians tombs show foreign warriors holding such weapons, clearly identifying them as Canaanites.

Probably the one cultural trait for which the Canaanites are remembered today was their religious practices. The Canaanites were a religious people, expressing their world view through gods and myths in which the forces of nature were personified and deified. The

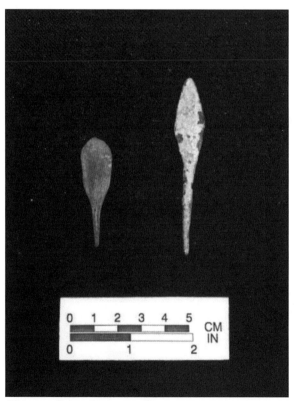

Figure 24. Bronze Canaanite arrowpoints from Northern Canaan (Late Bronze Age). (Wilson W. Crook, III Collection)

Figure 23. Bronze Canaanite sword from Jericho (Late Bronze Age). (Wilson W. Crook, III Collection)

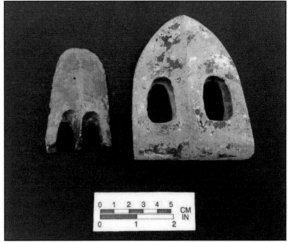

Figure 26. Bronze Canaanite "duckbill" axes from central Canaan (Late Bronze Age). (Wilson W. Crook, III Collection)

Figure 25. Bronze Canaanite socketed spear points from central Canaan (Late Bronze Age). (Wilson W. Crook, III Collection)

Canaanite pantheon of gods and goddesses included a large number of deities, principal among which were El (Patriarchal deity and once king of the Canaanite gods), Astarte / Asherah (El's wife), Baal – or more correctly Ba'al (the god of thunder, lightning and rain), Anat (Baal's sister), Yam (god of the sea), Mot (god of the underworld and death), Shapash (god of the sun), Lotan (seven headed serpent god), and Marqod (god of dance). The Canaanites' view of life focused on the forces of nature, both good and malevolent, against which they were helpless. The annual cycle of plant life in Canaan was often tenuous and subject to periods of drought or inadequate rainfall in a land lying between the desert and the sea. They knew the importance of winter rains for the fertility of the soil, and Baal was recognized as the source of fertility both for crops, animal flocks and the Canaanite family. While El was once the chief deity, by the second millennium B.C., he was replaced by Baal as Canaanite beliefs shifted more and more towards fertility. Interestingly, the Israelites later adopted the name "El", meaning "Lord" as one of the words to describe Yahweh (God). The use survives today in the name of Jewish synagogues (Temple Beth-El) and in personal names such as Daniel, Michael, and Samuel.

In the area of religion, the Canaanites created several epic myths, the most prominent one being the Baal epic. In this story, Baal challenges Yam, who as god of the sea is seen as the master of chaos. Baal slays Yam but then he himself is killed by Mot (death) and is taken to the realm of the underworld. Anat (or sometimes Astarte) travels to the underworld and through a very erotic sexual encounter, raises Baal from the dead to once again bring fertility and life to the land and its people.

The Canaanites practiced what is known as a "sympathetic" religion, in which the people (followers) reenacted the actions of the gods in order to help persuade the gods to perform like actions, ultimately bringing about the desired result. As such, Canaanite places of worship were filled with official temple prostitutes, both male and female, who reenacted the Baal epic among themselves and also with active petitioner participation. We do not know exactly how Canaanite temple services were conducted but there is archeological evidence that they included dancing, music, self-mutilation through cuts (this may have been done solely by the priests and temple prostitutes), and the eating of wine-soaked cakes – the latter having been proved by the discovery of apparent cake molds that typically had the form of a male or female deity on the surface. Clay incense stands have been found in a number of Canaanite temples indicating that the burning of incense was also a key component to their worship practices. These stands are frequently depicted with either the faces of deities on their sides or animals such as serpents.

Part of Canaanite participation in worship also involved the keeping of deity replicas in the home. As a consequence, Canaanite sites are filled with small bronze, or more commonly, clay artifacts which represent either Baal or Astarte / Anath (Figures 27 and 28). Baal is frequently depicted holding arrows (representing thunderbolts) or riding a horse as he was known as the "Rider of the Storm". Depictions of Astarte / Anath typically depict a female figure with either large breasts (typically the hands of the figurines are cupping the

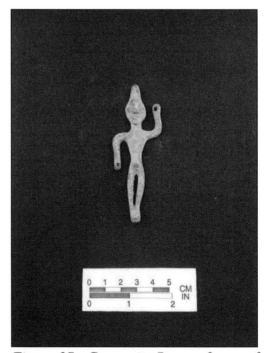

Figure 27. Canaanite Bronze figure of the god Baal (Late Bronze Age). (Wilson W. Crook, III Collection)

Figure 28. Canaanite clay figure of the goddess Astarte (Late Bronze Age). (Wilson W. Crook, III Collection)

Figure 29. Canaanite clay "Astarte Plaque" (Late Bronze Age). (Wilson W. Crook, III Collection)

breasts) and/or wide hips – both symbols of fertility. Astarte / Anath also had a number of other roles besides fertility as she was both the goddess of war and the "master of animals". As such, she is sometimes depicted standing on a bed of human skulls and holding the reins to either horses, ibex or some other animal. While most of these figures are three dimensional, there are also distinctive Astarte figures that are known as "Astarte Plaques" (Figure 29). These are clearly molded, flat-backed figures that show the female goddess lying on her back and typically completely nude. Archeologists believed these household deities were placed underneath the beds in residential houses in order to promote fertility.

One sad aspect of Canaanite religious worship was the practice of child sacrifice. While a true *tophet* or infant burial graveyard has never been found in a Canaanite site (as they have been in Carthaginian and Phoenician sites), a number of infant burials have been found beneath the cornerstones of houses. Invariably the infant is either a still-born or just born child that has been killed, placed inside a jar and buried beneath the house foundation (Figure 30). No physical evidence of injury is usually associated with the remains so it appears that the baby was either smothered or drowned prior to burial. It is believed that the practice was limited to the first born as an offering to the gods in order to bring later prosperity to the family.

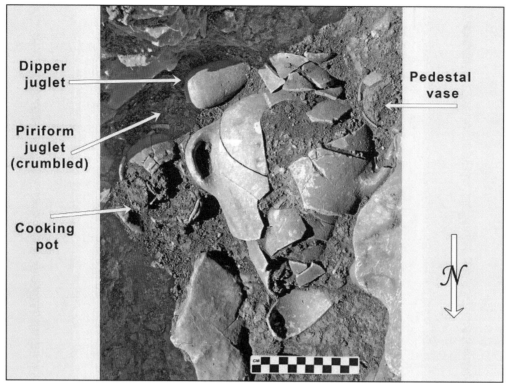

Figure 30. Canaanite infant jar burial, Khirbet el-Maqatir (Late Bronze Age).
(Courtesy of Associates for Biblical Research – www.BibleArcheology.org)

The Canaanites built large temples in their major cities and such structures have been excavated at Gezer, Beth She'an, Hazor, Lachish, Pella and other sites. In the second millennium B.C., Canaanite temples were generally elongate single rooms with a door on one of the long sides. During the Middle Bronze Age, temples tended to be square with a special portico over the entrance. In time, another room was added at the rear of the large square room. This inner cubicle was typically raised above the main room and reached by a platform of steps. The inner room was designated as a holy place and frequently contained either statues of deities, or more commonly, a single stone or series of standing stones known as "*masseboth*" (singular "*massebah*"). This architectural design, containing a porch, a long narrow central room, and an inner holy sanctum, became the prototype for all future temples in the Ancient Middle East, including the one built by Solomon in Jerusalem in the 10th Century B.C.

One question I am frequently asked about the Canaanites is how could a loving God sanction the total destruction of a people, including the deaths of the women and children? This is a difficult question and one which frequently results in people saying, "I only follow the New Testament God who is clearly a God of love and salvation; I don't believe in that Old Testament

God of vengeance and death". To this statement I always reply that the God of the Old Testament and the God of the New Testament are one and the same. God is the epitome of righteousness and abhors sin. In every aspect of the Bible, from Genesis to Revelation, God is depicted as balancing His love, mercy and grace against the consequences of rejecting His will and committing sin. People often ignore the Biblical truth of judgment but when Jesus came into the world, He stated, "For judgement I came into this world, so that those who do not see may see, and those that see may become blind" – John 9:39; and the second coming of the Messiah, as fully described in the Book of Revelation, also depicts Jesus as ultimate judge against sin as well as the bringer of salvation and everlasting life to those who believe in Him.

From the very beginning of their creation, God extended numerous chances for the Canaanites to stop their worship of idols and turn to Him. Even after a thousand years of allowing the Canaanites to worship false idols, God told Abraham that the Canaanites would still be given yet more time to change: "Your descendants will be strangers in a land that is not theirs, where they will be enslaved and oppressed for four hundred years . . . Then in the fourth generation, they shall return for the iniquity of the Amorites (Canaanites) is not yet complete" (Genesis 15:13, 16). The Canaanites were given yet another 400 years to change their practices and follow the one true God. When they failed to do so, God timed the arrival of His judgment with the fullness of the sin to be judged. Even so, God warned the Israelites (Deuteronomy 9:4-5) not to become arrogant or boastful over the destruction of the Canaanites because they had nothing to do with it; the victory was solely due to God's will and plan.

Lastly, God sees history on a higher plane than we can comprehend (Isaiah 55:9; Romans 11:30-36). He did not judge the Canaanite people out of cruelty but to prevent a greater evil occurring in the future:

> *"In the cities of the nations the Lord your God is giving you as an inheritance, do not leave anything alive that breathes. Completely destroy them – the Hittites, Amorites, Canaanites, Perizzites, Girgashites, Hivites and Jebusites – as the Lord God has commanded you. Otherwise they will teach you to follow all the detestable things they do in worshiping their gods, and you will sin against the Lord your God" (Deuteronomy 20:16-18).*

The Israelites did not completely exterminate the Canaanites and the admixture of Canaanite culture and religion into Israelite worship is exactly what happened. The Bible reflects the dangerous attraction of Canaanite culture for the Israelites. The monotheistic belief of the Israelites was in direct contrast and conflict with the seductive polytheistic beliefs of the Canaanites. Israel inherited the material culture of the Canaanites (cities, agricultural fields and vineyards, pottery techniques, etc.) along with their language and their system of writing. In changing from a nomadic tradition to a more sedentary agricultural lifestyle, it was difficult for the Israelites to resist the attraction of the Canaanite view of life, especially with its emphasis on fertility. Ultimately, the majority of the Israelites succumbed to Canaanite influences despite the repeated warnings from God and His prophets. Only a remnant survived in exile after the complete destruction of Israel by first the Assyrians and later the Babylonians. It was during the Babylonian exile that the Israelites were purged of the fatal attraction that had destroyed their forebears. From that time on the Jews did not worship idols.

4. ISRAELITES

The story of the Israelite people is a complex one which involves a number of changes and geographic movements over time. They are variously referred to in the Bible as "Hebrews", "Israelites" (children of Israel), "Judahites", "Judeans" and "Jews". Each of these terms refers to the same general people but at a different point in time in their history. For example, while the term "Hebrew" is used in a number of books of the Old Testament (and is the title of a New Testament epistle which subsequently never mentions the term), it is more heavily concentrated in the books of Genesis and Exodus, especially when the people are in Egypt and do not have a land of their own. It is therefore used as more of an ethnic term to describe a people as opposed to a country. The first mention of the people as Israelites begins with Jacob being renamed by God as "Israel" (Genesis 35:10); his family and their followers then adopt the term "Israelites". However, this term became more commonly used once the Hebrew people became free from Egyptian bondage and occupied a land of their own. When the United Monarchy split up into the Northern Kingdom of Israel and the Southern Kingdom of Judah after the death of King Solomon, the people were often referred to as either "Israelites" or "Judahites" as a means of referencing to which part of Israel they belonged. Lastly, during the Persian Period when the survivors of the Babylonian exile returned to the land of Israel, they were known as either "Judahites" after the Persian sub-province of Judah, or simply as "Jews" – a term derived from the Hebrew word "*Yehuda*". During the Roman period, the people of Israel were sometimes designated as "Judeans" or "Galileans" depending on which part of Israel they came from. More commonly the people were simply referred to as "Jews", indicating more of an ethnic origin than a country. Only after the establishment of the modern Jewish state of Israel in 1948, have its citizens returned to being called "Israelis" after the name of their country.

Accordingly, I have broken this chapter into eight sub-sections which follow the history of the Hebrew / Jewish people. These sections include (1) The Hebrew People in Egypt, (2) The Exodus, (3) The Conquest of Canaan, (4) The United Monarchy, (5) The Divided Kingdoms of Israel and Judah, (6) The Babylonian Exile, (7) The Persian Period (Judah after the return from the Babylonian exile), and (8) Palestine in the First Century A.D. (the Roman Period).

The Hebrew People in Egypt

The Bible portrays a strong linkage between the Israelites and Egypt, often as a result of a lack of water in Canaan. Even without its fertile, silt-bearing floods, the Nile River provided a constant and abundant source of water which has been utilized for millennia in the growing of food crops. The first mention of such a famine in Canaan was shortly after the patriarch Abraham's arrival. Genesis 12:10-20 tells of Abraham taking his family to Egypt until the life-giving rains returned. While Joseph was sold by his brothers into slavery to a group of caravan traders who in turn sold him in Egypt (Genesis 37:18-36), it was a severe famine in Canaan that brought the rest of his extended family to the Nile Delta region. There the Israelites, or Hebrews as they were called by the Egyptians, multiplied and prospered for over three centuries.

The term "Hebrew" occurs 34 times on the Old Testament and is used synonymously with the word "Israelite". In Genesis 14:13 Abraham is referred to as "*Avram Ha-Ivri*" (Abram the Hebrew), which literally means "Abram the one who stands on the other side". On Egyptian monuments there are two terms which scholars have tried to identify as meaning "Hebrews". The first is the similar sounding "*Habiru*" (or "*Apiru*") which has been found in 12th and 13th Century B.C. texts as referring to a people having once settled in Egypt. But it is unclear if the "*Habiru*" are actually the Hebrew people of the Bible despite the closeness in the sound of the two names. Other scholars argue that a name found in Hyksos Period inscriptions called "*Shasu*" (those who move on foot) is actually the name the Egyptians used for the Hebrews.

As noted in Chapter 2, there is little concrete archeological evidence for the presence of the Israelites in Egypt. The possibility of four-room Israelite-style houses at Tell el-Daba (Pi-Ramesses) and the one partial inscription recognizing a country called "I-S(h)R-IL" in the early part of the 14th Century B.C. on the base of a granite monument in the Egyptian Museum of Berlin constitute the sum total of all the archeological evidence we have to date.

The Jewish Encyclopedia states that the terms Hebrew and Israelite are largely synonymous, with Hebrew describing the people in the time before they had a country of their own and the name Israelite applying after the conquest of Canaan. Jewish scholars today say that the term "Hebrews" referring to a people (not a language) is rare and when used it describes Israelites in dangerous, precarious situations, as migrants or slaves.

The Exodus

If we accept the evidence presented in Chapter 2 that the Exodus did in fact take place and occurred during the reign of Amenhotep II near the middle of the 15th Century B.C., then the next questions commonly raised by scholars are (1) what was the route of the Exodus, and (2) where is the location of Mount Sinai where the Bible tells us that the people spent an important part of the 40 years of wandering prior to the Conquest of Canaan. The truth is that we just don't know for certain the answer to either of these questions but that has not stopped scholars from speculating on both issues for hundreds of years.

The Bible lists nearly 50 places between Egypt and the crossing of the Jordan River 40 years later. All we know for certain are the starting point (Pi-Ramesses), the mid-point (Ezion-Geber) and the ending point (Mount Nebo). Of all the wildernesses mentioned in Exodus through Deuteronomy, we only know for certain that the Wilderness of Shur is in the land of Midian. However, scholars even debate the precise location of Midian. As a result, over 15 places have been suggested as the location of Mount Sinai and almost as many for the location of the crossing of the Red Sea.

So let's start with what we know about the Red Sea crossing. Exodus tells us that the Israelites, once they left Egypt, did not travel the short route along the Mediterranean coast because of the fear of running into the war-like Philistines:

"God did not lead them by the way of the land of the Philistines, even though it was near; for God said, 'The people might change their minds when they see war, and return to Egypt" (Exodus 13:17-18)

Exodus further states that the Israelites traveled a considerable distance in the wilderness "in the land of Egypt" which then led to the Red Sea where they crossed over into Midian. This then led to the Well of Marah, the Springs of Elim, and eventually to Mount Sinai (Horeb).

The Hebrew words for Red Sea are "*yam suph*". "*Yam*", borrowed from the Canaanite sea god, clearly means sea; but the word "*suph*" can have multiple meanings including "red", "reed", or "seaweed". Many modern scholars have interpreted "*yam suph*" to mean the Sea of Reeds and thus they refer to the marshy area immediately east of the Nile Delta known as Lake

Timsah and the Bitter Lakes. The problem with this interpretation is that in Hebrew no freshwater body of water, even if brackish, is ever referred to "*yam*" (sea). The Gulf of Suez is referred to as "*yam*", as is the Gulf of Aqaba, as is the Red Sea. In fact, the Gulf of Aqaba, which has always been considered to be a part of the Red Sea, is referred to as "*yam suph*" in the books of Numbers, Deuteronomy, Judges, I Kings, and Psalms. Moreover, Lake Timsah and the Bitter Lakes are far too shallow to match the description given in Exodus:

"The sons of Israel went through the midst of the sea on dry land, and the waters were like a wall to them on their right hand and on their left" (Exodus 14:21-22)

When the Israelites crossed the Red Sea into Midian, they no longer feared the Egyptians, knowing they were indeed safe. Lake Timsah or the Bitter Lakes or even as some scholars have suggested, the northern end of the Gulf of Suez, just don't fit. Either they are not deep enough or the Egyptian army in their fast, mobile chariots would simply have gone around and caught the Israelites on the other side. So in my opinion, I believe the Red Sea (*yam suph*) actually does mean the Red Sea.

The Sinai Peninsula contains numerous copper mines which were actively guarded by Egyptian garrisons, a secure source of copper being critical for making weapons in the Late Bronze Age. The Sinai Peninsula was, and has always been, considered a part of Egypt. The traditional site for Mount Sinai, St. Catherine's Monastery, lies less than 40 miles from one of the larger of these mines which had a substantial military garrison to protect it. Does it make sense that Moses would lead the people away from Egypt only to camp out for weeks on end within close striking range of a significant Egyptian military outpost?

So, if St. Catherine's is not the location of Mount Sinai, then where are the real Mount Sinai and the place where the Israelites crossed the Red Sea in order to get to Midian? Even today, if you look at almost any map of the Ancient Middle East you will see that Midian is located in the northern part of what is now Saudi Arabia. Some maps will place the word "Midian" spanning the Gulf of Aqaba including a part of northern Saudi Arabia as well as the Sinai Peninsula simply because it is embarrassing to have the location of Mount Sinai, which the Bible tells us is in Midian (Exodus 4:19-25), located in the Sinai Peninsula which is not labeled as a part of Midian. Some modern researchers contend that Midian extends to the area north of the Gulf of Aqaba where Sinai and Arabia meet, and this could be true; but it still does not solve the question of the location of the Red Sea crossing.

The Biblical name for the Sinai Peninsula is the "Wilderness of Egypt" or the "Wilderness of the Red Sea" (Exodus 13:18; Judges 11:16; Ezekiel 20:36). The Exodus story further states that the Israelites traveled a "considerable distance" through the wilderness BEFORE crossing the Red Sea. This is one of the greatest problems with the Bitter Lakes-as-Red Sea theory in that they are so close to the Nile Delta region that there really isn't any wilderness to cross before coming to the water, let alone it being a "considerable distance" away from the Nile Delta. So, assuming *"yam suph"* means the Red Sea and Midian is in the northern part of Arabia, where are possible crossing points?

One theory which has been proposed recently is that the Straits of Tiran opposite the southern tip of the Sinai Peninsula could be a potential Red Sea crossing point. The basis for this theory lies in the fact that some sites which fit very well with the Biblical description of the Well of Marah and the Springs of Elim lie just opposite the strait in the northern part of modern Saudi Arabia. Moreover, it is suggested in Judges 11:16 that the distance between the Israelites leaving Egypt to the Red Sea (and then to Mount Sinai) is roughly equivalent to the distance that they later traveled from Mount Sinai to Kadesh Barnea (just south of Petra in Jordan) where they spent a number of years. If the Red Sea crossing point is assumed to be near the Straits of Tiran, the distance from Goshen in the Nile Delta to the Straits is approximately 220 miles; a mountain suggested to be Mount Sinai is but 30 miles away after the crossing; and from that Mountain (Jebel al-Lawz) to Kadesh Barnea is roughly 190 miles – very similar distances.

The Gulf of Aqaba is a deep fault-derived channel that ranges from 800-1,800 meters in depth (1,800-5,900 feet) and the crossing at the Straits of Tiran is approximately 12 miles across. However, large coral reefs that can be easily seen on Google Earth cover much of the Straits of Tiran such that in many places the bottom is only 13 meters (42 feet) deep. Moreover, the area has a very strong tidal system and at low tide each day parts of the reef are clearly exposed. Because of this extensive reef and tidal system, the area is littered with the wrecks of large ships stranded on the reefs which are also clearly visible on Google Earth. The area is also known for frequent strong winds blowing from east-to-west from Arabia ("Then Moses stretched out his hand over the sea, and the Lord caused the water to retreat by a strong east wind all night, turning the sea into dry land" Exodus 14:21). As mentioned above, we still do not know exactly where the Red Sea crossing took place, but there are some interesting hints for further exploration in the future.

Over 15 sites have been proposed over the years as the location of Mount Sinai. Unlike the Red Sea crossing location, the Bible is VERY specific about Mount Sinai's location and all the physical characteristics that should be found. These include:

- Located in Arabia, not in Egypt (Exodus 2:15, 19; 3:8, 10, 12; Galatians 4:25)
- Located in the northwestern part of Arabia in the land known as Midian (Exodus 4:19-25)
- The burning bush where God first appeared to Moses and the camp of the Israelites were located on the backside of the mountain, the side away from the homeland of his father-in-law Jethro (Exodus 3:1-2)
- There was room for a large number of people to camp (Exodus 12:37)
- Boundary markers were erected to prevent the Israelites from venturing up on the mountain (Exodus 19:23)
- Moses had an altar constructed of unhewn stones (Exodus 20:24-26)
- 12 pillars were set up around the edge of the mountain, one for each of the 12 tribes of Israel (Exodus 24:4)
- Mount Sinai had a brook (Deuteronomy 9:21)
- Mount Sinai had a habitable cave that was later used by Elijah (I Kings 19:8)
- The altar of the Golden Calf was set up within sight of Mount Sinai (Exodus 32:17-19)

There is no historical tradition for Jebel Musa, the traditional Mount Sinai in the Sinai Peninsula, before the 3rd-5th Centuries A.D. (Byzantine period). The mountain was "discovered" by the Emperor Constantine's mother, Saint Helena, somewhere around 330 A.D. After his conversion to Christianity, Constantine dispatched his mother to Palestine to find all the holy sites associated with Christendom and the Judeo-Christian heritage. His somewhat vague description regarding the location of Mount Sinai led her to the mountain in the Sinai Peninsula which she then proclaimed as "Mount Sinai". The Byzantine Emperor Justinian memorialized the site by building St. Catherine's Monastery and it has been known as the traditional site of Mount Sinai ever since.

The problem is that Jebel Musa has absolutely none of the characteristics described in the Book of Exodus for Mount Sinai. In particular: it has no water in the area for livestock; there is no large camping area near the mountain; it is very close to a major Late Bronze Age Egyptian military garrison; there is no cave on the mountain, no boundary markers, and no pillars. In fact, there is absolutely no archeological evidence for any Bronze Age occupation. When Israel defeated Egypt and captured the Sinai Peninsula in the 1967 Six Day War, the Israelis immediately sent teams of archeologists to conduct an extensive survey in the area of Jebel Musa. They found absolutely no artifacts, not even a single potsherd dating to the time of the Late Bronze Age.

So, if Jebel Musa is not the real Mount Sinai, where is it located? The largest mountain in northwest Saudi Arabia has a long-standing, local tradition as "the Mountain of Moses" – Jebel al-Lawz ("Mountain of Almonds"). In the late 1980's, two American businessmen, Larry Williams and Bob Cornuke, snuck into Saudi Arabia and visited Jebel al-Lawz twice. In the 1990's, an American couple working in Saudi Arabia, Jim and Penny Caldwell, visited the mountain eight times over a 15 year period. Williams, Cornuke, and the Caldwells found a number of features which appear to match the description given in the Book of Exodus. They found a number of piles of stones around the edge of the mountain, each about 400 meters apart (boundary markers). They also found 12 areas where flat circular stones had once been piled up to form pillars. A large altar of unhewn stone was located adjacent to the mountain which had an associated stone wall as if it were a pen for animals. Some distance away from this feature was a second large stone altar that had a number of petroglyphs on its side, including what appear to be lyre-shaped horned cattle as are found in Egypt. All around the base of the mountain were abundant pottery sherds and stone tools, some of the latter shaped like leaf-shaped knives known to occur in Egypt. There was a large cave (15 feet high and 20 feet deep) about halfway up the mountain and the entire top of the mountain was extensively blackened as if it had been thoroughly burned.

While Jebel al-Lawz continues to be the subject of hot debate amongst Biblical scholars, it certainly provides considerably more evidence for being Mount Sinai than does the traditional site of Jebel Musa. Moreover, until someone finds a better candidate that has so many of the specific features mentioned in Exodus, Jebel al-Lawz in northern Saudi Arabia has to be given serious consideration as one of the leading contenders for the Mountain of Moses.

The Conquest of Canaan

The Bible presents a rather straightforward account of the Israelites' conquest of the land of Canaan (Joshua 1-12). Moses, after leading the Israelites for 40 years, was allowed to look over the Jordan River from the summit of Mount Nebo (modern day Jordan) and see "the Promised Land". Before he died, he passed the mantle of leadership to his faithful lieutenant, Joshua, who led the people across the Jordan River at a place called Gilgal. Joshua then began a three-step military campaign which included first establishing a foothold in the central highlands (Jericho-Ai-Bethel), followed by a southern campaign that captured the largest Canaanite city in southern Canaan (Lachish), and finally a northern campaign that defeated the King of Hazor who was leading a confederation of Canaanite leaders in the area around and north of the Sea of Galilee. With this, the Book of Joshua proclaims that after conquering the whole land, Joshua divided Canaan, including territory east of the Jordan River, among the 12 tribes of Israel. Of course, with the opening lines of the Book of Judges, we find the Israelites are still at war with the Canaanites (and other peoples in the area) so the conquest was not quite as complete as stated in Joshua:

"These are the nations the LORD left to test all those Israelites who had not experienced any of the wars in Canaan (He did this only to teach warfare to the descendants of the Israelites who had not had previous battle experience): the five rulers of the Philistines, all the Canaanites, the Sidonians, and the Hivites living in the Lebanon mountains from Mount Baal Hermon to Lebo Hamath. They were left to test the Israelites to see whether they would obey the LORD's commands, which He had given their ancestors through Moses. The Israelites lived among the Canaanites, Hittites, Amorites, Perizzites, Hivites and Jebusites. They took their daughters in marriage and gave their own daughters to their sons, and served their gods". (Judges 3:1-6)

Additionally, there are some scholars (the Minimalists) who firmly believe that the entire Conquest of Canaan is pure fiction, invented by later writers of the Bible to give the nation a more glorious past. These scholars believe that not only were there no Exodus and no

Conquest, but the characters of Saul, David and Solomon are also the work of fiction and that the real history of Israel does not begin until sometime in the 9th Century B.C. Of course, if there is no Exodus, there cannot be a Conquest; and if there is no King David or King Solomon, then there is no Davidic lineage to Jesus and much of what we believe in the Bible crumbles away. Fortunately, there have been a number of recent archeological discoveries, all of which have confirmed the historicity of the Biblical account of the Conquest and the founding of the State of Israel, and the ranks of the Minimalists are steadily shrinking. There is still the controversy over the date of the Exodus, and thus the date of the Conquest of Canaan, but again new discoveries from Jericho and Biblical Ai (modern Khirbet al-Maqatir) have provided fresh evidence for the "Early" Exodus and Conquest dates.

Beginning the in the late 19th Century and continuing through the 20th Century to today, archeologists have tried to prove or disprove the Biblical account of the Conquest of Canaan. With regards to the conquest, probably the single most famous story is the account of Joshua's destruction of the city of Jericho – and that is where many Biblical archeologists have looked for proof of the historicity of the Israelite Conquest of Canaan.

Jericho lies on the western side of the Jordan River Valley near the base of the Judean highlands. The city is 670 feet below sea level making it the lowest city in the world. The ancient city, known as Tell es-Sultan, is on the northwest side of modern Jericho. The site was settled in antiquity because of a very prolific spring, Ein es-Sultan, which still produces over 1,000 gallons per minute of cool, fresh water today. As a result, Jericho looks like an oasis in the middle of the Judean desert (Figure 31).

Archeological interest in Jericho began as early as 1867-68, when Sir Charles Warren correctly identified Tell es-Sultan as the site of Biblical Jericho. Warren sank six vertical shafts and proved that the mound was man-made, not natural, and had occupational debris from the surface to the base of the shafts (Figure 32). The next excavation of Jericho came in 1906-07, and again in 1911, by the Austrian-German team of Ernst Sellin

Figure 31. Ein es-Sultan, the spring at Jericho and the lush oasis it creates in the middle of the Judean wilderness.

and Carl Watzinger. Their work uncovered a large outer city wall which extended around most of the outside of the tell (a "tell" or "tel" is a mound created by multiple human occupations each built on top of the other resulting in a small artificial mountain).

Figure 32. Tell es-Sultan, the still largely unexcavated occupational mound containing the ruins of ancient Jericho. Dimensions of the tell are approximately 350 x 150 meters.

The first major modern excavation of Jericho was conducted by the British archeologist John Garstang between 1930-36. Garstang found a number of features including several major collapsed walls and a series of fiery destructions. He also found that Jericho, like many other cities of the Ancient Middle East, was not one city but composed of as many as 20 cities, one built on top of another, and spanning a very long period of occupation. Based on the pottery types present in each city level, Garstang postulated that City IV, which had been completely destroyed in a huge conflagration, was the city that Joshua destroyed as recorded in the Bible (Joshua 6). He estimated that City IV dated to approximately 1400 B.C., which would fit with the "Early" Exodus theory. The onset of World War II prevented Garstang from completing his work at Jericho and he recommended that one of his students, Kathleen Kenyon, complete his work after the war. Kenyon worked at Jericho from 1952-58, excavating two large 26 x 26 foot squares (archeologists typically excavate in small, 5 x 5 foot squares, called "units", which they excavate vertically in controlled layers leaving smooth walls to observe site stratigraphy). She also put an immense vertical excavation through the side of the tell which she called her "Great Trench" (Figure 33).

Kenyon made a number of new discoveries at Jericho and obtained some of the first radiocarbon dates for the occupation. She found that the city had been first occupied around 10,400 years ago, which made Jericho the oldest organized city in world history. Despite this early age, the inhabitants of Jericho were surprisingly well-organized, building defensive walls and even a massive watch tower (Figure 34). Of the 20 Jerichos of the past, three had been destroyed in major conflagrations and 12 more in more minor destructions. Kenyon looked at City IV in detail and based on the pottery, dated its destruction at approximately 1500-1550 B.C. She also concluded that after this destruction, Jericho lay abandoned until about 1300 B.C., and then continued only as a very minor settlement until well after 1100 B.C. Thus she concluded that there was no walled city at the time of Joshua, whether at the "Early" date of ca. 1400 B.C. or the "Late" date of ca. 1200-1230 B.C. As would be expected, Kenyon's findings made head-lines all around the world and led some arche-

Figure 33. Remains of Kathleen Kenyon's "Great Trench" at Tell es-Sultan.

ologists to claim that "Jericho was the biggest disappointment in all of Biblical archeology".

There were several major problems with the validity of Kenyon's findings. First, even though she completed her excavations at Jericho, she never published any of her work. After her death in 1978, students and colleagues went through her notes and in 1981 published what she had written (you can purchase her three volume report online for about $1500). But her

Figure 34. Remains of the ancient watchtower at Tell es-Sultan. The original construction is believed to date to about 7000-8000 B.C.

personal writings also revealed a very different side of this world famous archeologist. Apparently Ms. Kenyon was a rabid anti-Zionist, and confirmation of the Joshua narrative only strengthened Israel's case for controlling all of Palestine including the West Bank. In the mid-1980's, Dr. Bryant Wood of the Associates for Biblical Research conducted his own excavation and review of Kenyon's work at Jericho, including going through all her ceramic artifacts and notes. Dr. Wood also went through the collections recovered by Garstang between 1930-36. Dr. Wood, a world-class expert on Bronze Age Canaanite pottery, found that (1) Kenyon had based her interpretation of the destruction of City IV of Jericho in 1500-1550 B.C. not on the presence of pottery but on the *absence* of imported Cypriot pottery – a known characteristic of Late Bronze Age Canaanite occupations (see Chapter 3); (2) she had conducted her major excavations (the two 26 x 26 foot squares) in what turned out to be a poorer section of ancient Jericho, which was not likely to have had expensive imported ceramics; (3) there were potential problems with the radiocarbon dates from City IV which had a very wide range from ca. 1347 to 1690 B.C.; and (4) a thorough examination of Kenyon's own pottery samples from Jericho showed an abundance of Cypriot-like imported pottery, but much of it appeared to be of local origin. Wood concluded that this was to be expected as Jericho was located a long distance from the Mediterranean coast and rather than have the expense of imported Cypriot ware, the people manufactured their own "knock off" version.

Wood also found a number of characteristics in both the artifacts and architecture of Jericho City IV which matched the descriptions given in the Book of Joshua:

- The city was strongly fortified, with an outer stone wall 15 feet high and an inner mud brick wall 12 feet in height with a plastered defensive glacis in between the walls (Joshua 2:5-15)
- The attack occurred just after harvest (excavated storage jars were full of grain) (Joshua 2:6, 3:15, 5:10)
- The inhabitants had no opportunity to flee (Joshua 6:1)
- The siege was short (Joshua 6:15)
- Sections of both the inner and outer walls were leveled, possibly by an earthquake (Joshua 6:20)
- The city was not plundered (Joshua 6:17-18)
- The city was extensively burned and totally destroyed; the heat being so great that mud bricks actually melted (Joshua 6:20)

New excavations begun in in the late 1990's and continuing to this day by a joint Italian-Palestinian team may reveal more about ancient Jericho. Observation of some of the exposed parts of this new excavation by the author showed the presence of a number of mud brick houses located in the space between the inner and outer walls (Figure 35). This fits with the description of the prostitute Rahab's house as mentioned in Joshua 2. Population growth in Jericho, necessitating the construction of small houses in between the inner and outer defensive walls, would have neutralized the effectiveness of a defensive glacis and made the city's defenses weaker.

After the successful battle at Jericho, Joshua moved the Israelite army to besiege the Canaanite city at Ai (Arabic for "heap of ruins"). The hills of Jerusalem can be seen from Ai and thus it likely served as a military outpost and was allied to the Jebusites. For years archeologists believed that the small hill known as Et Tel was the Biblical city of Ai.

Figure 35. Remains of mud brick residential structures in the space between the inner and outer walls at Tell es-Sultan.

Excavations at Et Tel showed it had been destroyed around 2200 B.C. and never reoccupied. The Bible is very specific about what should be found at Ai, both geographically and archeologically (Joshua 7-8):

- Ai was strategically important, located at a major N-S, E-W crossroad
- It was located immediately east of the city of Bethel
- There should be a hidden ambush site to the west of Ai used by Joshua
- There should be a large, militarily significant hill to the north of Ai
- A shallow valley should be between this hill and Ai
- The city should be small; more of an outpost than a city
- There should be fortified walls and a large fortified gate on the north side of the city
- The city should date to the Late Bronze Age (ca. 1400-1500 B.C.)
- It should be burned by fire
- The city remained a ruin "forever"; no succeeding occupation

The work at Et Tel found virtually none of these features. When Kenyon made her announcement that Jericho had not been occupied at the time of Joshua, the lack of evidence at Et Tell further moved the archeological community toward the belief that the entire Joshua narrative was a work of fiction.

Since 1995, Dr. Bryant Wood and the Associates for Biblical Research have been conducting an extensive excavation at a small hill adjacent to Et Tel known as Khirbet el-Maqatir. Examination of the site shows that all the major topographic features mentioned about Ai in the Book of Joshua are present at Khirbet el-Maqatir. Moreover, excavations to date have found that (1) the city is fairly small, covering only about 2.5 acres (1 Hectare), (2) it has massive fortified walls that were as much as three meters in height and up to four meters in thickness, (3) there are the remains of a large fortified gate, estimated to have been five meters in height, (4) the city was extensively burned and destroyed, (5) the pottery in the destruction layer is from the Late Bronze Age (ca. 1400-1500 B.C.), and (6) after the city's destruction, the hill was never reoccupied, even to this day. In 2013, near the end of the field season, a small Egyptian scarab measuring just 7/10 of an inch in length was recovered in association with Late Bronze Age pottery. The scarab depicts a falcon-headed sphinx with both an ankh (life) to the right and a netjer (god) sign above it (Figure 36).

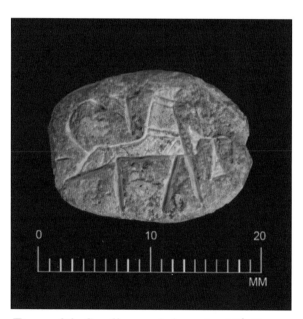

Figure 36. Small scarab from the 15th Century B.C. found at Khirbet el-Maqatir (Ai). (Courtesy of Associates for Biblical Research – www.BibleArcheology.org)

Dr. Wood has made an extensive study of scarabs with similar symbols through all the Egyptian collections in Egypt, the U.K. and the U.S. and has found analogues only occur during the reigns of Thutmosis III, Amenhotep II and Thutmosis IV or roughly the period between 1485-1400 B.C. This adds strong evidence that Khirbet el-Maqatir is the Biblical city of Ai and was occupied and then destroyed by the Israelites toward the end of the 15th Century B.C. A further find in 2014 of a small bronze

Canaanite deity with its head cleanly cut off as if by a sword cut. This also would support the Joshua narrative of destroying Canaanite idols.

The last piece of archeological evidence for the Conquest of Canaan comes from the city of Hazor, located just north of the Sea of Galilee. Since 1990, the site has been extensively excavated by the famous Israeli archeologist Amnon Ben-Tor of Hebrew University in Jerusalem. Professor Ben-Tor has found a major destruction layer at the site which has been radiocarbon dated to approximately 1220-1230 B.C. This data point has been used by one group of the Maximalists to demonstrate that the Conquest of Canaan by Joshua occurred much later than 1400 B.C.

However, there is a second significant destruction layer at Hazor which lies well below the 1220-1230 B.C. level. The Bible relates that Hazor was destroyed by the Israelites twice, once by Joshua (Joshua 11) and a second time during the period of the Judges by Deborah and

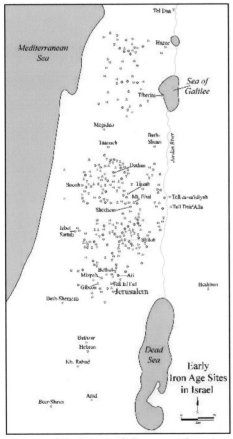

Figure 37. Map of Canaan showing new sites dating to the Early Iron Age (1200-1400 B.C.).
(Map illustrated by Lance K. Trask)

her general Barak (Judges 4-5). It is possible that the destruction layer dated by Amnon Ben-Tor could be from the time of the Judges and the older layer from Joshua. Time and more research will tell.

Assuming a Conquest of Canaan by Joshua at the end of the 15th Century B.C., what other evidence is there of an early settlement throughout Canaan by the Israelites? During the period between 1400 and 1200 B.C. (Early Iron Age), there was a major influx of new habitations in the central highland area of Canaan (Figure 37). These sites differ from the traditional Canaanite occupations in a number of ways. Chief among these is the presence of "Four-Room Houses", so named because they consist of four basic rooms usually arranged with three rooms parallel to one another with a fourth room perpendicular to the other three at the rear (Figure 38). The central room was usually an open courtyard where meal preparation also took place. One or both of the side rooms could be sub-divided and used

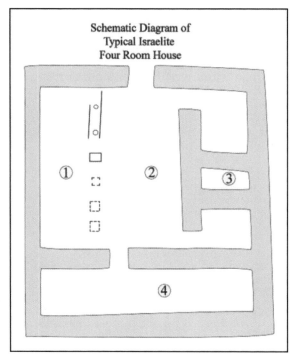

Schematic Diagram of
Typical Israelite
Four Room House

Figure 38. Schematic diagram of a basic Israelite Four-Room House (after a house found at Hazor, Northern Israel). (Figure drawn by Lance K. Trask)

as stables for livestock at night. The family lived either in the back room, or more commonly, a second floor was added on top of the back room and the inhabitants slept there or on the roof when the weather was warm. This style of house is absolutely unique to the Israelites and is found nowhere else in the Ancient Middle East. Thus its appearance after 1400 B.C. in the Early Iron Age in Canaan is significant.

The new settlements were also characterized by cruder, thicker pottery, storage jars that have distinctive "collared rims" (completely absent in Canaanite storage wares) (Figure 39), stone-lined storage pits, and cisterns carved out of the native limestone and plastered with slaked lime. The last are very significant as while the Canaanites also had water collecting cisterns, they did not use slaked lime to plaster the sides. This appears to be a purely Israelite invention and one which probably stemmed from having spent 40 years in the wilderness between Egypt and Canaan where water was always at a premium. Lastly, some of the new settlements were built on top of older Canaanite occupations but were more rural in nature, consisting of a few houses clustered together instead of forming larger towns or cities. While not yet definitive, all of these characteristics point to the new inhabitants of central Canaan as being Israelites following a conquest of the land at the end of the 15th Century B.C.

Joshua's last act before his death was to divide the land of Canaan amongst the 12

Figure 39. Examples of crude, early Israelite pottery from Lachish (ca. 1200 B.C.). (Wilson W. Crook, III Collection)

tribes of Israel (Figure 40). Note that Levi, the Priestly Tribe, did not receive a specific land allocation but instead was granted special cities within each tribal territory. Also there was no allocation for Joseph: his land was given as a "double portion" to his two sons, Manasseh and Ephraim. The tribe of Manasseh was so large that it was given land on both sides of the Jordan River. As is told in the Book of Judges, not all of the land was able to be settled because of the presence of the remaining Canaanites as well as the Philistines. Gradually over the next several hundred years, either through conquest and/or assimilation, Israel moved to occupy all of the land of Canaan.

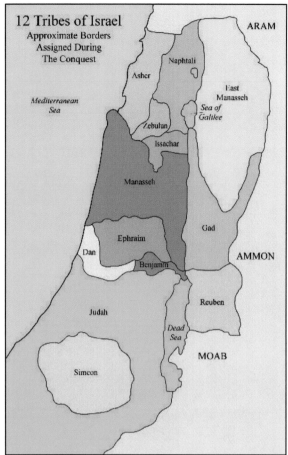

Figure 40. Map of Canaan as divided amongst the 12 Tribes of Israel. (Map illustrated by Lance K. Trask after Ralph F. Wilson, www.jesuswalk.com)

The United Monarchy

The so-called "United Monarchy" refers to the time when Israel decided to move from the period of the Judges to having its own King ("like the other nations" – I Samuel 8:4). This period, which lasted only about a century, had three main figures, Saul – the first King of Israel, David, and David's son, Solomon. Upon the death of Solomon, the ten tribes in the northern part of the kingdom broke away and founded their own kingdom (Northern Kingdom of Israel) while the two southern tribes took the name of the Kingdom of Judah. The aerial size of Israel reached its maximum extent during the reigns of David and Solomon including the regions of the Edomites (south of the Dead Sea), the Moabites (opposite the Dead Sea in modern Jordan), the Ammonites (modern northern Jordan) and parts of Syria.

We do not know exactly when Saul became the first King of Israel but the Bible says that Saul ruled for 42 years (I Samuel 13:1), David ruled for 40 years – 7 years in Hebron over Judah and 33 years over all of Israel (I Kings 2:1), and Solomon also ruled for 40 years (I Kings 11:42). Some scholars doubt the kingships of David and Solomon were exactly 40 years each as the number 40 was often used to express "a generation". David's death traditionally has been ascribed to 970 B.C. Therefore working backwards, David would have become King of Judah in Hebron around 1010 B.C. and King of all Israel in 1003 B.C. Saul ruled for 42 years and David did not become King of Judah until Saul had been killed at the battle of Gilboa. Thus, Saul would have ruled Israel from approximately 1052 to 1010 B.C. Solomon's reign would then have been from approximately 970 to 930 B.C. (Table 2).

Table 2. The United Monarchy of Israel

Name	Reign
Saul	ca. 1052-1010 B.C.
David	ca. 1010-1003 – Hebron ca. 1003-970 – Israel
Solomon	ca. 970-930 B.C.
Total Years	122 Years

Despite the fact that David and Solomon are two of the most famous figures from the Old Testament, prior to the 1990's there was no evidence of their existence outside the Bible and the Quran. The lack of extra-Biblical evidence was of course seized upon by the Minimalists as "proof" that all of early Israelite history was fiction, the product of later writing in order to give the nation a romantic sense of a glorious past:

"Joshua, Saul, David and Solomon are the stuff of legends, like King Arthur and the Knights of the Round Table" (David Ussishkin, Tel Aviv University)

In 1993, this all changed when a worker at an excavation of Tel Dan in extreme northern Israel stopped on his way home from the site and turned over a flat looking rock. The rock turned out to be part of a stela, or monument stone that had been inscribed on one side in Aramaic with part of a story of the victory of the Syrians over the armies of northern Israel. In the description of the defeated Israelites, the stela noted that their King's victory was over a

King from the "House of David" (*"bqtdwd"*). A replica of the Tel Dan inscription is shown in Figure 41 with a close-up of the words "House of David" in Figure 42. Clearly, if David had been a fictional character of a much later invention, there would be no mention of his name, let alone a reference to the "House of David". Moreover, the inscription implies the significance of David's stature as the Kings of the Northern Kingdom did not descend from his line; only those from the Southern Kingdom of Judah did. The victor wanted it known that he had beaten not just any King, but one from a great line of warrior Kings.

Figure 41. Exact replica of the Tel Dan inscription showing the words "House of David". (Wilson W. Crook, III Collection)

Figure 42. Close-up of the words "House of David" from the Tel Dan inscription. (Wilson W. Crook, III Collection)

After the discovery of the Tel Dan inscription, even the most ardent of the Minimalists had to admit the existence of a King named David, but they downplayed the degree of his importance saying that, at best, he was a local chieftain of a small tribe living in the hills of Judea.

In 1995, Dr. Eilat Mazar of Hebrew University set out to try and locate David's palace in the Old City of Jerusalem. She started by looking at II Samuel 5:17 which states that David went "down to the fortress" to meet the Philistines. Down from where? Perhaps his palace? So she looked in the area between the Temple Mount and the Old City and soon found some column capitals that were completed in the Phoenician style. This is significant as King Hiram of Tyre was known to have worked on David's palace. She expanded excavations in the area and six meters below the surface, she encountered Byzantine ruins from the 4th-6th Centuries A.D. Below this level were artifacts (mainly pottery) that dated from the Persian Period

(539-331 B.C.); and below that, she encountered a large rock foundation with many rooms. The walls of this structure were 2 meters thick, far greater than any other structure found inside the walls of the Old City. In the upper layers within the large building she found several clay bullae (inscribed pieces of clay used to seal a written document), one of which had an impression that read "Jehucal, son of Shelemiah, son of Shivi". Jehucal was a member of the court of King Zedekiah of Judah and is mentioned in the 37th and 38th chapters of the Book of Jeremiah. Below this level were pottery sherds which dated to the 10th Century B.C. – the time of King David. Nowhere in all the levels of this structure, from the 10th Century to the time of the Babylonian destruction, did she find a single idol, strengthening the conclusion that the structure was likely the residence of monotheistic Jewish kings.

Dr. Mazar was faced with the fact that she had an extraordinarily large structure that was at the right place to be a palace, was at the right time (lowest levels dated to the 10th Century B.C.), with Phoenician column capitals nearby, no idol statues, and a clay bulla that indicated the area had been used as a Royal Palace during the early 6th Century B.C. She thus concluded that it was highly likely that she had indeed found King David's palace (Figure 43).

Figure 43. Dr. Eilat Mazar's excavations of what is believed to be the palace of King David in Jerusalem. The large square structure in the middle of the photo is the base of a large tower.

More recently, Yosef Garfinkel of Hebrew University has been excavating a site located about 20 miles southwest of Jerusalem in the Judean Shephelah (lowlands) at a place known as Khirbet Qeiyafa. Khirbet Qeiyafa is a relatively small site (5.7 acres) that sits on top of a bluff overlooking the Valley of Elah (the traditional site where David defeated Goliath). The site oversees the main road between Philistia and Jerusalem and may be the Biblical city of Shaaraim ("Two Gates") (I Samuel 17:52). Khirbet Qeiyafa has an outer wall that stretches for 600 meters made up of very large stones (1.5 meters thick weighing up to 4 tons each). There is a thinner inner wall which is attached to the outer wall in a casement structure (rooms between the two walls which could be filled in to strengthen the outer wall during attacks). Two "four chamber" gates are present, one on the western wall facing Philistia and one on the southern wall facing Jerusalem. Ancient city gates were often constructed in a series of defensive chambers making it much more difficult for invaders to fight their way into the city. David is believed to have invented the "four chamber" gate and his son, Solomon, improved it to a massive "six chamber" gate system. A major administrative building is situated in the middle of the walled city with walls thicker than any other structure found in Early Iron Age Israel. A total of 28 radiocarbon dates on olive pits and one grape seed yielded an average date of ca. 961-1006 B.C. (68% probability). Animal bones are present throughout the ruins but pig bones are conspicuously absent. All the ceramics found at the site as well as the bronze weapons are consistent with a date in the early part of the 10th Century B.C. The site appears to have been occupied for only a short time, was destroyed and then abandoned.

The construction of Khirbet Qeiyafa appears to have been carried out in a single well-planned operation that involved considerable amounts of labor as well as expense. As the site dates almost precisely to the reign of King David, it must be assumed that it was built on David's instruction. The sheer size and magnitude of the fortifications were well beyond the capabilities of someone who was merely a "local tribal chieftain". Only a King, and a King of some magnitude, could have built Khirbet Qeiyafa.

Lastly, one of the great discoveries from the site was that of an "ostracon" which had some 70 characters on it arranged in five lines (an "ostracon" is a broken piece of pottery which was then used as a writing tablet). The writing is in "Proto-Canaanite" and is the oldest known piece of Hebrew writing. While there have been several translations, the generally accepted one is as follows:

Line 1: *You shall not do [it], but worship El*

Line 2: *Judge the slave and the widow; judge the orphan*

Line 3: *and the stranger. Plead for the infant, plead for the poor*

Line 4: *and the widow. Rehabilitate the poor at the hands of the King.*

Line 5: *Protect the poor and the slave; support the stranger.*

The passage sounds very "Biblical" and could either have been a practice tablet used by someone learning to write or by a scribe writing down a law given by an official or even the King. A reproduction of the ostracon is shown in Figure 44.

While there has now been considerable archeological evidence found to support the

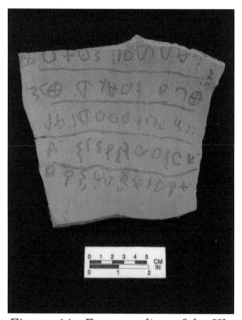

Figure 44. Exact replica of the Khirbet Qeiyafa ostracon – the earliest known Hebrew writing. (Wilson W. Crook, III Collection)

presence of King David in the manner described in I & II Samuel and I Kings, there has yet to be much concrete evidence for the extra-Biblical existence of King Solomon. In I Kings 3, the Bible tells us that when asked what he wanted from God, Solomon chose wisdom instead of fame and fortune. Pleased by Solomon's request, God grants him wisdom but then also great wealth as well (I Kings 10:23). Scholars have speculated about the exact source of King Solomon's great wealth. The quest for Solomon's riches led the English writer, H. Ryder Haggard, to pen his famous novel *King Solomon's Mines* in 1885, and people have been searching for Solomon's mines ever since.

At Timnah, about 15 miles north of the Israeli port city of Eilat at the head of the Gulf of Aqaba (Biblical Ezion-Geber), the remains of extensive copper workings can be found all across the region, some dating back as far as 6,000 years ago. Further north at Khirbet en-Nahas ("ruins of copper" in Arabic) in the Arabah Valley of Jordan, is another large group of ancient copper mines. Dr. Erez Ben-Yosef of Tel Aviv University has been excavating Timnah and since 2002, Dr. Thomas Levy of the University of California at San Diego has been working at

Khirbet en-Nahas. Both men have made some remarkable discoveries that may shed light on the reign of King Solomon.

At Khirbet en-Nahas, Levy has discovered 20 foot thick mounds of copper ore slag covering hundreds of acres. The volume of slag is so great that given an average copper content of 1-2 percent, over 100,000 tons of copper must have been extracted from this one area. Excavations have also uncovered a 24 acre city which has over 100 building structures. Several of the buildings are classic Israelite four-room houses. At one end of the complex is a 240 x 240 foot fortress that has a four-chamber gate, identical in structure to those found at Khirbet Qeiyafa. Collared-rim storage jars, carinated bowls and bronze arrowheads – all characteristic of Iron Age Israelite occupations – have been found throughout the fortress and house structures. Levy has obtained 37 radiocarbon dates from olive pits and charcoal found at the site ranging from the 12th Century B.C. to the 9th Century B.C. with the biggest cluster being in the middle of the 10th Century. There appears to have been a major spike in copper production around 950 B.C. The site was destroyed near the end of the 10th Century, possibly by the Egyptians.

At Timnah, Dr. Erez Ben-Yosef has found extensive copper deposits in the Cambrian age Nehustan and Mikhrot Formations, with copper occurring in ore grade quantities in 12-25 foot thick zones. Copper mineralization consists exclusively of secondary copper silicates and carbonates such as chrysocolla ($Cu_2(H_2Si_2O_5)(OH_4) \cdot nH_2O$), malachite ($Cu_2CO_3(OH)_2$), pseudomalachite ($Cu_5(PO_4)_2(OH)_4$), plancheite ($Cu_8Si_8O_{22}(OH)_4 \cdot H_2O$), and bisbeeite ($(Cu,Mg)SiO_3 \cdot nH_2O$) (Figure 45). No primary copper sulfides have been found at the site. Large copper smelters which are oriented east-west in order to take advantage of the prevailing easterly winds have been uncovered. Artifacts characteristic of both Israelite and earlier Edomite occupations have been recovered. Most recently, a number of small pieces of woven fabric,

Figure 45. Secondary copper minerals from the ancient mines at Timnah, Israel. (Wilson W. Crook, III Collection)

mainly from sheep's wool, were recovered, giving an indication of the types of simple clothing, bags and tents the mine workers must have had.

Solomon was known to have had a number of ocean-going ships at his disposal (I Kings 9:26). Given the apparent increase in copper production at both Khirbet en-Nahas and Timnah in the middle of the 10th Century B.C., perhaps these are the real "King Solomon's Mines" and Solomon was the copper king of the Ancient Middle East.

While there remains much more work to be done to define the full extent of the United Monarchy, the discoveries over the past 25 years are beginning to show that the reigns of David and Solomon were real and probably in the same terms as described to us in the Old Testament.

The Divided Kingdoms of Israel and Judah

In approximately 930 B.C., King Solomon died and the kingdom was given to his son, Rehoboam. Solomon's reign was marked by a large number of building projects both in Jerusalem and throughout Israel. This included the great Temple, a new palace, palaces for his many wives and concubines, and major new fortifications at the cities of Gezer, Megiddo and Hazor. To accomplish all of these projects, Solomon needed not only all of his wealth but also extensive taxes and conscripted labor. After 40 years of massive public works, the people were weary and asked Rehoboam if he could relax the financial pressure. Rehoboam did not listen to his elder counselors

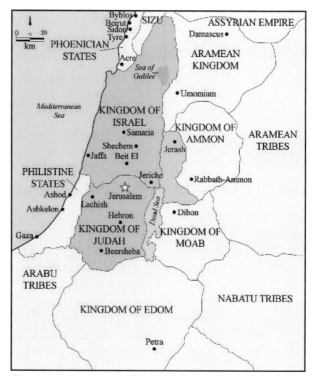

Figure 46. Map of the Divided Kingdom. (Map illustrated by Lance K. Trask)

but instead to his younger companions who did not want to see their life of luxury in Jerusalem diminish. When he refused the people's request, the 10 northern tribes revolted and formed their own kingdom which became known as the Northern Kingdom of Israel. Only the tribes of

Judah and Benjamin stayed with the original Davidic monarchy and formed the Southern Kingdom of Judah. The tribe of Simeon, originally granted a territory in the southern part of Israel surrounded by Judah, seems to have dwindled over time and became absorbed into Judah (Figure 46).

The first King of the Northern Kingdom of Israel was Jeroboam, who originally had been one of Solomon's chief overseers for building projects in Jerusalem. Jeroboam was seen as the leader of the revolt against Solomon and Rehoboam's oppressive taxation, a move that was initially supported by God (I Kings 11:31). However, immediately after assuming the throne of the Northern Kingdom, Jeroboam's first action was to set up cultic worship places in the new country, one in the north at Dan and one in the south at Bethel. Both places had long been centers of cultic worship during Canaanite times and thus there was already a tradition that established them as "holy places". The reason for Jeroboam's actions was his fear that with the Temple in Jerusalem in the Southern Kingdom of Judah, people in the Northern Kingdom might revert to their former center of worship in Jerusalem. The Bible states that Jeroboam built temples at both Dan and Bethel and installed a golden calf at each site as the worship deity (I Kings 12:25-33). Jeroboam made Shechem, located in the middle of Israel, his new capital.

The Biblical accounts of the histories of both the Northern Kingdom of Israel and the Southern Kingdom of Judah are given in the latter half of I Kings (Chapters 12-22) and in II Kings, as well as the books of I & II Chronicles. In both Kings and Chronicles, the reigns of the various Kings are given a Biblical assessment: either the King "did evil in the sight of the Lord" or he "did what was right in the sight of the Lord". In other words, there is a judgment given by the writers of both Kings and Chronicles on the success or failure in the sight of God of the Kings of the Divided Kingdom. Sadly, all of the 19 Kings of the Northern Kingdom of Israel received a failing grade (Jehu sometimes receives a "mixed" report) and only Asa, Jehoshaphat, Uzziah, Jotham, Hezekiah and Josiah were considered good Kings of the 20 rulers in Judah during the time of the Divided Kingdom (Joash and Amaziah both started out doing good in the early part of their reigns but then did evil) (Table 3). Equally sad is that the moral direction of each nation mirrored that of its leadership.

Table 3. List of the Kings of the Divided Monarchy ca. 1030 B.C. to 586 B.C.

Kings of Judah	Reign	Kings of Israel	Reign
Rehoboam	930-911 B.C.	Jeroboam	930-907 B.C.
Abijah	911-908	Nadab	907-906
Asa*	908-867	Baasha	907-883
Jehoshaphat*	867-846	Elah	883-882
Jehoram	846-843	Zimri	882
Ahaziah	843-842	Omri	882-871
Athaliah	842-836	Ahab	871-852
Joash	836-798	Ahaziah	852-851
Amaziah	798-769	Jehoram	851-842
Uzziah*	769-733	Jehu	842-814
Jotham*	758-743	Jehoaz	814-800
Ahaz	743-727	Joash	800-784
Hezekiah*	727-698	Jeroboam II	784-748
Manasseh	698-642	Zechariah	748
Amon	642-640	Shallum	748
Josiah*	640-609	Menahem	748-737
Jehoahaz	609	Pekahiah	737-735
Jehoiakim	609-598	Pekah	735-733
Jehoiachin	598-597	Hoshea	733-721
Zedekiah	597-586		
Babylonian Destruction		Assyrian Destruction	

Led by the example set by Jeroboam, worship of one god (monotheism) apparently never really occurred in the Northern Kingdom of Israel. There is some thought that in the beginning, worship of Yahweh (God) may have been retained but was corrupted by adding a Canaanite female deity as His consort (similar to Baal and his consort Astarte). However, if worship of Yahweh ever existed, it did not last long and worship quickly moved to the full Canaanite pantheon of gods and goddesses. King Ahab (ca. 871-852 B.C.) is thought to have been the leader that brought in full worship of the Canaanite deities as his wife, Queen Jezebel, daughter of King Ethbaal of Sidon (Phoenicia), was a devout follower of Baal and Astarte. Even her name is derived from *"Izevel"* meaning "Where is the Prince?" – a cry shouted at ceremonies honoring Baal. Her influence over the kingdom's religious practices led to the Prophet Elijah's challenge to the 400 priests of Baal which ultimately resulted in their slaughter by the prophet. Jezebel was so infuriated by this that Elijah had to flee the country to take refuge in the cave on the side of Mount Sinai (I Kings 18:16-46; I Kings 19:1-8).

The lack of moral leadership also led to lack of respect for the position of the King. Unlike the Southern Kingdom of Judah, where all of its rulers continued an uninterrupted line from King David, frequently the ruler of the Northern Kingdom of Israel came to the throne via assassination or military revolt (Table 4). God's reaction to the moral swing of the Israelites

Table 4. List of the Kings of the Northern Kingdom of Israel and the Manner they Assumed the Throne

King	Manner of Succession	Reign (Years)
Jeroboam I	Led Israel's revolt of Judah	23
Nadab	Son of Jeroboam	1
Baasha	Assassinated Nadab and entire royal family	23
Elah	Son of Baasha	1
Zimri	Assassinated Elah	<1
Omri	Proclaimed King over Zimri	11
Ahab	Son of Omri	19
Ahaziah	Son of Ahab	1
Jehoram	Son of Ahab	9
Jehu	Assassinated Jehoram	28
Jehoahaz	Son of Jehu	14
Joash	Son of Jehoahaz	16
Jeroboam II	Son of Joash	36
Zechariah	Son of Jeroboam II	<1
Shallum	Assassinated Zechariah	<1
Menahem	Assassinated Shallum	11
Pekahiah	Son of Menahem	2
Pekah	Assassinated Pekahiah	2
Hoshea	Assassinated Pekah	12

was to send a series of prophets including Elijah, then Elisha, and finally Amos and Hosea. The prophetic warning by these last two prophets to turn back to the worship of God came during the latter part of the reign of King Jeroboam II. This was a time of great prosperity in the Northern Kingdom. Jeroboam II had conquered Moab and Ammon and had defeated the Syrians and controlled part of their territory. King Uzziah was in self-exile in Judah and the

Southern Kingdom was largely subservient to Israel. However, with growing prosperity also came less focus on worship of God. There were abundant rituals but little real practice or sincere worship. Moreover, the reign of Jeroboam II was also a period of growing social injustice at all levels. Taxes on the poor were high; those who could not keep up with tax payments had their property confiscated and sometimes were even thrown into indentured servitude. High usurious lending rates were common and people on the margin were encouraged to borrow. As a result, there was a great disparity between the "haves" and the "have nots"; the rich got richer and the poor got poorer. The Northern Kingdom's predilection for luxury items was well known since the reign of King Omri and his son Ahab. Ahab's father, Omri, moved the capital of Israel to Samaria and there built a magnificent palace for himself. The Bible states that Ahab's own palace in Samaria was "adorned with ivory" (I Kings 22:39), a fact verified by archeologist who continue to find thousands of fragments of ivory at the site today.

While things appeared to be going well, the Northern Kingdom was unprepared to meet a new threat coming from Mesopotamia. The rise of Emperor Tiglath-Pileser III (Biblical "Pul") in 745 B.C. would see Assyria grow into the dominant power in the Ancient Middle East in just a few short years. Too late, the Northern Kingdom tried to form a military alliance with Syria but when Tiglath-Pileser III crushed Damascus and the Syrian city-states in 732 B.C., Israel was obliged to surrender and pay tribute. In an effort to appease the Assyrians, the Israelites also adopted many of the Assyrian gods and began to worship them as well as the Canaanite deities. When King Hoshea attempted to form an alliance with Egypt to counter Assyria, the Assyrians marched on Israel, besieged the capitol of Samaria for three years, captured King Hoshea and carried him and many of the citizens off into captivity, putting an end to the Northern Kingdom (721 B.C.). The removal of the Israelites into Assyrian captivity is the origin for the story of the "Lost Tribes of Israel". The captives were resettled across the Assyrian Empire, most likely as slave labor and Israel ceased to be a recognized entity. Those who were not removed intermixed with new settlers from Assyria and over time became known as the Samaritans of New Testament infamy.

The story of the Southern Kingdom of Judah is not much better than its northern counterpart. Scholars now debate whether Judah was ever truly monotheistic until after the return of the exiles from the Babylonian captivity in 539 B.C. It seems that while worship of Yahweh (God) continued in the Temple, the people adopted the concept of a female consort.

Worship of a female goddess alongside Yahweh seems to have been prevalent in Judahite households, possibly led by women who felt somewhat disenfranchised by the male-dominated society of the time. Thousands of so-called "pillar figures" have been found in excavations of Judean households from the period between 600-800 B.C. These figurines differ from those of traditional Canaanite worship as they are devoid of any anatomical detail from below the waist (Figure 47) but clearly accentuate the breasts which are a recognized symbol of fertility.

Figure 47. "Pillar Figurine" from Judah (600-800 B.C.). (Wilson W. Crook, III Collection)

Another distinctive artifact of the period of the Divided Kingdom is a new type of ceramic vessel known as a "Pilgrim's Flask". These vessels are flattened juglets that have two carrying handles near the mouth (Figure 48). The volume of liquid that they could hold is relatively small so they are thought to have been carriers of special oils or spices to be used in a religious ceremony, probably as an offering.

The general time period of the Divided Kingdom, and certainly the period between ca. 900-750 B.C., was one of general weakness in the traditional powers of the region – Egypt and Assyria. Both nations went through periods of internal turmoil and as a result, were more inwardly focused rather than worrying about the minor states in Palestine. Relations between the two Israelite states varied but were never truly friendly. There was an occasional "war" (usually a small, short-lived dispute) but no great amount of territory ever changed hands. Regional power either in the North (Israel) or the South (Judah) waxed and waned but conflict was more concentrated on control of neighboring nations such as Edom, Moab, Ammon and the Syri-

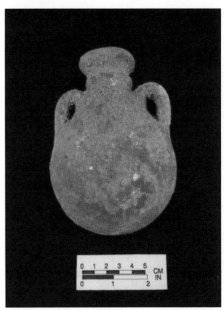

Figure 48. "Pilgrim's Flask" from Judah (600-800 B.C.). (Wilson W. Crook, III Collection)

an city-states than against each other. By and large, both Israel and Judah remained agrarian societies focusing on production of the "Seven Fruits of Israel" – wheat, barley, olives, figs, grapes, pomegranates and honey.

As mentioned above, when Tiglath-Pileser III created the modern Assyrian state (Neo-Assyrian Empire) in 745 B.C., Judah became a vassal state to Assyria, the latter not wishing to destroy Judah but to take advantage of the lucrative olive (oil) trade. After Tiglath-Pileser died,

Figure 49. A portion of Hezekiah's "Broad Wall" preserved in Jerusalem today.

his sons Shalmaneser V (727-722 B.C.) and then Sargon II (722-705 B.C.) assumed the Assyrian throne. Sargon II was a superior military leader and when he died in 705 B.C., many vassal states, especially those on the outer fringes of the Assyrian Empire, saw this as their opportunity to revolt. King Hezekiah of Judah (ca. 727-698 B.C.) formed an alliance with Phoenicia and Philistia and stopped paying tribute to the Assyrians. The new Assyrian King, Sargon's son and Tiglath-Pileser's grandson, Sennacherib, was enraged but had to put down revolts all around the empire before he could concentrate on the rebellious Palestinian states. This gave Hezekiah the time he needed to shore up the defenses of Jerusalem and elsewhere in Judah. In particular, he greatly expanded Jerusalem's defensive walls by as much as 21 feet. This has become known as "Hezekiah's Broad Wall", parts of which can still be seen preserved underneath modern Jerusalem (Figure 49).

The other major defensive work Hezekiah undertook in Jerusalem was the protection of the city's water supply which has become known as "Hezekiah's Tunnel" or the "Siloam Tunnel".

"When Hezekiah saw that Sennacherib intended to attack Jerusalem, he planned with his civil and military officers to stop up the water of the springs outside the city; and they helped him. They gathered together a large number of people and stopped up all of the springs and the stream which flowed through the land.

'Why should the King of Assyria come here and find much water?' they asked. Hezekiah closed the upper outlets of the waters of Gihon and directed them down to the west side of the City of David" (II Chronicles 32:2-4)

The old city of Jerusalem was located on a small limestone hill separated on three sides by steep valleys. As such, it was a very defensible position but suffered from the drawback that its major source of fresh water, the Spring of Gihon, lies outside the city walls on the slope of the hill facing the Kidron Valley. Fearing that Jerusalem would be besieged by the Assyrians, Hezekiah had surface access to the spring walled up and then initiated the construction of a long, sub-surface tunnel from the Spring of Gihon to a natural low spot in the city called Siloam, at which point he created a water reservoir ("Pool of Siloam"). Construction of the tunnel was initiated in 705 B.C. with teams starting at each location and digging toward one another. Digging of both tunnels was apparently directed from the surface as the excavation was as much as 130 feet below ground near the Spring of Gihon. The completed tunnel was approximately 1,750 feet in length and constructed with a 12 inch (0.6%) gradient from the Gihon Spring (high point) to the Pool of Siloam (low point). The tunnel averages about 5 feet in height (2 feet wide) but expands to nearly 16 feet in height at the Pool of Siloam due to natural fissures in the limestone (Figures 50-53). In 1880, an Arab boy explored the then-forgotten tunnel and found an inscription in the wall where the two digging teams finally met. He removed the inscription and tried to sell it on the antiquities market. Ottoman Empire officials, who controlled Palestine at the time, found out about the artifact, confiscated it and placed it in the Topkapi Palace in Istanbul where it resides today. The inscription tells the story of the meeting of the two tunnels:

"And this is the account of the breakthrough. While the laborers were still working with their picks, each toward the other, and while there were still three cubits to be broken through, the voice of each was heard calling to the other, because there was a crack in the rock to the south and to the north. And at the moment of the breakthrough, the laborers struck each toward the other, pick against pick. Then the water flowed from the spring to the pool for 1200 cubits.

And the height of the rock above the heads of the laborers was 100 cubits."
(Inscription at the meeting place of the two tunnels)

Figure 50. Entering Hezekiah's Tunnel at the Spring of Gihon.

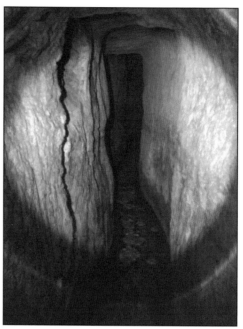

Figure 51. Inside Hezekiah's Tunnel.

Figure 52. The author, his wife Ginny, and friend Gary Schwantz exiting Hezekiah's Tunnel at the Pool of Siloam.

Figure 53. The Pool of Siloam.

The tunnel was completed in 701 B.C., just before Sennacherib laid siege to Jerusalem. After crushing the Phoenicians and the Philistines, Sennacherib destroyed 46 cities throughout Israel (Micah 1:8-16; II Kings 18:9-15), of which the most violent attack was the siege and total destruction of Lachish in southern Judah. Detailed depictions of this battle were carved onto long slabs of gypsum and placed in the royal palace at Nineveh and they can be seen today in their entirety in the Assyrian rooms at the British Museum in London. Jerusalem was indeed besieged by the Assyrians but God sent a plague which destroyed 185,000 of their troops and the siege was ended. Hezekiah agreed to pay tribute to Assyria and released some of its allies which he held captive (II Kings 19:35).

King Hezekiah died in ca. 698 B.C. and his eldest son, Manasseh, assumed the throne. Manasseh ruled Judah for 56 years and was known as both the longest-lived ruler and by far the most wicked in the history of the Divided Kingdom. Unlike his father, Manasseh did not hold to the worship of Yahweh (God) but instead not only reverted to the Canaanite fertility deities, but additionally brought in worship of the Ammonite chief god, Milcom (Molech), and the principal Moabite deity, Chemosh. Worship of these two gods demanded child sacrifice, not in the manner of the Canaanites, but by throwing the child alive into sacrificial fires. Apparently this practice became so common that one section of the Hinnom Valley on the south side of Jerusalem became known as *"Tophet"* because of the sacrifice of so many children. *"Tophet"* is derived from the Hebrew words *"toph"* meaning drum and *"taph"* meaning to burn, evidently derived from the priests' use of drums to drown out the sounds of the burning children. This abominable practice was continued by Manasseh's son, Amon, during his two year rule. When Amon died in ca. 640 B.C., he left his nine year old son Josiah on the throne. It appears that Manasseh's and Amon's advisors largely ruled for the young King until the priests of Yahweh "discovered" the "Scroll of the Law" (probably the Book of Deuteronomy) hidden away inside the Temple. It is unknown if the location of the scroll had been known all along or was actually found by the priests, but when it was read to the King, Josiah realized how badly deviated the worship in Judah had become from God's standards. He immediately instituted a series of wide-sweeping reforms which resulted in the destruction of many of the pagan worship places as well as the reinstitution of worship of the one God, Yahweh. Archeological evidence that Josiah's reforms did indeed take place comes in the form of destroyed pagan deities, many of which show clean cut marks from having been destroyed by a sword (Figure 54).

Figure 54. Cleanly severed head of a Pillared Figurine goddess. (Wilson W. Crook, III Collection)

In 612 B.C., the rising Neo-Babylonian Empire captured the Assyrian capital of Nineveh and sent what remained of the Assyrian army west into Anatolia and Syria. Seizing an opportunity to finally rid his kingdom of the Assyrian yoke, King Josiah made an alliance with the Babylonians. The Assyrians, realizing that they were truly in danger, made the unprecedented move to form an alliance with their traditional enemy, Egypt. The Egyptians, who had been in a prolonged period of non-influence over Palestine, saw a chance to regain control over the entire Levant and moved north to join with the Assyrians. The Babylonians assigned Josiah the task of stopping the Egyptians from joining up with the Assyrians and thus he moved his army north into the Jezreel Valley. In 609 B.C., the two armies met at the Battle of Megiddo (Armageddon) where Judah stopped the advance of the Egyptians but King Josiah lost his life as a result of an arrow to the eye. Josiah's followers quickly placed his third son, Jehoahaz, on the throne. No reasons are given why the elder sons were bypassed but Biblical scholars have speculated that the 18 year old Jehoahaz was a devout follower of Yahweh and would have continued his father's religious reforms. The Egyptian Pharaoh Necho II refused to accept this, marched on Jerusalem, placed Josiah's eldest son Eliakim on the throne, and carried Jehoahaz off to captivity in Egypt. Although he was defeated, Josiah's brave actions prevented the union of the Egyptians with the Assyrians in time and the latter were ultimately completely destroyed by the Babylonians.

Eliakim took the throne name of Jehoiakim and ruled Judah for 11 years. Jehoiakim reverted to the ways of Manasseh and Amon and once again permitted open worship of all the pagan deities of Canaan, Ammon and Moab. Initially siding with the Egyptians, he switched his allegiance to Babylon when King Nebuchadnezzar of Babylon marched on Jerusalem after his victory over the Egyptians at Carchemish in 605 B.C. However, in 598 B.C., Jehoiakim revolted against Babylon believing that Egypt would come to his aid. As Nebuchadnezzar's army approached Jerusalem, Jehoiakim died and his 18 year old son, Jehoiachin (also known as "Jeconiah" or "Coniah") was placed on the throne. The young King stayed on the throne for three months until the Babylonian army arrived, at which time he surrendered and was carried off into captivity. Nebuchadnezzar placed Jehoiachin's uncle (Josiah's youngest son) Mattaniah on the throne who took the King-name of Zedekiah. Interestingly, Jehoiachin was apparently treated well in Babylon as he is listed in their records as being invited to a royal dinner in his honor some 35 years later.

Zedekiah initially was loyal to Babylon but later he too was convinced to revolt in 588 B.C. After a brutal, two year siege, the Babylonians captured Jerusalem and burned the entire city to the ground, including the Temple built by Solomon. Zedekiah tried to escape the doomed city but was captured. His family was dragged before him and Zedekiah was forced to watch them killed, one by one, before his eyes. He was then blinded by hot pokers and carried off into captivity, never to be heard of again. The destruction of Jerusalem and the Temple ends the story of the Divided Kingdom of Israel and Judah.

The Babylonian Exile

No period of time has had as much influence on the Israelite people as the Babylonian Exile. Traditionally, the dates of the exile start from the fall of Jerusalem in 586 B.C. to the capture of Babylon by Cyrus the Great of Persia in 539 BC. (47 years). However, in reality there was not one but three exiles from Judah to Babylon. The first came in approximately 605 B.C. when King Nebuchadnezzar marched on Jerusalem after annihilating the remaining part of the Assyrian army at the battle of Carchemish. At that time, Nebuchadnezzar took as "captives" a few of the youngest "rising stars" of Judean society. Babylonian policy was to take these young men from captured parts of the empire, bring them to the court in Babylon, train them in Babylonian language, laws, religion and policy, and then place them back in their native lands as "Babylonianized" leaders. The prophet Daniel and his friends Shadrach, Meshach and Abednego were believed to have been taken as part of the first Babylonian exile.

When Nebuchadnezzar had to march again on Jerusalem to put down King Jehoiakim's revolt in 597 B.C., more Judeans were taken into captivity including the prophet Ezekiel. The last deportation occurred when Jerusalem was destroyed in 586 B.C. Scholars estimate that about 10,000 people in total were taken to Babylon including all the skilled craftsmen, political, religious and military leaders, and anyone else who could either be of service to the Babylonians or could potentially cause another revolt. People in the rural countryside of Judah were largely left alone, although much of their crops were either taken or burned. Survivors of the Babylonian conquest of Judah endured a number of famines during the years of the exile.

Contrary to popular Jewish writings at the time, the exile was not as severe as was recorded in Psalm 137:

> *"By the waters of Babylon we sat and wept when we remembered Zion.*
> *There on the poplars we hung our harps, for there our captors asked us for songs, our tormentors demanded songs of joy; they said, "Sing us one of the songs of Zion! "How can we sing the songs of the Lord while in a foreign land! If I forget you, O Jerusalem, may my right hand forget its skill. May my tongue cling to the roof of my mouth if I do not remember you, if I do not consider Jerusalem my highest joy. Remember, O Lord, what the Edomites did on the day Jerusalem fell. "Tear it down", they cried, "Tear it down to its foundations!" O Daughter of Babylon, doomed to destruction, happy is he who repays you for what you have done to us,*
> *He who seizes your infants and dashes them against the rocks".*

In fact, life in Babylon was so prosperous that when the exiles were allowed to return to Judah in 539 B.C., only a small number of those in exile chose to do so; the remainder stayed in Babylon and continued on in their businesses for centuries. Babylonian society was organized into three tiers: (1) Babylonian citizens who could vote and hold political office, (2) a middle class made up largely of foreigners who did not have as many rights as ethnic Babylonians but nonetheless could own property, set up businesses, and even own slaves, and (3) the lower class made up of true slaves. The exiles brought to Babylon from Judah were assigned this middle class status. Some of the exiles were actually brought to the capital city of Babylon but most were apparently settled in a community called "Tel Abib" ("Spring Mound" or the "Mound of the Deluge") located about 50 miles southeast of Babylon near Nippur on the

Chebar Canal (Ezekiel 3:15). The Israelites in exile referred to themselves as *"gola"* (exiles) or *ben-gola* (children of the exiles).

Also contrary to popular thought, Babylon, unlike Assyria, was not built on a society of war and conquest. Babylon was a huge center of commerce – the New York or London of its day – and had major businesses for banking, insurance, money lending, currency exchange, and jewelry, especially in precious stones. Before the Babylonian exile, the state of Judah was largely an agrarian society. When the exiles returned, Judah became a mixture of agriculture and commerce. New commercial districts sprung up in Jerusalem, even immediately adjacent to the Temple. The Jews themselves became very adept at certain businesses, such as banking, insurance, money lending and jewelry – all industries associated with the Jewish people today.

Without the presence of the Temple, worship services moved to the synagogues which the exiles were allowed to build and worship in while in Babylon. Rabbinic thought, interpretation of the scriptures, and leadership became increasingly important. This would ultimately sow the seeds of the emergence of the Pharisees which would later compete for power and influence with the priestly and royal leadership of the Sadducees. The exiles further adopted a number of Babylonian beliefs and customs. While in exile, the people reorganized themselves by clans instead of tribes, something that carries on to this day (the exception is the priestly tribe of Levi). The Jewish calendar, still in use today, is almost identical to the Babylonian calendar (Table 5). The exiles began celebrating monthly feasts on the 15th of each month – which coincided with the monthly celebrations to the Babylonian goddess Ishtar. Before the exile, angels were depicted as human-like creatures; after the Babylonian exile, all angels are pictured with wings, mirroring the winged messengers of the Babylonian gods. There was also the rise in the belief in demons, especially the demon, "Lilith".

According to Jewish tradition which probably started in Babylonia, Lilith (from *"layil"* or night) was Adam's first wife, created from the same earth as Adam (Genesis 1:27). Lilith considered herself equal to Adam and refused to be submissive to him (notably during sex); she then fled from the Garden of Eden. A second wife (Eve) was then created from Adam's rib (Genesis 2:21-23). Infuriated that another woman had taken her rightful place, Lilith changed into a demon that was said to haunt the mothers of newborn children. The legend may have been created as a means to explain the tragic nature of Sudden Infant Death syndrome but it has survived to this day through a cradle song sung to children at night which originally went

Table 5. Comparison of Modern Jewish Calendar to Babylonian Calendar

Jewish Month	Babylonian Month	Julian Calendar
Nisan	Nisanu	March - April
Iyyar	Ayaru	April - May
Sivan	Simanu	May - June
Tamuz	Du-uzu	June - July
Ab	Abu	July - August
Elul	Elulu	August - September
Tishri	Teshritu	September - October
Marcheshvan	Ara-samma	October - November
Chislev	Kislimu	November - December
Tebeth	Tebitu	December - January
Shebat	Shabatu	January - February
Adar	Adaru	February - March

"Lilith go bye (go away)" and has come down to us as "lullaby". The Lilith tradition spawned an entire genre of artifacts known as "incantation bowls" which are known from Babylon (later

Persia) from the 4th Century B.C. to the 6th Century A.D. These bowls (sometimes even human skulls are used) have circular "spells" written on them to ward off evil spirits of all kinds, but notably Lilith (Figure 55).

After the death of Nebuchadnezzar in 562 B.C., the Babylonian Empire went through a series of progressively weaker rulers. Cyrus the Great of Persia was able to enter Babylon in 539 B.C. almost unopposed and the former Neo-Babylonian Empire was annexed into Persia. One of Cyrus'

Figure 55. Jewish incantation bowl from Babylon (4th Century B.C.).
(Wilson W. Crook, III Collection)

first actions as the ruler of Babylon was to issue an edict of freedom for all the captives. People would be allowed to return to their respective homelands, rebuild their cities, and live in peace as long as they remained loyal to Cyrus and the Persian Empire. This edict, which has survived to this day, is known as the "Cyrus Cylinder," and is the first known document relating to basic human freedoms. As such, a copy of it now resides in the antechamber of the United Nations building in New York while the original is in the Persian Room of the British Museum in London (Figure 56). With the issuance of freedom by Cyrus the Great, the Jews were allowed to return to Judah and the Babylonian Exile was over.

Figure 56.   Replica of the Cyrus Cylinder from 539 B.C. (Wilson W. Crook, III Collection)

The Persian Period (Judah After the Babylonian Exile)

The Persian Period began with Cyrus' defeat of Babylonia in 539 B.C., and ended when Alexander the Great conquered the Persian Empire in 331 B.C. (208 years). During this time, a portion of the Jews (the term used by the Persians to denote citizens of Judah) returned to Israel and began to rebuild Jerusalem and the Temple. Judah was designated as a sub-province called "*Yehud Medinata*" within the larger Satrap (Province) of "*Eber-Nari*" (Beyond the River). The new Judah was considerably smaller than the Israel of the United Monarchy or even the Judah of the Divided Kingdom. The province was a relatively small, 30 x 30 mile area that stretched from the southernmost part of the River Jordan in the east to the edge of the Judean highlands in the west and included Jerusalem near its center (Figure 57). What was once the

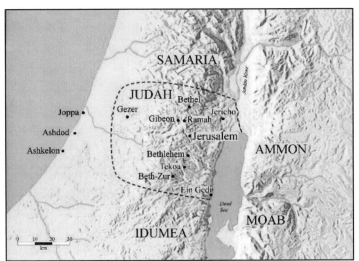

Figure 57. Map of Persian Sub-Province of Judah. (Map illustrated by Lance K. Trask)

southern part of Judah had been settled by Edomites who had moved to the west as they were gradually displaced from their native homeland south of the Dead Sea. The area to the north was called "Samaria" and consisted of the remnants of the Northern Kingdom of Israel intermixed with Assyrians, Babylonians and other peoples.

When Cyrus issued his famous edict of freedom (Ezra 1:1-6; 6:1-5) not all of the Jews living in the now Persian Empire wanted to return to Israel. The second chapter of the Book of Ezra details all of the people who participated in the "*Aliya*" – the return. The total number listed (by clan and not by tribe with the exception of the Levites) is 42,360 Jews, 200 male and female singers, and 7,337 slaves for a total of 49,897 people. Cyrus appointed Zerubbabel ("Born in Babylon"; Sheshbazzar was his Babylonian name) as the governor of the sub-province of Judah. Zerubbabel, while not a "King", was of the lineage of David and thus maintained the line of Davidic leadership. A search of the Babylonian temples retrieved 5,400 articles of gold and silver, which had been part of the Temple treasury. Cyrus also allowed these items to be transported back with the exiles. Those remaining in Persia, estimated by scholars to be several times the number of those that returned, donated a considerable sum of silver and gold to help with the rebuilding (Ezra 2:69).

We do not know precisely when Zerubbabel led the exiles back to Israel; scholars variously place the journey as early as 538 B.C. and as late as 535 B.C. The journey back up the Tigris-Euphrates Valley and down from Syria (~900 miles) would have taken several months to complete. Once back the returnees would have found a devastated land that had been beset by a series of famines. None of the major cities had been rebuilt and Jerusalem still lay in ruins. With no defensive infrastructure, the returnees were subject to constant raids by their neighbors, especially those from Edom. Zerubbabel spent roughly two years laying the large foundation stones for rebuilding the Temple. However, the work then stopped as the pressing needs of building houses, putting the fields back in order, planting and raising crops began to take precedent. After a period of about 15 years, God sent two prophets, Haggai and Zechariah, to support Zerubbabel and get the people back to work completing the Temple. Work restarted in ca. 521 B.C. and was completed in 516 B.C. There was a large celebration at the rededication of what became known as the "Second Temple"; however, those old enough to remember the beauty of Solomon's Temple cried as apparently the Second Temple, built by the unskilled hands of the returnees, was only a shadow of the original structure.

The Persians granted the returnees a fair amount of autonomy, provided that they remained loyal to the empire and the King. It was during the Persian Period that the first coins of the Jewish State were minted (coins did not gain popularity as a form of currency until the reign of King Darius I – 522-486 B.C.). The coins were typically of a rough oval shape, were made of either silver or bronze, and were stamped with the letter Y-H-D for Yehud (Judah) (Figure 58)

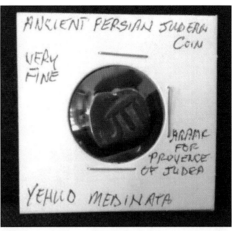

Figure 58.   Jewish coin with the stamp "Yehud" from the Persian Period.
(Wilson W. Crook, III Collection)

Fifty-eight years after the completion of the Second Temple, a second group of exiles returned led by the scribe Ezra in ca. 458 B.C. Ezra found the people were once again beginning to stray from the pure worship of one God so he implemented a series of religious reforms that are the foundations of what has become known as "Jewish Legalism". Since the time of Moses, Jewish law was separated into the "Written Law" – namely the five books of the Torah (Genesis, Exodus, Leviticus, Numbers and Deuteronomy), and the "Oral Law" which was composed of additional laws given to Moses by God on Mount Sinai which were separate from the Ten Commandments. This second part of the law was passed down through oral tradition within the Temple priests. With the rise of the synagogues during the Babylonian Exile, there was a growing amount of interpretations of the laws by various Rabbis (teachers) as a means to help the people live their lives as they believed God would have them live. The Rabbis would write interpretations of how the laws were to be applied to daily life, especially life in exile without the Temple. Ezra took all of this material and codified it into the *Mishna* and the *Gemara.* The *Mishna* contained the 613 additional laws (known as "*Mitzvots*") which were divided into 6 Orders covering (1) agriculture, (2) the Sabbath, (3) marriage and family law, (4) criminal and civil law, (5) Temple worship, and (6) ritual purity. The *Gemara* contained the teachings and interpretations made by both the priests and the Rabbis regarding how to put the law into practice in daily life. Together, these two bodies of law formed what is known as the "Talmud", which even to this day continues to be supplemented. The new codified law, especially the 613 *Mitzvots*, became the basis of the laws that fueled so many of the later confrontations between Jesus and the Pharisees.

In 445-444 B.C., the Persian Emperor Artaxerxes I (465-425 B.C.) allowed his cup-bearer, Nehemiah ("the Lord Strengthens") to return to Judah to assist the people in their defense of Jerusalem. While Ezra had provided some moral strength to the community, the walls and gates of Jerusalem were still not fully repaired and the people were in constant danger from raiding bands of bandits. Nehemiah supplied much needed leadership, re-organized the people into effective work parties, and in an amazing 52 days completely rebuilt Jerusalem's walls (Nehemiah 6:15). Some of this work required the moving and re-setting of larger stones but much of the work consisted of filling in the holes with smaller stones and rubbish such as broken pottery. The effectiveness of Nehemiah's wall can still be seen today where some of the original Jerusalem defensive walls have been exposed (Figure 57).

Figure 59. Original Jerusalem wall from the 6th Century B.C. Note all the small stones placed in the crevices to repair the wall's structure.

Often overlooked by both Biblical scholars and Pastors (when was the last time you heard a sermon from the Book of Nehemiah?), Nehemiah offers some of the best examples of true Godly leadership that can be found anywhere. These traits not only applied then, but I can personally attest to their superior application to the business world of the 21st Century. I will conclude this section by listing the top leadership lessons that can be found in the writings of this amazing man from the Persian Period.

Leadership Lessons from Nehemiah

- A Leader is keenly interested in the welfare of God's people (Nehemiah 1:2)
- A Leader pays attention to details and gathers all the correct information before acting (Nehemiah 1:3)
- A Leader has a heart for his people and his country (Nehemiah 1:3)
- A Leader is devoted to prayer and consults God with sincere prayer before acting (Nehemiah 1:4-10)
- The prayer of a Leader should demonstrate respect and a relationship with God including praise, confession of sin, call for a re-establishment of God's purpose, and a request for what is needed (Nehemiah 1:4-10)
- A Leader is willing to be patient and wait for God's timing (Nehemiah 2:3)
- A Leader is willing, for a time, to bear the burden of his people alone (Nehemiah 2:1)
- A Leader seeks wisdom and guidance from God before making the presentation of his project (Nehemiah 2:2-4)
- A Leader plans out all the essential details before the meeting (Nehemiah 2:5-8)
- A Leader has knowledge and awareness of the obstacles and opposition (Nehemiah 2:10)
- A Leader makes a personal assessment of what needs to be accomplished (Nehemiah 2:11-15)
- A Leader is not easily discouraged by obstacles or opposition (Nehemiah 2:14-15)
- A Leader motivates followers by sharing with them what God has done (Nehemiah 2:18)
- A Leader gives the people an opportunity to "own" the decision for the action (Nehemiah 2:18)
- A Leader allows for mutual support among the people to do the work (Nehemiah 2:18)
- A Leader inspires trust in God during times of trouble (Nehemiah 2:20)
- A Leader provides an organized plan so that everyone has a part and understands the objectives clearly (Nehemiah 3:1)

- A Leader assigns the best people for each task and holds them accountable for their completion (Nehemiah 3:1)

- A Leader keeps track of who does their job and who does extra – with both being rewarded accordingly (Nehemiah 3:4-4, 21)

- A Leader will recognize that some may feel they are "too important" for the work and has a ready plan to respond (Nehemiah 3:5-6, 12, 17-19)

- A Leader recognizes the group's success is in part due to a good attitude (Nehemiah 4:6)

- A Leader sets the tone for regular prayer to God (Nehemiah 4:9)

- A Leader remains vigilant for opposition (Nehemiah 4:9)

- A Leader exhorts the people to trust God for their defense but also makes preparation for battle as needed (Nehemiah 4:14)

- A Leader protects his people and is alert and prepared for all eventualities (Nehemiah 4:16-17, 23)

- A Leader knows how to effectively delegate authority (Nehemiah 4:18-19)

- A Leader has concern for those who have been unjustly treated (Nehemiah 5:1-6)

- A Leader takes time to reflect on the situation before confrontation; he does not act in anger but acts with Godly conviction and authority (Nehemiah 5:7-8)

- A Leader is willing to use the power available to him to right a wrong; he does not permit abuse (Nehemiah 5:7-13)

- A Leader identifies with the common person and is willing to do all the things he asks his people to do including working side-by-side (Nehemiah 4:23; 5:14)

- A Leader refuses to get distracted from the task for the sake of personal gain (Nehemiah 5:16)

- A Leader does not quit until the job is completed (Nehemiah 6:1-4)

- A Leader is prepared to handle all forms of opposition, including the questioning of his motives (Nehemiah 6:6-11)

- A Leader does not succumb to blackmail; he quickly refutes lies and goes to God for strength in prayer (Nehemiah 6:7-9)

- A Leader fears God but has no fear of man (Nehemiah 6:10-13)

- A Leader is able to discern when a man is not speaking the word of God (Nehemiah 6:12-14)

- When God ordained Leadership is involved, even the opposition will recognize the success of the venture (Nehemiah 6:16)

- A Leader recognizes that teaching God's Word and promotion of worship are the ultimate goals of any project (Nehemiah 8:6-8)

- A Leader makes the appointments for all responsible tasks including the handling of money (Nehemiah 12:44)

- A Leader makes a thorough review of the work after completion of the tasks (Nehemiah 13:7-11)

- A Leader will perform his role with one overriding motivation: to receive a commendation from God (Nehemiah 12:31)

Palestine in the First Century A.D.

After the death of Artaxerxes I in ca. 425 B.C., the Persian Empire went through a gradual period of decline ending with its complete collapse at the hands of Alexander of Macedon. After conquering the Persians, Alexander lived only eight more years, dying in Babylon in 323 B.C. His empire was divided amongst his generals ("Companions") with Ptolemy being given Egypt and Palestine, including Judah. A long period of civil war between Alexander's generals followed, ultimately leading to Palestine falling under the control of Seleucus, another of Alexander's boyhood friends and generals.

The Seleucids increasingly tried to Hellenize Judah, going so far as to bring pigs into the Temple and using the Temple Mount area for a gymnasium complete with naked athletes. These acts finally pushed the Jews to revolt against their Seleucid overlords in 167 B.C. ("Maccabean Revolt") resulting in an ultimate Jewish victory and the establishment of the first Jewish-controlled state since the Babylonian Exile. Independent Jewish rule lasted for a century until Palestine and Jerusalem were captured by Pompey the Great for Rome in 66-63 B.C. Rome, and its successor, the Byzantine Empire, would rule the region for the next 700 years.

Initially Rome allowed limited Jewish rule but the persistence of revolts against the empire led to Rome placing its own King on the throne of Judea. This action began the succession of the family of Herod the Great, who, along with Rome procurators, controlled Palestine for the next century.

Herod the Great was born in ca. 71-74 B.C., the second son of Antipater the Idumean, a high-ranking official under the Jewish King Hyrcanus II; his mother was Cypros, a Nabatean Princess (from Petra). At age 25 he was appointed the Governor for Galilee by the Roman Governor of the region. The brutality of Herod's rule was condemned by the Sanhedrin (the governing body of the Jewish people) and he was generally despised for being an Idumean (descendant of the Edomite people) and not an ethnic Jew. In the aftermath of the assassination of Julius Caesar, the young Herod was forced to choose which side in the Roman civil war he would pledge his allegiance to. Initially siding with the conspirators, he quickly changed sides as the war began to favor the side of Marc Anthony and Octavian (later Augustus Caesar). Octavian appointed Herod to be Tetrarch of Galilee but the Jewish people forced him to flee to Rome in exile. There, Octavian and the Roman Senate made Herod "King of the Jews" in 37 B.C.

Herod returned to Palestine with his Roman allies, routed the opposing forces and claimed his throne. He became close friends with both Marc Anthony and with Cleopatra. However, when Augustus defeated the forces of Anthony and Cleopatra at Actium and became the first Roman Emperor, Herod quickly switched sides again and pledged loyalty to the new Caesar. He was rewarded by Augustus by being confirmed King of Judea in 30 B.C. While Herod adopted all of the worship practices of his Jewish subjects, he continued to suffer from the fact that most of the Jews did not consider him to be one of them. To help remedy this, Herod married Mariamne, the granddaughter of the last Jewish King, Hyrcanus II. Herod already had one wife, Doris, at the time and he would marry another seven women in his lifetime, at least seven of which would bear him children. Herod was completely paranoid about losing his throne and he constantly perceived plots from his wives, and more especially from his sons, to replace him. As a result, he had three of his sons killed between 7 B.C. and 4 B.C. So ruthless was Herod towards his family that the Emperor Augustus once remarked. "It is better to be Herod's pig than son".

Herod the Great was known as a great architect and builder having built the fortress on the mountain top at Masada, the fortress at Herodium, a palace at Jericho, and the port of Caesarea Maritima with its artificial harbor (the construction done with revolutionary quick-drying cement under the sea). But his greatest building achievement was the complete rebuilding of the Second Temple in Jerusalem. To enlarge the Temple grounds, Herod's builders constructed a new platform that completely spanned all of Mount Moriah. The Second Temple itself was covered in gold, ivory and cedar, with a series of outer courts built on top of the new platform. The initial work on expanding the Temple Mount was completed between 20 B.C. and 10 B.C., but the final completion of all the rebuilding was not finished until ca. 60 A.D. Some of the stones used in building the platform's foundation weighed over 500 tons – the heaviest known building stones ever used (the great "Western Stone" is 48.6 feet in length by 9.8 feet height with an estimated width of 10.8 feet; it weighs an estimated 570 tons) (Figure 60). So impressive was the new structure that it was widely considered to be the single most impressive building in the entire Roman world. Today, all that remain are the stones making up part of the western side of the Temple Mount, known as the "Western" or "Wailing" Wall (Figures 61-62).

Herodian architecture wasn't always about massive projects. Some of the most beautiful art work has been found in the mosaics that frequently adorned floors and walls of palaces, synagogues and even private

Figure 60. The great "Western Stone" in the western wall of the Temple Mount, Jerusalem.

Figure 61. The "Western Wall" today at the Temple Mount, Jerusalem.

Figure 62. Massive stones making up the Western Wall in Jerusalem.

homes. In the 1970's, Mr. Robert Russell of Katy, Texas was invited to spend the summer with friends in the small town of Ein Kerem (Karem), located about 5 miles southwest of Jerusalem. Ein Kerem was the home of Zechariah and Elizabeth, the parents of John the Baptist. It is also the location where upon greeting her cousin Elizabeth, Mary was moved to sing the *Magnificat* (Luke 1:46-55). While there, Mr. Russell assisted the family he was staying with in some remodeling work

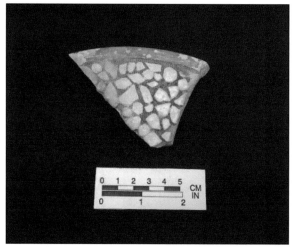

Figure 63. Herodian mosaic wall tile from Ein Kerem. (Wilson W. Crook, III Collection)

of their home. During this work, they discovered that the house was built on the ruins of a First Century A.D. home that had several rooms, a kitchen and a *"mikveh"* ritual bath. They also recovered a number of mosaic tiles. The Israeli Antiquities Authority identified the tiles as being Herodian (First Century A.D.) and from their thinness, suggested they were probably

Figure 64. Map of First Century A.D. Palestine. (Map illustrated by Lance K. Trask after The American Bible Society)

wall decorations as opposed to floor tiles. Mr. Russell kindly gave me his piece so that I could use it in my teaching (Figure 63).

Suffering from extreme depression and paranoia, Herod the Great died in ca. 4 B.C. from kidney failure brought on by painful gangrene of the genitals ("Fournier's Gangrene"). There is some controversy as to the actual date of Herod's death. The Roman historian Josephus recorded that Herod died shortly after a lunar eclipse. There was an eclipse in the spring of 4 B.C., but it was very minor and difficult to see. A much more prominent eclipse occurred in December, 1 B.C., which could be the actual date of Herod's death. With his passing, the Emperor Augustus divided Judea among Herod's surviving sons. Archelaus, son of Herod and Malthace the Samaritan, became "Ethnarch" (not King) of Judea and Samaria; his full brother, Herod Antipas, became "Tetrarch" of Galilee and Perea; and his half-brother, Herod Philip (son of Herod and Cleopatra of Jerusalem) became "Tetrarch" over the northeastern part of the kingdom including Ituraea and Trachonitus (Figure 64). The division followed Jewish tradition wherein the eldest son received a double portion of the inheritance (Ethnarch versus Tetrarch).

Archelaus was renowned for his cruelty – putting to death 3,000 Pharisees in a single day. He was considered so cruel that the Romans themselves found him unfit to rule and in 6 A.D., he was banished to Gaul where he died 12 years later. The Bible tells us that after Joseph had taken Mary and Jesus to safety in Egypt, he received a dream in which he learned that Herod had died. An angel told him that Archelaus had assumed the throne in Judea so Joseph returned to Nazareth (in Galilee under Herod Antipas) rather than to Jerusalem or Bethlehem (Matthew 2:22). With Archelaus gone, the Romans placed Judea and Samaria under direct Roman government, creating the position of "Procurator of Judea and Samaria". A Roman Procurator (Prefect) was a sub-governor; the Governor of the province that included all of Palestine and Syria was located in Damascus. Thus, the Judean Procurator reported directly to the regional Governor. This system lasted for the next 60 years until the region was placed under military governorship during the Jewish War (66-70 A.D.) (Table 6). Of these Procurators, at least three including Pontius Pilate (Luke 23; John 18:28-38; Mark 15:1-5; Matthew 27:1, 19), Felix (Acts 23-24) and Festus (Acts 25-26) are prominently mentioned in the New Testament.

Herod Antipas, full brother to Archelaus, ruled Galilee and Perea (the latter on the eastern side of the Jordan River) from 4 B.C. until he was exiled by the Emperor Caligula for treason. He died in Gaul in 39 A.D. Herod Antipas divorced his first wife and then seduced and married his half-brother Philip's wife, Herodias. This action brought condemnation from John the Baptist whom Herod later had imprisoned and executed (Mark 6:14-18; Matthew 14:1-11). Salome of "dance, Salome, dance" infamy, was Herodias' daughter and Antipas' step-daughter. Herod Antipas was the Herod spoken of in the gospels to whom Pilate handed Jesus over to be judged as Jesus had been most active in Herod's province of Galilee.

Herod Philip, half-brother to both Archelaus and Herod Antipas, ruled the extreme northeastern part of the kingdom until his death in 34 A.D. By all accounts he was a fair and just ruler unlike his brothers.

Herod Agrippa I was the favorite grandson of Herod the Great. He was sent to Rome as a young boy for his education and became a favorite of both the Emperor Tiberius and more especially, his successor, Caligula. With the death of Herod Philip and the exile of Herod Antipas, Caligula made Agrippa King of Iudeae (Judea), Galilee and Perea – a territory almost as large as his grandfather's. Agrippa was also known for his extreme cruelty. He had the apostle Peter arrested (Acts 12:1-19) and was responsible for the death of the apostle James. Acts 12:20-23 says that Herod Agrippa was killed (eaten by worms) by an angel of the Lord for his cruelty and blasphemy of God. Upon his death in 44 A.D., the Emperor Claudius re-instated the system of Roman procurators in Judea which had been temporarily suspended by Caligula (see Table 6).

Table 6. Roman Procurators of Judea and Samaria, 6-70 A.D.

Procurator	Dates	Office
Coponius	6-9 A.D.	Procurator
Marcus Ambivulus	9/12/2016	Procurator
Annius Rufus	12/15/2016	Procurator
Valerius Gratus	15-26	Procurator
Pontius Pilate	26-36	Procurator
Marcellus	36-37	Procurator
Marullus	37-41	Procurator
Herod Agrippa I	41-44	King of Judea
Cuspius Fadus	44-46	Procurator
Tiberius Julius Alexander	46-48	Procurator
Ventidius Cumanus	48-52	Procurator
Marcus Antonius Felix	52-60	Procurator
Porcius Festus	60-62	Procurator
Lucceius Albinus	62-64	Procurator
Gessius Florus	64-66	Procurator
Titus	66-70	Military Governor

The last member of the Herodian family to rule in Palestine was Herod Agrippa's son, Herod Agrippa II. Like his father, Agrippa was sent to Rome for his education. His father died when he was only 17 so the Emperor gave him a small territory north of Samaria known as Chalcis to rule. In 55 A.D., Claudius made him ruler of Galilee and Perea but also granted him oversight of the Temple in Jerusalem. This allowed Herod Agrippa II to appoint the High Priests and effectively oversee Jerusalem's administration which brought him into direct conflict with many Jews. According to the Roman historian Josephus, Herod Agrippa II lived in an incestuous relationship with his sister Bernice (also Berenice). He is recorded as being the judge over the initial trial of the apostle Paul (Acts 25 & 26) where he is pictured arriving with his sister Bernice. Herod Agrippa II ruled in Palestine until his death in approximately 100 A.D.

The other part of First Century Palestine is the so-called "*Decapolis*" – Greek for the "Ten Cities" (see Figure 60). These cities (and there were closer to 18-19 rather than just 10) were grouped together as a semi-autonomous unit after Rome conquered the region in 66 B.C. They remained a center of Roman-Greek culture and trade well beyond the First Century A.D. The most important cities in the Decapolis included Jerash, Pella, Scythopolis (Beth She'an), and Philadelphia (modern day Amman, Jordan).

Rome was the unquestioned power not only in the region of Palestine in the First Century A.D. but over most of the known world. According to the great Pharisee teacher Gamaliel (Paul's religious teacher), "No corner of the earth escaped the Romans, unless heat and cold made it of no value to them". As mentioned above, a Roman Procurator governed Judea, including Jerusalem, for most of the First Century A.D. The Governor made his home in Caesarea Maritima on the coast, traveling to Jerusalem only during important festivals and in times of public disorder. As a Procurator or Prefect, he did not have significant military forces at his disposal; that power was kept by the Governor for the region who was located in Damascus in Syria. During the First Century A.D. the Romans maintained three Legions in Syria (roughly 18,000 men plus auxiliaries); in Judea, the local Procurator would typically have had between 1,500-3,000 soldiers at his disposal, mostly auxiliaries or soldiers who were of regional origin.

The Romans kept order in Palestine through brute force and intimidation. In reality, the only importance of Palestine to the Romans was the payment of taxes and protection of valuable commerce, especially trade in olive oil and balsam. The latter was almost exclusively controlled through the southern Judean town of Ein Gedi. Balsam was the basis for many perfumes and as such, was an extremely lucrative trade item. This is ultimately the reason that the Romans decided to besiege the Judean citadel of Masada in 72-73 A.D. as the rebels camped out on the mountain were raiding Ein Gedi and threatening the lucrative balsam trade.

Within the Jewish population of Judea and Galilee, local administration came from the Sanhedrin ("Sitting Together"), composed of 71 members in an Upper and Lower House structure with the Temple's High Priest as its chair. There was no separation of church and state in Jewish Palestine so the Sadducees (Upper House) and the Pharisees (Lower House) controlled daily life, with Roman approval. The Sadducees (the name seems to derive from "Zadokites" – Solomon's High Priest) as a political organization were founded in the Second Century B.C. and lasted until the destruction of Jerusalem and the Temple by the Romans in 70 A.D. They were an elitist group composed of members of the priestly order and the descendants of the Jewish royal family. The focus of the Sadducees centered on Temple rituals and worship in the Temple (and on increasing their wealth as generated by Temple worship). They believed in a strict interpretation of the written law (Torah) and rejected any of the oral Torah tradition. The Sadducees further rejected the belief in angels and demons as well as the concept of the soul and the resurrection of the body. As such, their entire focus was on what could be accomplished during one's earthly life.

In direct contrast to the Sadducees were the Pharisees. This group also stems from the Second Century B.C., but from people who refused to accept any form of Hellenization by the Seleucid Greeks (the name "Pharisee" means the "separated ones"). The Pharisees were from more common stock but were highly educated, ultra-religious and legalistically focused. Rather than worship in the Temple, the Pharisees focused their attention on knowledge of the scriptures and worship in the local synagogues. They believed in both the written law as well as the oral tradition (Talmud). They believed in both angels and demons and in an afterlife in which God punishes the wicked and rewards the righteous, of which the most righteous of all, of course, were the Pharisees. Not all the Pharisees were bad, but in the end, they could not reconcile Jesus' actions and claims with their own understanding of piety and godliness which led to the many encounters between Jesus and the Pharisees as recorded throughout the gospels.

Even though these two groups effectively ruled together, there were many areas of conflict between the Sadducees and the Pharisees including:

- Class: wealthy vs. middle class
- Cultural: acceptance of Hellenism vs. strict opposition
- Religion: importance of the Temple vs. the synagogue
- Doctrine: written letter of the Law vs. Rabbinic tradition and interpretation of how to apply the law to life

In addition to the Sadducees and the Pharisees and their differences, there were several other religious and political groups which were active during First Century A.D. Palestine. One of these was the group we now know as the "Essenes". The Essenes emerged in the late Second Century A.D. largely in disgust at the actions of both the Sadducees and the Pharisees. They believed the Sadducees had corrupted the Temple and the Pharisees had corrupted the synagogues and the people. As a result, they withdrew to the wilderness in a self-imposed exile from society in order to contemplate worship of God and await deliverance of the Jewish people by the promised Messiah. The best known settlement of the Essenes was on the northern edge of the Dead Sea at Qumran (Figure 65). There they

Figure 65. Ruins of the Essene community at Qumran near the Dead Sea.

practiced an extreme form of religious purity and celibacy which demanded that they continually keep themselves "ritually clean" by immersing themselves periodically in a ritual bath or *mikveh* (Figure 66). Oddly, this practice, coupled with their extreme toilet restrictions, may have ultimately led to the downfall of their society. The Essenes believed that all toilet activities must be carried out away from eyesight of the community. After relieving themselves, they then had to immerse themselves in a *mikveh* before they could re-enter the Qumran society. Researchers studying both the toilet area of the Qumran community as well as the skeletons of the Qumran cemetery have found that many people suffered from diseases probably brought on by spreading fecal matter into the body by walking into these ritual baths.

Figure 66. A Mikveh or ritual bath at Qumran.

Despite their reclusive lifestyle, the Essenes have left us one great treasure: the earliest known texts of the books of the Old Testament which are now known as the "Dead Sea Scrolls". In the caves in and around the Qumran community, a total of 931 documents have been found which represent 38 of the 39 books of the Old Testament (only the Book of Esther is not represented). In addition to Biblical literature, the scrolls contain many of the beliefs and rules of the Essene community, including a great many documents dealing with the coming global apocalypse which involves the great battle between the "Sons of Light" and the "Sons of Darkness". The most prolific cave at Qumran, Cave 4, contained over 15,000 fragments of texts including 122 copies of books in the Bible (Figure 67). While many of the scrolls are still being

Figure 67. The prolific Cave 4 at Qumran, location of the discovery of many copies of the Dead Sea Scrolls.

reassembled and translated, those copies of the books in our Bible have been shown to be more than 95 percent compatible word-for-word with our modern texts.

The Romans used Qumran as a military camp after the destruction of Jerusalem in 70 A.D. All the Essenes either fled or were killed and the sect completely disappeared from history until Bedouin shepherds found the scrolls in the caves in 1946.

The last political groups operating in Palestine in the First Century A.D. were the revolutionaries – the Zealots and the Sicarii. Both groups emerged during the First Century, largely in opposition to the Roman Empire. The zealots were a largely a non-violent group; the apostle "Simon the Zealot" may have belonged to this group prior to joining Jesus' ministry. The Sicarii ("Dagger Men") were not only ultra-nationalistic but openly advocated the use of terror against their Roman rulers. They were named for the short knives ("sicae") they carried concealed under their cloaks. They would dash forward out of crowds and attempt to assassinate high Roman or Jewish officials who were seen as being Roman sympathizers (Figure 68). Eleazar ben Jair, leader of the Jewish rebels who occupied Masada, was believed to have been a Sicarii. Some scholars believe that the apostle Judas Iscariot also may have been a member of this sect as the suffix "*iot*" means membership or belonging to ("Judas of the Sicarii").

There were other groups of people living in Palestine in the First Century A.D. which also had interaction with the Jews, notably the Samaritans. The Jews hated the Romans but they hated the Samaritans even more. The Samaritans lived in the region north of Jerusalem but below Galilee in what had once been the heart of the Northern Kingdom of Israel. The people living there were the descendants of the people not deported by the Assyrians in 721 B.C. who had admixed with Assyrian and Babylonian settlers over

Figure 68.   Iron sicae dagger from First Century A.D. Palestine.
(Wilson W. Crook, III Collection)

the following centuries. The Samaritans were often called "a herd" by the Jews because they were considered to be a collection of undesirable people who had no right to call themselves "a nation". The capital of Samaria, Shechem, was referred to by the Jews as "Sychar" (drunkenness). So unclean were the Samaritans that pious Jews coming from Galilee to Jerusalem would circumnavigate the region rather than walk on Samaritan roads. This is one of the reasons Jesus used the parable of the "good Samaritan", because to a Jew of the First Century A.D., there was no such thing.

Only two things were certain in First Century A.D. Palestine – death and an abundance of Roman taxes. Life in Roman Palestine was strongly divided between the "haves" and the "have nots"; a middle class was not well developed. The people lived with a lot of filth in their lives as sanitation was relatively poor. In cities like Jerusalem, daily waste would have been dumped in the space between houses. It was then collected and taken out through the Dung Gate to an area outside of the city where it was dumped and burned in a continual fire. The locals referred to this area as "*Gehenna*" or "hell" because of the perpetual stench. As a result, home owners always placed their windows on the second floor of the buildings – above the smell of the waste. Spices were used to perfume houses, although the smell of olive oil would have been pervasive. Perfumes were popular to cover up body odor; there is little hard evidence the people of Palestine either made or used much soap. A common First Century A.D. ceramic piece is known as an "unguentarium" or perfume bottle and likely contained either special oils or perfume (Figure 69). Hair styles were typically short and beards were well trimmed. Judging from burial inscriptions found outside the city (cemeteries were always placed "in the wilder-

ness" beyond city walls because of disease and the law that stated that corpses were ritually "unclean"), the typical life expectancy of a male in First Century A.D. Palestine was only about 29 years of age.

Figure 69. First Century A.D. Herodian unguentarium or perfume bottle. (Wilson W. Crook, III Collection)

In both large cities and small villages, such as Nazareth, almost all household items were made locally (grinding stones, storage jars, cooking vessels, looms, oil lamps, etc.). Many drinking vessels were made out of the local limestone (known as "Herodian stoneware") as stone from the earth was considered more ritually clean than a clay pottery vessel (a human product) (Figure 70). That being said, pottery production, especially of cooking pots and storage jars, was very important. Trace element geochemical studies of ceramics across First Century A.D. Palestine show that the pottery used by most people came from only a few major production centers, the largest of

Figure 70. First Century A.D. Herodian stoneware vessel from the area south of Jerusalem.
(Wilson W. Crook, III Collection)

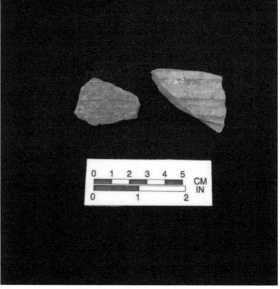

Figure 71. First Century A.D. pottery sherds from Capernaum. The ribbed texture on the outside of the pottery indicates that it likely came from a cooking pot. (Wilson W. Crook, III Collection)

which was at Kefar Hananya in the Upper Galilee region. Almost all of the common pottery used by people across Galilee, especially in Nazareth, Cana, and the Sea of Galilee cities such as Capernaum, came from Kefar Hananya (Figure 71).

Typical foods included olives, olive oil, figs, dates, pomegranates, legumes (lentils, peas), cheese, butter, yogurt, onions, garlic, wild greens, nuts and berries. On rare occasions a family might have a little meat – either mutton, fish (if they lived close to the sea) or roasted fowl. Wine was ubiquitous but was consumed heavily watered down. Consumption of undiluted wine or milk was considered barbaric. An astonishing 70 percent of the average person's daily caloric intake came from bread. Because it was that critical to survival, it is the reason that the first petition Jesus makes to God in the Lord's Prayer is "give us this day our daily bread". Bread came from both barley (planted in November and harvested in April) and wheat (planted in January and harvested in May). Grain harvest celebrations began with the Feast of Unleavened Bread (immediately following Passover) and ended with the Festival of Pentecost.

Equally important to daily life in Palestine was olive oil. It was used to cook virtually every meal and was consumed daily as a dip for bread. It also provided the fuel used in oil lamps which supplied the only lighting inside most houses (windows being rare). Oil lamps, like pottery, changed styles over the years and thus can be used by archeologists as time indicators. The most common oil lamp of the First Century A.D., known as a "Herodian lamp", has a very distinctive triangular-shaped spout where the wick was inserted (Figure 72). Literally tens of thousands of such lamps have been recovered as every house used several at a time.

The Sea of Galilee region was extremely important economically, both as a source of fresh water and for its fish. The sea, which is the product of a down-thrown graben fault at the northern end of the Great African rift system, is shaped like a frying pan – relatively wide and shallow (it is 13 miles long by 8 miles wide and averages only 84 feet in depth). As a result, winds funneling through valleys from the eastern side of the lake (the Golan Heights) can cause sudden

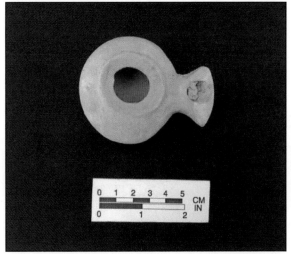

Figure 72. First Century A.D. Herodian oil lamp. (Wilson W. Crook, III Collection)

and violent storms. Fishing was typically done at night when the sea was more quiet and net and boat repair work was done during the day (Figure 73). Sea of Galilee fish were placed on leaf-covered racks and smoked and dried, then shipped over the entire Roman world (evidence of Sea of Galilee fish has been found in places as far west as Spain). Cities, especially Capernaum which was located at the northern end of the Sea of Galilee along a major east-west trade route, were major gathering places for a wide range of peoples including fishermen, merchants, Rabbis and Pharisees, Roman soldiers and tax collectors. This is one reason that

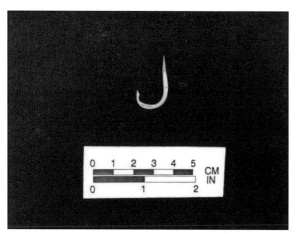

Figure 74. Ruins of First Century A.D. Capernaum, Jesus' home along the Sea of Galilee.

Figure 73. First Century A.D. bronze fish hook from the Sea of Galilee region. (Wilson W. Crook, III Collection)

Figure 75. Remains of house foundations in Capernaum.

Figure 76. Black basalt foundation of First Century A.D. synagogue below the white limestone of a later 4th Century A.D. structure. This was the synagogue used by Jesus.

Jesus made Capernaum his home during his ministry in Galilee and is the setting for so many of his miracles, parables and the assembling of His Apostles (Figures 74-76).

In 1986, after an extended period of drought which significantly lowered the water level of the Sea of Galilee, two workers from the Kibbutz Ginosar on the northwestern shore of the sea discovered the remains of an ancient wooden boat. A coffer dam was built around the boat and the area surrounding it drained and excavated. Shelley Wachsmann, then of the Israeli Department of Antiquities and Museums and now a professor at Texas A&M University, in conjunction with volunteers from the U. S. Embassy and from Kibbutz Ginosar, excavated the boat. The boat, which took 12 days and nights to carefully excavate, measured 27 feet in length, 7.5 feet wide and had a preserved height of 4.3 feet. In order to preserve the fragile remains, the wood was soaked for seven years in a chemical bath. Radiocarbon dating of the wood yielded a date of 40 B.C. +/- 80 years and pottery found inside the boat was estimated to be from the period of 50 B.C. to 50 A.D. Since these dates cover the period of time that Jesus was active along the Sea of Galilee and the boat's location was only five miles from Capernaum, it was dubbed by the press as "the Jesus boat" (although there is absolutely no proof that Jesus ever came near the boat). It is now on exhibit in a special museum at Kibbutz Ginosar.

During the excavation, one of the volunteers from the U.S. Embassy in Tel Aviv was Karen Sullivan. Karen (who later married archeologist Shelley Wachsmann), received a small group of wooden pieces that could not be refitted into the boat. She gave three of those fragments to her U.S. Embassy colleague, Mr. Sebastian Failla. Mr. Failla has since donated two of the fragments to museums in the United States and upon hearing of my teaching of Biblical archeology, agreed to give me one of the small fragments which is shown in Figure 77.

One question I am frequently asked in my Sunday School classes is if Jesus Christ did live on the earth, why is there no evidence for his life outside that of the Bible? The answer to this question is two-fold: first, Jesus came from Judea, which was a backwater in the Roman Empire, and then from Galilee, which was a

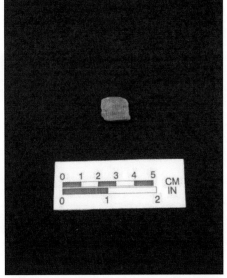

Figure 77. Small wooden fragment from the "Jesus Boat" which has been dated to the First Century A.D. (Wilson W. Crook, III Collection)

backwater inside Judea. His ministry was but three years in length and with no television, CNN or FOX News at the time, there was little reporting of anyone from there to those outside of that region. Second, despite these obvious handicaps, there actually is some substantial evidence to His existence outside of the Bible.

Caius Gaius Publius Cornelius Tacitus, or just Tacitus (ca. 55-118 A.D.), was a noted Roman Senator, orator and ethnographer, and was arguably the best of all the Roman historians (his name means "silence" from which we get the word "tacit"). Tacitus' last major work, his "*Annals*", was published in ca. 116-117 A.D. and includes the story of the burning of Rome:

> *"Neither human effort nor the Emperor's generosity nor the placating of the gods ended the scandalous belief that the fire had been ordered by Nero. Therefore, to put down the rumor, Nero substituted as culprits and punished in the most unusual ways those hated for their shameful acts, whom the crowd (mob) called "Christians". The founder of this group named "Christus", had been executed in the reign of Tiberius by the Procurator Pontius Pilate. Suppressed for a time, the deadly superstition erupted again not only in Judea, the origin of this evil, but also in the city [Rome] where all things horrible and shameful from everywhere come together and become popular".*

Tacitus gives us four pieces of accurate historical information about Jesus in this story: (1) He was referred to by his followers as Christ, (2) He was associated with the beginning of a religious movement whose name derived from His, (3) He was executed by the Roman Procurator of Judea, Pontius Pilate, and (4) the death occurred during the reign of the Emperor Tiberius (14-37 A.D.). All four of these facts are presented in the Gospels.

Another Roman historian, Flavius Josephus, gives further evidence for the life of Jesus. Josephus was a Jewish priest who grew up as an aristocrat in First Century A.D. Palestine. He was educated in Rome and was a noted political leader. During the Jewish War of 66-70 A.D., Josephus surrendered to the Romans rather than fight to the death. He prophesied that General Vespasian would become Emperor and when this happened in 69 A.D., he was freed, given Roman citizenship, and moved to Rome where he enjoyed Imperial patronage. Josephus wrote two great historical works – "*The Jewish War*" and "*Jewish Antiquities*". In the latter he wrote about Jesus:

"Around this time there lived Jesus, a wise man, if indeed one ought to call him a man. For he was one who did surprising deeds, and a teacher of such people as accept the truth gladly. He won over many Jews and many of the Greeks. He was the Messiah. When Pilate, upon hearing him accused by men of the highest standing among us, had condemned him to be crucified, those who in the first place came to love him did not give up their affection for him for on the third day, he appeared to them restored to life. The prophets of God had prophesied this and countless other marvelous things about him. And the tribe of Christians, so called after him, have still to this day not died out".

Three copies of this text exist, all in Greek, and are identical with no additions or deletions. It should also be noted that Josephus was writing before any of the Gospels had been compiled and made public. In *"The Jewish War"* Josephus further mentions the story of the death of James, the brother of Jesus. He specifically identified James as "the brother of Jesus – who is called Messiah". James was a common name in First Century A.D. Palestine so the identifier with Jesus was used because Jesus was a known man of some repute. So what do we take from these references? First, Jesus was a known man; His followers and His brother James were contemporaries with Josephus and first-hand accounts of His life were available. Second, His personal name was Jesus and He was called the Messiah in Hebrew, Christos in Greek, and Christus in Latin – a title that meant the anointed one. Third, He had a brother named James (Jacob) who was killed in Jerusalem in the First Century A.D. Fourth, He won over many Jews and Greeks to His beliefs and teachings. Fifth, the Jewish leaders of the day expressed an unfavorable opinion of Jesus. Sixth, Pontius Pilate, the Roman Procurator of Judea from 26-36 A.D., rendered judgment that He should be executed and His execution would be by crucifixion. Seventh, Jesus was executed under Pontius Pilate's procuratorship and during the reign of the Emperor Tiberius. Eighth, some of Jesus' followers did not abandon Him, even after His death. Lastly, Jesus rose from the dead on the third day after His death and appeared to His followers in accordance with ancient prophecies.

Absolutely all of these facts coincide directly with the accounts in the Bible.

5. PEOPLES SURROUNDING ISRAEL

A number of smaller nations surrounded Israel throughout much of its history. These included, counterclockwise from the south, the Kingdoms of Edom, Moab, Ammon, the Aramean Kingdom of Syria, Phoenicia and Philistia (Figure 78). Some of these nations, such as Edom, Moab and Ammon, were related to the Israelites; Phoenicia was part of the Canaanite peoples; the people from Syria were related to other Mesopotamian Semitic peoples and the Philistines appear to have been later migrants to the region, possibly coming from the Greek Aegean islands and/or Crete. Israel had interactions, both friendly and otherwise, with all of these peoples, so this chapter will briefly touch on each of the six nations surrounding Israel.

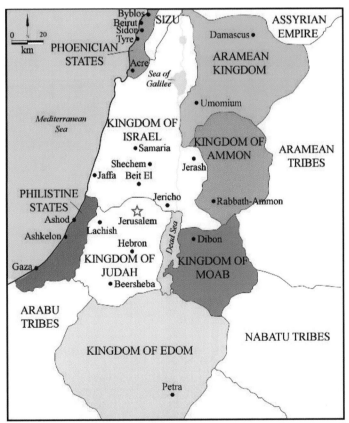

Figure 78. Map of the nations surrounding Israel including Edom, Moab, Ammon, the Aramean Kingdom of Syria, Phoenicia and Philistia.
(Map illustrated by Lance K. Trask)

THE EDOMITES

Of the many peoples that inhabited Palestine in the first and second millennia B.C., perhaps none were more closely related to the Israelites than the Edomites. The Bible states that the Edomites stemmed from the descendants of Jacob's brother Esau (Genesis 36:1-8) and in fact, Esau's nickname was "Edom" meaning reddish (Genesis 25:30). When the Israelites were wandering in the wilderness and encountered the Edomites, they referred to them as "brother" (Numbers 20:14).

Edomite history is somewhat vague as there are few surviving records of their culture. The Egyptians referred to the Edomites as *"Shasu"*, a term meaning wandering nomads. The Egyptians made mention of two types of Shasu, those from Edom and those from Seir. Both were located south of Israel (Canaan) and below the Dead Sea. The Bible frequently treats the references to "Edom" and "Seir" as one region. The environmental character of Edom is forbidding, with rocky crags towering four thousand feet over desert floors. In Jeremiah 49:16 it makes mention that the Edomites "nested with the eagles". Archeological evidence has now shown that the region inhabited by the Edomites contained substantial deposits of copper which were apparently exploited by the Edomites and later by the Israelites under David and Solomon.

The Bible records that David was the first Israelite King to defeat the Edomites and bring them under direct Israelite control. David further established military garrisons through-out the country (II Samuel 8:13-14). This initiated a period of about 150 years of Israelite dominance until Edom was able to regain its independence from Judah. Over the next several centuries, a pattern followed of Judah being able to regain control of Edom for a short period only to have the Edomites throw off their Israelite overseers and become independent once again. Apparently Edom sided with King Rezin of Damascus in his revolt against the Assyrian Empire which resulted not only in Syria being destroyed by King Tiglath-Pileser III in 732 B.C., but Edom then falling under general Assyrian control. When Judah was attacked and destroyed by the Babylonians in 586 B.C., the Edomites apparently moved both westward and northward into the southern part of Judean territory (Ezekiel 35:10-12). This movement to the west away from the traditional Edomite homeland was also the result of the entrance of a new people from the Arabian Desert who migrated into southern and western Jordan. These peoples, known as the Nabateans, skillfully adapted to the arid conditions of the region and turned the region into one of the most prosperous trading centers in the Ancient Middle East (Petra).

During the independent Jewish rule of Judah from ca. 167-63 B.C., the Edomites, now known as the "Idumeans", were forced to nominally adopt Jewish religion and customs. It was from this group of people that the Herodian Dynasty which controlled Judea and most of Palestine (under Roman oversight) from 37 B.C. to ca. 100 A.D. arose.

The Edomites spoke their own language, which was closely related to the other regional Semitic languages including Hebrew. However, in written form Edomite apparently had some unusual letter forms which today provide scholars with the surest means of determining if an inscription is actually Edomite. The religion of the Edomites is also a bit of a puzzle. There are a number of inscriptions which mention a principal god named "Qos" (Figure 79). The name

Qos is similar to the Arabic word "*qaus*" which means bow. In the religions of many of the peoples in the region of Palestine the storm god Baal is frequently depicted with arrows as his "lightning bolts". Consequently, Qos may have been a similar storm god associated with rain and fertility. Only one verifiable Edomite temple at Horvit Qitmit has been found. The shrine has podiums for several deities and it is unclear if Qos had a female consort as the Canaanite god Baal had. Some scholars argue that the Bible never mentions any of the "abominations" associated with Edomite worship as it does for all of the other surrounding nations. As such, they argue that worship of Yahweh may have continued and that Qos could either be Yahweh or possibly another god that was worshiped alongside Yahweh.

Figure 79. Edomite ceramic goblet from Ein Gedi with what is believed to be the face of the god Qos.
(Wilson W. Crook, III Collection)

THE MOABITES

Over the last 70 years there has been a substantial increase in our knowledge of the ancient cultures of Palestine, especially those that occupied the western parts of modern day

116   The Peoples of the Bible

Jordan. The Moabites, however, much like the Edomites, still remain somewhat of a mystery. The name "Moab" refers to that part of the TransJordanian Plateau that lies immediately east of the Dead Sea. While Moab's southern border was historically fixed with Edom at the Zered Brook (modern Wadi el-Hesa), its northern border fluctuated over time depending on the strength or weakness of Moab's rulers at any given period. Moab's eastern desert was both a blessing and a curse as while it offered a forbidding terrain and therefore some measure of protection, there was also nothing to effectively block marauding desert raiders from coming into Moab. Most of the region's population lived in a narrow north-south trending fertile strip that lies sandwiched between the Dead Sea escarpment and the Syrian Desert, a zone that only extends east for about 15 miles (see Figure 78).

Due to rainfall near the Dead Sea escarpment, the land of Moab has traditionally been known for its excellent pasturage, notably for sheep and goats (II Kings 3:4). Not to be overlooked, there is also an excellent Mediterranean-like climate along the escarpment which allows for the growing of wheat and barley along with fruit trees and vineyards (Figure 80). Average precipitation is only about 14 inches per year but this is supplemented by fresh water springs, a few rivers and cisterns cut into the limestone bedrock.

Figure 80. Fertile region along the Dead Sea escarpment in Moab.

According to the Bible, the Moabites descend from Moab, son of the illicit liaison between Lot and his eldest daughter following the destruction of Sodom and Gomorrah (Genesis 19:37). Moab is next mentioned in connection to the "King's Highway" ("*derek hammelek*") which traversed the TransJordanian Plateau from end to end (Numbers 20:17; Deuteronomy 21:22) (see Figure 78). The Moabites, along with the Edomites and the Amorites did not wish to let the Israelites pass through their land during the Exodus, resulting in conflict between these nations and Israel. Much like Edomite history, the story of Israel and Moab is a series of seemingly never-ending conflicts in which Israel periodically gained oversight of the land only to have Moab later rebel and regain its independence.

Most of our knowledge about ancient Moab outside of the Bible comes from a single monument stone (stela) placed by the Moabite King Mesha (II Kings 3). The "Mesha Stela" or "the Moabite Stone" tells of how, in about 840 B.C., King Mesha overcame the oppression of the Northern Kingdom of Israel and re-established Moabite independence, all due to the intervention of the Moabite god, Chemosh (Kemosh). Mesha, and apparently many of the other Moabite Kings, came from the city of Dibon in central Moab, which appears to have been the region's capital.

According to the Roman historian Josephus, Moab was largely destroyed by the Babylonians under King Nebuchadnezzar in 582 B.C. Following the Babylonian conquest, Moab ceased to become a recognized national entity. The region came under Persian control but there did not seem to be any real central authority or leadership.

The Moabite Stone refers to the people of Moab as "the children of Chemosh", who appears to have been their national god (Number 21:29; Jeremiah 48:46). Chemosh, variously translated as "the destroyer" or "the subduer," is believed to have been a fertility god similar to Baal. It is claimed that the worship of Chemosh demanded child sacrifice by throwing children into a sacrificial fire. Solomon married a princess of Moab and later set up a temple to her "abomination" (I Kings 11:7). The wicked King Manasseh of Judah is said to have made his "sons pass through the fire" which may also be a reference to instituting the worship of Chemosh in the Temple at Jerusalem (II Kings 21:3-9). As a result of this worship, the Israelites were specifically forbidden to marry Moabite women for fear of introducing the religious contamination of Chemosh worship (Deuteronomy 23:3). The great exception to this is Ruth, who, as a Moabitess, was not only allowed to enter Israel, but also married Boaz and ultimately became the great grandmother of David (Ruth 4:17) and is therefore in the lineage of Jesus. The reason for this exception appears to have been Ruth's complete acceptance of Yahweh as the one true God and her unwavering faith in God (Ruth 1:16-17).

THE AMMONITES

The Ammonites were a people who inhabited the central part of the TransJordanian Plateau from the middle of the second millennium until the middle of the first millennium B.C. Their country was known as Ammon and their capital was Rabbah-Ammon (modern day

Amman, Jordan). The boundaries of Ammon were vague; most references in the Bible stress the region of the Jabbok River (Deuteronomy 3:16; Joshua 12:2) but a definitive set of boundaries did not exist. The Jabbok River essentially forms a circle around a considerable area surrounding Amman and it could be that this is the land referred to in the Bible as the "land along the course of the Jabbok" (Deuteronomy 2:37) (see Figure 78).

According to Genesis 19:38, the ancestor of the Ammonite people was Ben-Ammi, son of the incestuous relationship between Lot and his youngest daughter after their escape from Sodom. The name "Ammi" means "son of my paternal father" and seems to have been used as a popular description of the relationship between Israel and the Ammonites. A number of Ammonite names refer to Ben-Ammi and it is very possible that the Ammonites did indeed have an ancestor of that name. All that is really known is that the Ammonite people had settled in the central TransJordanian Plateau sometime prior to the arrival of the Israelites. Some scholars believe that they may have migrated into the region from either Northern Syria or Southern Anatolia during the widespread socio-economic collapse that occurred throughout the Ancient Middle East in the Late Bronze Age, but this remains speculative.

Like the Moabites, the Ammonites appear to have been largely a pastoral people, raising sheep and goats, who supplemented their diet by minor agriculture in the region immediately adjacent to the Jabbok River. Ammonite history is also very similar to that of the Moabites in that it involved a series of conflicts with the people of Israel. The earliest record of hostilities is in Judges 3:12-14 where the Ammonites are said to have joined forces with the Moabites and Amalekites against Israel. This coalition subjugated Israel for a period of 18 years. An unnamed Ammonite King was confronted by the Israelite Judge Jephthah in Judges 11. The first recorded name of an Ammonite ruler is that of Nahash who crossed the Jabbok River and besieged Jabesh-Gilead. His command to put out the right eye of every Israelite warrior spurred the Israelites to rally around King Saul who then led them to victory (I Samuel 11:1-11). David captured the Ammonite capital of Rabbah-Ammon (II Samuel 12:26-31) and Ammon remained under Israelite control during the remainder of the United Monarchy. Solomon married an Ammonite princess, Naamah, who became the mother of Rehoboam, who later inherited the throne of Israel (I Kings 14:21). Much like the Edomites and the Moabites, the Ammonites variously fell under control of either Israel or Judah and periodically gained their independence during the period of the Divided Kingdom. Sometime during this period, the Ammonites evidently became one of the wealthiest kingdoms in the entire Palestine region as they had the dubious honor of paying the highest tribute to the Assyrian coffers (assuming the amount of tribute is emblematic of their wealth and not a measure of disloyalty). Ammon joined the general revolt against Babylon and a punitive expedition led by Nebuchadnezzar in ca. 582-81 B.C. resulted in the almost complete destruction of the Ammonites.

We are told in I Kings 11:5 that the Ammonite national god was Milcom (derived from the Hebrew root word "*mlk*" meaning "the King"). Milcom is also equated with the word "Molech" and both are used in describing child sacrifice by fire (II Kings 23:10). Rabbinic tradition states that Molech was a large bronze statue in the shape of a horned bull inside which sacrificial fires constantly burned. The Bible further mentions that the Ammonites practiced circumcision but it is unknown what significance this practice meant in term of Ammonite religion (Jeremiah 9:25-26). Small clay figurines have been recovered from Ammonite sites which most frequently depict a male rider, either on top of a horse or a bull, or a female figure often holding a tambourine. The latter is represented either in the form of a plaque or as a pillar figurine. Baal was sometimes referred to as the "Rider of the Storm" and the mounted figures could reflect this representation. Baal's symbol was often the bull so these figures may represent a general storm god deity. Similar tambourine carrying figures have been found in Canaanite sites and are generally ascribed to be the Baal consort, Astarte/Anath/Asherah.

THE ARAMEAN KINGDOM OF SYRIA

The Arameans were a large group of linguistically related peoples who spoke a dialect of a Semitic language known as Aramean. They lived over a large part of Upper Mesopotamia including much of what is today Syria. Aram, the eponymous ancestor of the Aramean people, is a grandson of Abraham's brother Nahor (Genesis 22:21). Abraham's relatives, Bethuel and Laban, are identified in the Bible as Arameans (Genesis 25:20; 31:20). However, the precise origin of the Aramean people remains a mystery. They are not mentioned in Mesopotamian documents until the late 12th Century B.C., settling all across the northern Euphrates River Valley and into southern Syria, especially in and around Damascus. It was this southern group of the Arameans that had the most contact with the peoples of the Bible and is the focus of this discussion.

One of the problems in fully assessing the ancient Arameans is that they were not truly a single people per se, and did not have a single country with defined borders. Instead, much like the Canaanites, the Arameans tended to form city-states which from time to time would bind together in order to face some common enemy. Also like Canaan, different Aramean city-states would become the dominant power for a period of time only to subsequently relinquish the leadership role to another city-state.

The Arameans had a prolonged relationship of conflict with the powers in Mesopotamia, primarily the Assyrians. The first recorded conflict occurred during the reign of the Assyrian King Tiglath-Pileser I (ca. 1114-1076 B.C.) who recorded encountering Aramaic tribes during his westward expansion of the first Assyrian Empire. The first mention of Syria in the Bible comes in II Samuel 8-10 which recounts three battles fought between the Aramean state of Zobah under its ruler, Hadadezer, and Israel under King David. Zobah, not Damascus, seems to have been the dominant city-state in southern Syria during the early part of the Iron Age.

However, it is Aram Damascus, usually just called Aram in the Bible (or just "Syria"), that had the greatest effect on Israel. It was regularly seen as being the most powerful Aramean city-state bordering on Israel and the two nations had a long and complex relationship. In the 9th Century B.C., Aram under the leadership of King Bir Hadad I (Biblical Ben Hadad) staged a major attack on the Northern Kingdom of Israel and temporarily captured a number of important towns (I Kings 15:16-22). However, the peak of Damascus' power came in the latter part of the 9th Century B.C. when a coalition of 12 city-states led by Hadad-idr of Damascus met and stopped the westward advance of the Assyrian King Shalmaneser III at the battle of Qarqar. Shalmaneser apparently returned twice more to northern Syria and each time was repulsed by the Arameans. This was one of the few times in history that the Assyrians were effectively stopped and markedly increased Aram Damascus' influence across the region.

It is in this general time period (ca. 850 B.C.) that the Bible tells us the story of Namaan, a "Captain" (General) under the King of Syria, who came to Elisha the prophet to be cured of leprosy (II Kings 5). Although a pagan, Namaan saw the power of Elisha's God and while he did not convert to monotheism, he was greatly impressed by Israel's God.

A century later, Aram's last King, called Rezin in the Bible but probably more properly pronounced "Radyan" in Aramaic, tried to form an anti-Assyrian coalition of Palestinian states

(Syria, Tyre, Ashkelon and Israel). Tiglath-Pileser III completely defeated the coalition, besieged Damascus in 733-732 B.C., and utterly destroyed it, killing Rezin. By the time of the Neo-Babylonian Empire, very little of the Syrian city-state structure remained.

As mentioned above, it is difficult to distinguish a true Aramean "culture" as each city-state had its own distinct characteristics. Much of what can be seen archeologically appears to have been borrowed from other Western Semitic cultures, the Phoenicians in particular. The Arameans seem to have had a similar fertility type religion with Hadad being the principal deity (Hadad more or less equals Baal as a storm god). Hadad is often referred to as Hadad-Rimmon (probably pronounced "Hadad-Rammain") which means Hadad the Thunderer. Other common Ancient Middle East deities were also present including El, Astarte, the moon god Sin and the sun god Shamash.

Without a doubt, the major legacy of the Aramean civilization was its language and writing. In this regard, they had an extraordinary impact on the entire region of Mesopotamia and Palestine – well beyond their political or military legacy. While the Arameans seemed to have borrowed the alphabet from the Phoenicians, the Arameans were the first to assign specific consonants to indicate long vowel sounds ("*maatres lectionis*" or "mothers of reading"). This important contribution to writing was then adopted by most of the other cultures in the region, including the Israelites (Hebrew). Because of the Assyrian doctrine of deporting peoples from conquered lands to Assyria, by the 8th Century B.C. there was a huge Aramean-speaking population throughout Mesopotamia. By the time of the Persian Empire, Aramean was the single most widely spoken language in the Ancient Middle East. As a result, it became the *lingua franca* of the Persian Empire. Aramaic, alongside Hebrew, also became the principal language of Judea. Translations of the scriptures were produced in Aramaic and read alongside Hebrew texts in the synagogues. Thus Aramaic was probably one of, and may have even been the principal language spoken by Jesus. Today, it is largely a dead language except to scholars, although there remains a small enclave of people inside Syria that still speak Aramaic as it was spoken over 2,000 years ago.

THE PHOENICIANS

The Phoenicians occupied a narrow coastal strip of land stretching from the island of Aradus (modern Arwad) in the north to Tyre in the south. The Lebanon mountain range to the east throughout history has created a political and cultural barrier between the coast and inland Syria (see Figure 78). Due to rains coming off the Mediterranean, the area along the coast is a rich agricultural region which helped support the major cities, all of which were centered in and around natural harbors. In terms of the Bible, only Iron Age Phoenicia is discussed (ca 1200-331 B.C.) but the Phoenicians themselves have a substantial history that stretches back to the third millennium B.C.

The Phoenicians were largely a Canaanite culture with most of the same gods and goddesses and customs of the other Canaanite tribes to the south. To this traditional culture, the Phoenicians melded a strong culture of sea travel and trade. In fact, by adopting a dominant merchant role rather than that of warriors, the Phoenicians periodically adopted a vassal-like role rather than threaten the existence of their far-flung commercial interests. Given their key coastal location, the Phoenicians found themselves at a natural crossroad of trade and thus established a commercial network that stretched from Persia across the Mediterranean to Gibraltar and from the Caucasus to Nubia. The invention of coinage, first at Sidon and later at Tyre, Byblos, Aradus and other cities, greatly facilitated this international trade.

Realizing that they could take advantage of the production of foreign products in addition to transportation and sale, the Phoenicians began to establish colonies all across the Mediterranean. Settlement initially began in Cyprus to take advantage of the island's rich copper mines, but soon spread to other parts of the Mediterranean such that by the 8th Century B.C. there were Phoenician colonies in North Africa, Sicily, Sardinia, Malta and Spain. The North African colony, which later became the nation of Carthage, was particularly successful.

Phoenician culture must be viewed from two perspectives – that within its homeland and that which is associated with its western colonies and foreign trade. In Palestine, the Phoenicians were well known for being superior craftsmen, with skill in fine woodworking, masonry finish, and metals. The initial Biblical contact was between David and King Hiram of Tyre to send cedar wood (from the "Cedars of Lebanon"), carpenters and stone masons to build David's palace in Jerusalem (II Samuel 5:11). Later, David would purchase the materials from the Phoenicians to build the Temple (I Chronicles 22:2-5) which Solomon subsequently used for its completion (I Kings 5). Solomon provided annual payments in wheat and olive oil to the Phoenicians under Hiram who then supplied the skilled artisans needed to complete the work on the Temple. Solomon also used Phoenician ships to move copper from the mines near Eilat (Ezion-Geber) across the Levant (I Kings 9:26-27).

Phoenician is a dialect of Canaanite, akin to Aramaic and Hebrew. Phoenician is written in a consonantal alphabet, and it is for the transmission of this alphabet throughout the Mediterranean that the Phoenicians are mostly remembered ("Phonetics" comes from Phoenician). By the 8th Century B.C., Greek inscriptions were clearly borrowing from the Phoenicians and the modern alphabet we use today was passed down from Greece. As would be expected from a nation that came into contact with so many different cultures, Phoenician culture was a blended style, taking bits and pieces from across the known world and adding a Phoenician touch to it. The Phoenicians were well known for producing purple dyes and dyed cloth, as well as fine metal work and jewelry. After the 8th Century B.C., Phoenician glass became one of their major exports. Glass-blowing was unknown at the time so the Phoenicians produced glass vessels and beads using a process known as "core forming". A core, usually composed of a clay shape on the stick, was produced first and then viscous glass was draped around the core until the dimensions of the vessel were complete. Later, handles or other external pieces could be added and the clay core carefully drilled out and removed. The core-forming glass process allowed the Phoenicians to produce glass vessels with many colors and blended layers of colors which were instantly in great demand throughout the Ancient Middle East (Figure 81).

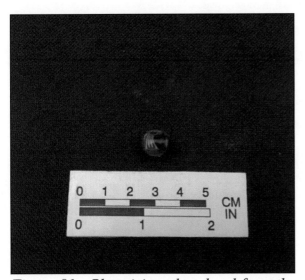

Figure 81. Phoenician glass bead from the Iron Age. (Wilson W. Crook, III Collection)

The gods and goddesses worshiped by the Phoenicians were a mixture of older Canaanite deities (El, Baal, Astarte/Anath/Asherah) plus some new ones adopted along the way. Many of the deities also seem to have been city-specific; for example, Baal in Sidon was known as

Baal-Sidon. The most important deity of Byblos was Baalat Gubla, or "the Mistress of Byblos" (= Astarte/Anath). At Tyre, the city god was "Melqart" or "King of the City". All of these deities filled the same role as the traditional Canaanite gods and goddesses, being primarily centered on fertility of the land, the people, and of trade and commerce. Wherever the Phoenicians went, they took their deities with them. At many Phoenician colonies, and at Carthage in particular, the goddess "Tannit" seems to have been particularly important. Depictions of Tannit, unlike Astarte or Anath, are typically clothed, the mother goddess usually draped in a scarf that covered the head and shoulders. However, just because the goddess was depicted as clothed, did not mean that the Phoenicians did not actively practice temple prostitution and other forms of Canaanite sympathetic religion. The worst of these practices was, of course, child sacrifice. At Carthage in modern Tunisia, archeologists have found an immense *tophet* or child graveyard where the remains of over 20,000 children have been found. At one time, apologists for the Phoenicians said that this was a Carthaginian practice and was not something inherited from the Phoenicians. However, the discovery of a large *tophet* near Tyre in 1991, introduced an entirely new dimension into the debate over Phoenician civilization.

THE PHILISTINES

The Philistines occupied the southwestern coast of Canaan, notably in the region of their five dominant city-states of Ashkelon, Ashdod, Ekron, Gaza and Gath (see Figure 78). According to the Bible, the Philistines came to Canaan from the islands of the Aegean Sea, including the island of Crete (Ezekiel 25:15-16; Zephaniah 2:4-5). They are particularly associated with "Caphtor," a term in several languages referring to the area in and around Crete. The term "Philistine" (from which we get Palestine) comes from the Hebrew word "*pelisti*", which occurs 288 times in the Old Testament. In modern times, being referred to as a "Philistine" is an insult, meaning uncultured and is clearly an exaggerated extrapolation based on the way the Philistines are depicted in the Bible.

Outside the Bible, the Philistines are first mentioned in Egyptian records from the time of Pharaoh Ramesses III (ca. 1184-1153 B.C.). Ramesses' accounts tell of a series of battles with a group of invaders called "the Sea Peoples". One of the groups of these Sea Peoples is referred to as the "Peleset", which most scholars identify with the Biblical Philistines. Other groups within the Sea Peoples include the Sherden, Lukka, Ekwesh, Teresh and the Shekelesh – most of which we know little to nothing about. The Philistines appear in Ramesses III's annals in the year 1176 B.C. Archeologists have observed that there were major socio-political disturbances throughout the Mediterranean world shortly after 1200 B.C., which led to a series of large-scale population migrations. It is entirely plausible that the Philistines' migration to Palestine was a result of this yet not completely understood movement.

From the Egyptian records, it appears that the Philistines initially tried to settle in the Nile Delta but after being defeated by the Egyptians they moved eastward along the coast to Canaan. While Egyptian victories are always depicted as being crushing defeats of the enemy, the accounts of the Philistine military prowess – both on land and on the sea – indicate that this battle may actually have been a very close run thing. As a result, the Egyptians did not wish to have such a potentially dangerous force on their doorstep so they helped the Philistines move and settle in southern Canaan adjacent to the Sinai Peninsula (again reinforcing the fact that the Egyptians have always considered Sinai as part of Egypt). Being from the Greek world, the Philistines were accustomed to the concept of city-states and thus established the Philistine Pentapolis described above, each one of which was headed by a "*seren*" (Lord).

During the period of 1150-1000 B.C., the Philistines were the major adversary of the Israelites. The "five Lords of the Philistines" was one of the groups of the peoples left by God to test Israel (Judges 2:6-3:6). The conflict between the two peoples came to a head during the time of Samson (Judges 14-16). Despite his less than stellar personal character, Samson defeated the Philistines on a number of occasions including ultimately at the time of his death when he brought down the Temple of Dagon on a great number of Philistines (Judges 16:19). Philistine temples have now been excavated at Tel Qasile and at Ekron. Interestingly, the temple architecture has shown two major central support pillars which are reminiscent and supportive of the Samson narrative.

King David is given credit for battling and defeating the Philistine threat. His first encounter with the Philistines comes in his battle with the Philistine giant and champion, Goliath of Gath in the Valley of Elah:

"He had a bronze helmet on his head and wore a coat of scale armor of bronze weighing five thousand shekels; on his legs he wore bronze greaves, and a

bronze javelin was strung on his back. His spear shaft was like a weaver's rod, and its iron point weighed six hundred shekels. His shield bearer went ahead of him." (I Samuel 17:5-7)

The description of Goliath's spear, helmet, shield, armor and especially his greaves sounds very typical for Greek warriors of the day from the Aegean region. Of particular importance is the mention that his spear point was constructed of iron. While iron was known by this time, bronze was still the predominant metal used in warfare, especially among the Israelites. In fact, the Philistines were known to have controlled the manufacture and production of iron. While the Philistines would allow the Israelites to purchase iron implements from time to time, they did not allow them to work in iron (I Samuel 13:19-21). This changed when David became King and iron production rapidly spread throughout Israel. As David was known to have taken refuge from Saul with the Philistines, some scholars believe that he learned the secret of iron technology while living in Philistia and then brought it to the Israelites. Depictions of the Philistines on Egyptian monuments show them wearing a distinctive headdress made of either very short stiff feathers or possibly dyed horsehair in an upright arrangement; the latter was popular among Greek warriors and would have been logical for the Philistines to have adopted.

After their defeat by David, the Philistines became largely peaceful neighbors of Israel, their soldiers even being used as mercenaries within the Israelite army. The Philistines were conquered by the Assyrians when they invaded Judah in 701 B.C., and were largely destroyed by the Babylonians under Nebuchadnezzar such that after about 580 B.C. they ceased to be a recognized national entity.

As to be expected, Philistine culture borrowed a great deal from the Aegean region, especially in the design and manufacture of its pottery. Philistine ceramics are known for having been made from very fine clays which were fired at higher-than-average temperatures. Vessels were often covered with fine slips prior to firing which resulted in exquisite, thin-walled vessels. Philistine pot-

Figure 82. Philistine pottery sherds from the Early Iron Age. (Wilson W. Crook, III Collection)

tery was more often buff-colored but then painted with glossy red, purple and brown patterns. Concentric circles laid out on horizontal bands are a common Philistine ceramic motif (Figure 82). While the Philistines produced plates, jars, goblets, jugs, storage jars and other vessels, one characteristic vessel type is readily identifiable with the Philistines – the strainer spouted "beer pot" (Figure 83). This large vessel had a spout on one side with a punched hole strainer on the vessel wall above the spout (Figure 84). Beer at the time was relatively crude and often contained the husks of grain. A strainer spout would help eliminate the husks from being poured into a drinking cup.

Figure 83. Philistine "beer pot" showing side spout.
(Wilson W. Crook, III Collection)

Figure 84. Philistine "beer pot" showing detail of strainer inside the spout.
(Wilson W. Crook, III Collection)

It is uncertain what language the Philistines spoke; only one word, "*seren*" (Lord) has survived and it is not of a Semitic language. A few examples of Philistine writing, known as "Linear B", have been recovered but they have yet to be fully deciphered. Linear B was a form of writing known to the Mycenaean Greeks, which again would make sense, given an Aegean origin for the Philistines.

Little is known of Philistine religion other than they worshiped a pantheon of gods, worshiped in temples, and were uncircumcised – the latter setting them apart from their neighbors and becoming a point of derision with the Israelites. The Philistines also used soothsayers and diviners, as did most of the peoples around them. The chief Philistine god was believed to be "Dagon" who figures in several stories in the Bible (Judges 16:23-25; I Samuel 5:1-5). Little is known about Dagon other than in some regions of the Ancient Middle East, he is said to have been Baal's father. Depictions of the god show a man's head with the body of a fish. Dagon's consort in the Philistine pantheon was Ashtoreth, a known goddess of love and war and comparable to Inanna, Ishtar, Anat, etc. Baal-zebub (or possibly Baal-zvev) was a Philistine deity associated with the city of Ekron (II Kings 2:2-3, 6, 16). His name was possibly originally Baal-zebul (Lord of the Heavenly Dwelling) but was corrupted by the writers of the Old Testament to Baal-zebub meaning "the Lord of the Flies"; and yes, this is where the English novelist William Golding got the inspiration for his book of the same name. We also derive the nickname of the devil, Beelzebub, from this Philistine deity.

High ranking Philistines were buried in unique clay, anthropoid coffins which had a molded face, presumably of the occupant, on the coffin's head. The heads often have indications of the short feathered headdress which instantly identifies them as being Philistine in origin.

In summary, the Philistines left an indelible imprint on the Israelites, not the least of which was that their military threat resulted in the people of Israel demanding a King which started the entire monarchy period of Israelite history from Saul to the destruction of Judah by Babylon.

6. ASSYRIANS

The Assyrians were an ancient people that have a well-deserved reputation for being one of the cruelest civilizations in the history of mankind. Ancient Assyria's geographical location greatly influenced its cultural attitudes and actions. Assyria is located in the northern part of modern day Iraq where it straddled the upper Tigris River Valley and its two major tributaries, the Greater (upper) Zab and the Lesser (lower) Zab. The region is surrounded by a number of imposing mountains: the Zagros to the east, the Armenian to the north, the Hamrin Hills in the south, and a major ridge that separated the Assyrian heartland from the Jazira Steppe to the west. The Assyrians were continually confronted by invasions from mountain tribes attacking through passes from the north and the east, and migrations of people from the west looking for new lands to settle. As a result, the Assyrians adopted a belligerent lifestyle with a civilization that was almost constantly on a wartime footing.

It is uncertain where the original settlers into what became Assyria came from. Scholars have variously proposed Iran, Armenia, the Syrian Desert or even southern Mesopotamia. Whatever their early origins, there can be no doubt that by the time of the Late Bronze Age, the people that inhabited Assyria were of Semitic origin. The land of Assyria received sufficient rain to grow cereal crops (wheat, barley) without the need of irrigation. Vegetables (especially lentils), fruit and vines were also plentiful. While originally an agrarian culture, several major cities began to emerge. The first was Ashur, named for the Assyrian's principal god, located about 60 miles south of modern Mosul on the west bank of the Tigris River. Nineveh, which ultimately became the last capital of the Assyrians, was located on the east bank of the Tigris directly across the river from Mosul. The ruins of Nineveh cover over 1,800 acres and were one of the first parts of ancient Assyria to be discovered by explorers in the 19th Century. The third major Assyrian city, Calah, was also located on the east bank of the Tigris about 20 miles south of Nineveh.

Much of what we know about ancient Assyria comes from the great library of King Ashurbanipal (ca. 668-627 B.C.) which is now housed in the British Museum as the Kouyunjik Collection. The library contains thousands of cuneiform tablets which detail almost every aspect of Assyrian history. Chief among these is the so-called "Assyrian King List" which records the name of every Assyrian King from the third millennium B.C. to Sargon II (721-705 B.C.). The first 17 Assyrian Kings are listed as "Kings living in tents". This is followed by a group of 10 Kings who traced their lineage to the last king of the first group, then a further list of 6 Kings that are listed with no patronage. Thereafter every king listed has his name, his relationship to the previous ruler, and the number of years that he ruled. The library also provides descriptions of the conquests of some of these Kings adding a great more color and texture to the history. From these records we can see that the Assyrians went through several periods of power followed by periods of weakness. From a Biblical perspective, the most relevant period of Assyrian history was that of its last great period of greatness known as the Neo-Assyrian Empire (ca. 745-608 B.C.) (Table 7).

Table 7. Kings of the Neo-Assyrian Empire 745-608 B.C.

King	Years of Reign
Tiglath-Pileser III	745-727 B.C.
Shalmaneser V	727-722
Sargon II	721-705
Sennacherib	705-681
Esarhaddon	681-669
Ashurbanipal	669-627
Ashur-etil-ilani	631-627
Sin-shumu-lishir	626
Sin-shar-ishkun	626-612
Ashur-uballit II	612-608

In the years prior to 750 B.C., Assyria had once again retreated inward after several stunning defeats at the hands of a coalition led by the Aramean city-states. Power in Assyria was not concentrated at the level of the King; instead regional governors more or less did as they pleased, living as feudal lords. There was no central army to back up the power of the King. Into this vacuum, the Governor of Calah, a general by the name of Pulu (Biblical "Pul"), led a revolt and became King in 745 B.C., taking the throne name of Tiglath-Pileser III (II Kings 15:19). He immediately instituted a series of wide-sweeping reforms which completely transformed the Assyrian state. These reforms included:

- Strengthening the central government by placing all power with the King
- Replacing all existing governors with eunuchs loyal to the King

- Instituting unannounced visits by royal "inspectors"; if they were not treated by the same standards accorded to the King, the local officials would all be put to death
- Formalizing a standing army
- Reorganizing the army into units of cavalry, heavy infantry, light infantry, sling throwers and chariots
- Redesigning the Assyrian chariot into a massive four horse-drawn, four-man fighting vehicle with one driver, one shield protector and two archers
- Designing massive siege engines capable of destroying any city wall

With the completion of the above reforms, Tiglath-Pileser III instituted a major expansion of the empire. All newly conquered lands were to be largely depopulated with the native population either killed or resettled within Assyria; the new lands were then to be repopulated by ethnic Assyrians. Besieged cities were given three days to surrender; if they surrendered on day 1, no one would be killed; if they did not surrender on day 2, all the city leaders would be executed upon capture of the city by means of public impalement on sharpened stakes; if the city did not surrender on day 3, the whole city would be destroyed and the entire population either killed or sold into slavery. As can be seen in Figure 85, Tiglath-Pileser III's military campaigns were extremely successful, subjugating the rest of Mesopotamia (Babylon) first, followed by Anatolia and Syria, and ultimately all of Palestine in less than 50 years (II Kings 15:19-20).

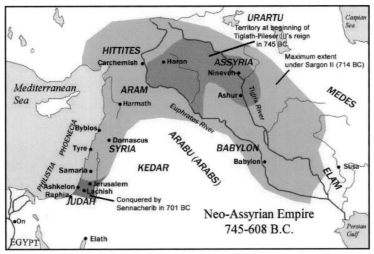

Figure 85. Map of the Assyrian Empire under Tiglath-Pileser III (ca. 745-727 B.C.).
(Map illustrated by Lance K. Trask after Ralph F. Wilson)

The Assyrian weapon of choice was the bow and arrow. All Assyrian cavalry men carried a bow as did the two armed men in the four-man heavy chariot. The light infantry, which was typically composed of non-Assyrians, also had bowmen. As a result, bronze arrowpoints were produced in the millions (Figure 86). Most ethnic Assyrians (cavalry, chariot forces and the heavy infantry) wore bronze helmets for protection. The heavy infantry was additionally equipped with spears and swords, bronze helmets, shields and bronze chest armor, the latter being constructed from dozens of plates approximately 2 1/2 x 3/4 inches sewn together in an overlapping arrangement. Behind the infantry would be the "peltists" who were armed with light javelins, bows and slings. Assyrian slingers were apparently particularly lethal and thousands of very heavy sling stones can be found at the sites of major Assyrian battles or sieges (Figure 87).

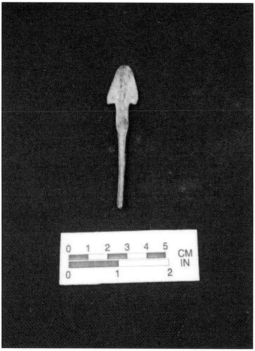

Figure 86. Assyrian bronze arrowhead from the period of the Neo-Assyrian Empire. (Wilson W. Crook, III Collection)

Figure 87. Assyrian sling stone from the siege of Lachish, Judah (701 B.C.). (Wilson W. Crook, III Collection)

Tiglath-Pileser III formulated a relatively simple but effective order of battle. In the center of the line was his heavy infantry made up exclusively of ethnic Assyrian veterans. These men were the toughest soldiers in the army. Flanking the heavy infantry was the light infantry, armed with an assortment of weapons but usually not equipped with the same plated armor worn by the heavy infantry. The light infantry contained both Assyrian and non-Assyrian soldiers, the latter usually conscripts and mercenaries from conquered lands. Behind this line of infantry were the peltists. On either flank of the infantry was the cavalry, also composed of ethnic Assyrians who were expert bowmen. As the two armies would line up, Tiglath-Pileser would move his heavy chariots to the front of the line. These vehicles acted as the tanks of their day and would charge the enemy line. Long curved scythes were added to the wheels of the chariots which would smash through the enemy's line, the horses trampling men, the wheel blades cutting a wide swath through the opposition while the bowmen in the chariots cut down the enemy with arrows. If the opposing force broke and ran, Tiglath-Pileser would release the cavalry to run them down and complete the rout. If they withstood the chariot charge, the infantry would move forward, the light infantry first, followed by the heavy infantry. Before the two lines engaged, the peltists would assail the enemy with javelins and sling stones. The heavy infantry would be reserved for the final *coup de grace*. Interestingly, the effectiveness of the battle plan devised by Tiglath-Pileser stood the test of time and was used with some minor modification by Napoleon 2,500 years later.

In addition to the above information which is preserved in Assyrian cuneiform tablets, virtually all of the military reforms described above can be verified from the discovery of a treasure trove of carved gypsum slabs that once adorned the palace walls in Nineveh. These priceless artifacts were recovered by early archeologists working in Nineveh in the 19th Century and have been exquisitely preserved and are on display today in the various Assyrian rooms in the British Museum in London. The scenes depict the army on maneuvers with troops crossing rivers using animal bladders as floats. The depiction of the siege of the Judean city of Lachish in 701 B.C. is particularly well preserved and shows in detail every aspect of the Assyrian army, including the large siege engines, captives being impaled on sharpened stakes, and captives being tortured by being skinned alive. Enemy prisoners were especially cruelly treated, often being carried off by the use of hooks through the nose or lips.

"And I will turn you back, and put hooks in your jaws, and I will bring you forth, and all your army, horses and horsemen." Ezekiel 38:4

After conquering Syria and placing the Northern Kingdom of Israel and the other rebelling states in Palestine under Assyrian overlordship, Tiglath-Pileser III returned to Assyria. He died in 727 B.C. and was succeeded by his eldest son, Shalmaneser V. Shalmaneser continued the policies of his father and when Israel rebelled yet again against Assyria, he led the army in a three year siege of the capital of Samaria, destroying both the city and the entire Northern Kingdom of Israel (II Kings 18-19). It is unclear if Shalmaneser himself completed the destruction of Israel, which is generally listed as occurring in 721 B.C. He may even have died during this campaign and was succeeded by his younger brother, Sargon II. Sargon is recorded as carrying out the deportation of 27,290 Israelites which has led to the story of the "Lost Ten Tribes of Israel". As was frequently the case in ancient times, when an oppressive foreign King died, especially if he was away from home, there were frequent revolts following his death by the conquered peoples. As a result, Sargon II spent much of his reign putting down revolts in Babylon, then in the western provinces of Anatolia, and later in the northern part of the empire near Armenia. Sargon II died in battle in Tabal, a province in central Anatolia in 705 B.C. after a 16 year reign. He was succeeded by his son, Sennacherib (grandson of Tiglath-Pileser III) who may not have been Sargon's eldest son. Sennacherib's date of succession is variously given in Assyrian records as 705, 704 or even 703 B.C., so the succession may not have been a smooth process.

It was the death of Sargon II and the confusion that followed that spurred King Hezekiah of Judah to form an alliance with Ashkelon and Egypt and refuse to pay tribute to Assyria. It took Sennacherib several years to put down local revolts before he could march on Judah. Several accounts of the campaign have been preserved. The Biblical account is in II Kings 18-19 which states that after destroying 46 cities in Judah, Sennacherib came to besiege Jerusalem but was stopped when a plague swept through the Assyrian army and killed 185,000 soldiers. A large clay cylinder, known as the "Sennacherib prism", tells the Assyrian side of the story in which Sennacherib destroyed 46 cities in Judah and then hemmed up Hezekiah "like a bird in a cage" and forced him to pay a great deal of tribute in gold.

The remainder of Sennacherib's reign was spent trying to solve "the Babylonian problem". The Babylonians, especially the people from the southernmost part of Babylon (known as "Chaldea") always strongly resented Assyrian rule. After a series of punitive campaigns, Sennacherib completely destroyed the city of Babylon in 689 B.C. This action resulted in even greater resentment against the Assyrians which, in part, led to the end of the Assyrian Empire 77 years later.

In 681 B.C. Sennacherib was assassinated under mysterious circumstances. It seems that he had designated a younger son, Esarhaddon, to be his heir. Sennacherib's eldest son, Arda-Mulissi, was accused of the murder and Esarhaddon had him killed. The assassination is recorded in the Bible (II Kings 19:37) and in both Babylonian and Assyrian records. Recent research has shown that Sennacherib's true eldest son, Assur-nadin-sumi, had been captured and killed earlier by the Babylonians. One of Sennacherib's wives (and mother of Esarhaddon), Naqia, convinced her husband that Esarhaddon should be the heir designate instead of his second son, Arda-Mulissi. Esarhaddon was apparently somewhat sickly and not very popular with the people, so by assuming the throne, Arda-Mulissi thought he would gain the support of the King's advisors. Esarhaddon turned out to be a much stronger person that his half-brother supposed and Arda-Mulissi was quickly eliminated.

Esarhaddon apparently disagreed with his father's policies against Babylon and spent considerable effort to rebuild the Babylonian capital. Esarhaddon led a number of military campaigns both to Anatolia as well as into Egypt. He died in 669 B.C. and divided the empire between his two sons, one ruling over Babylon and the other, Ashurbanipal, ruling the rest of Assyria. Ashurbanipal (ca. 669-627 B.C.) was the last great King of the Neo-Assyrian Empire and it is from the discovery of his great library at Nineveh that we know so much about Assyrian history. Following Ashurbanipal's death, a series of very weak Kings tried to rule the empire but much of the decisive leadership and military prowess so evident in Tiglath-Pileser III and his sons and grandson were gone. Sensing an opportunity to finally throw off the Assyrian yoke, the Babylonians revolted in 626 B.C., and eventually destroyed the Assyrian Empire in a series of decisive battles that took place in 612, 608, and finally 605 B.C.

We owe much of our understanding of the Neo-Assyrian Empire and its Kings, history and culture to the exploits of three British scholars and explorers of the 19th Century. The first was Sir Austen Henry Layard who traveled to Mosul in Iraq, and seeing the vast mounds across the Tigris River, crossed over and spent the next two years excavating parts of Nineveh. He published two great volumes on his work, "*Nineveh and its Remains*" in 1848 followed by "*Illustrations of the Monuments of Nineveh*" in 1849. Layard was the explorer who discovered and catalogued the great library of King Ashurbanipal which contained over 22,000 cuneiform tablets covering every aspect of Assyrian life. Layard sent all of his discoveries to the British Museum (where they are to this day) and for his efforts he was knighted and is known as the "Father of Assyriology".

The second great Assyriologist was a British army officer, Sir Henry Rawlinson. Rawlinson traveled extensively through Persia and Assyria between 1827 and 1855. He surveyed many ancient Assyrian cities (mounds of ruins) but his greatest contribution was the discovery of the "Behistun Inscription", a large Persian monument which was inscribed in Persian, Elamite and Akkadian (Babylonian). By comparing the three languages, he was able to begin to decipher the cuneiform script which led to the reading of all the Assyrian tablets. The third member of this trio of British scholars was George Smith, an engraver with the treasury in London. Smith was an avid amateur archeologist and spent every lunch hour at the British Museum studying the cuneiform tablets from Assyria. He became more knowledgeable on cuneiform than anyone on the staff of the British Museum, so at the recommendation of Sir Henry Rawlinson, Smith was hired full time. He led several expeditions to Iraq and is credited with translating many of the great Assyrian epics, including the famous *Epic of Gilgamesh*.

Why is understanding Assyrian history and literature so important? The translations of the Assyrian histories written by the Kings of the Neo-Assyrian Empire provided the first extra-Biblical sources for material contained in the Old Testament. Several examples of the congruence between the Bible and the Assyrian chronicles are shown below:

Fall of Damascus

"The King of Assyria went up against Damascus, and took it and carried the people of it captive to Kir, and slew Rezin." II Kings 16:9

"His noblemen I impaled alive and displayed this exhibition to his land. All his gardens and fruit orchards I destroyed. I besieged and captured the native city of Rezin of Damascus. Eight hundred people with their belongings I led away. Towns in sixteen districts of Damascus I laid waste like mounds after the flood." Tiglath-Pileser III, 733 B.C.

The Fall of the Northern Kingdom of Israel

"In the days of Pekah King of Israel, came Tiglath-Pileser, King of Assyria and took . . . Hazor and Gilead of Galilee, all the land of Naphtali and carried them captive to Assyria. And Hoshea . . . made a conspiracy against Pekah and slew him and reigned in his stead." II Kings 15:29-30

"Israel all of whose cities I added to my territories on my former campaigns, and had left out only the city of Samaria . . . the whole of Naphtali I took for Assyria. I put my officials over them as governors. The land of Israel, all of its people and their possessions I took away to Assyria." Tiglath-Pileser III, 733 B.C.

"They overthrew Pekah their King and I made Hoshea to be King over them." Tiglath-Pileser III, 733 B.C.

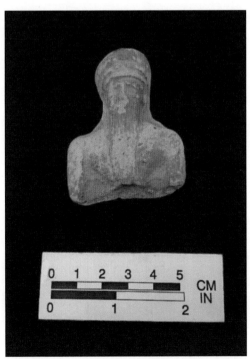

Figure 88. Clay statue of the principal Assyrian god Ashur. (Wilson W. Crook, III Collection)

In terms of their true cultural contributions, it is difficult to discern what is Sumerian, what is Babylonian and what is actually Assyrian culture. The Assyrians largely borrowed what we would describe as "culture" from every people and land they conquered. The one aspect of Assyrian culture that is truly indigenous is their belief in the principal deity of Ashur (Figure 88). Ashur is variously depicted but is most traditionally shown as the upper half of what is clearly an Assyrian bearded male (almost all Assyrian men had extensive beards, often combed in ringlets) who is within a winged disc and is holding a bow and arrows. Some scholars believe the disc is representative of the sun while others believe it is a chariot wheel. Ashur was the national god of Assyria and was generally treated more like the king of the gods as well as being the god of war. The Assyrians believed that all the other gods were forced to recognize Ashur as the supreme deity. Worship of Ashur in Assyria dates to the third millennium B.C., but was particularly revived during the time of the Neo-Assyrian Empire. Other gods worshiped by the Assyrians included most of the known Mesopotamian pantheon including Shamash (sun god), Sin (moon god), and Inanna/Ishtar (fertility).

The Assyrian Kings also carried the title of "High Priests" and were expected to oversee the religious observances of the Assyrian High Holy Days which occurred during the last two months of the year and the first month of the New Year. Conquered peoples were made to take an oath ("*ade*") to the Assyrian gods, especially to Ashur. This may account for much of the introduction of the Assyrian deities into both Israel and Judah during the time of the Divided Kingdom. The Assyrians, like all their neighbors, lived in a world populated by many gods and goddesses, demons, spirits and ghosts of the dead – both good and malevolent. They were a superstitious people as evidenced by the large number of cuneiform tablets which deal with incantations and spells.

In summary, the Assyrians left a legacy of military prowess and savage cruelty all across the Ancient Middle East. Attesting to this legacy, much of what remains as "Assyrian art" are scenes of battle, death, killing and the torture of prisoners. They were God's instrument to bring about the destruction of the Northern Kingdom of Israel but ultimately they themselves were judged and completely destroyed by the Babylonians. Had it not been for the efforts of men like Layard, Rawlinson and Smith in the 19th Century, the Assyrians would have been consigned forever to the dust bin of history.

7. BABYLONIANS

The Babylonian people originally came from what are today Kuwait and the southern half of Iraq in the land between the Tigris and Euphrates Rivers and their delta ("Mesopotamia"). The exact boundaries of Babylonia varied over time but the central Babylonian heartland lay in the fertile plains between the two rivers south of Baghdad. All the major Babylonian cities were either located on the Euphrates River or on one of its canals. The Babylonians are notable in the Bible because they (1) originated and passed on much of the original cultural and religious foundations for the entire Ancient Middle East, (2) they were God's chosen instrument to destroy Judah and the Temple and place the Israelite people into exile for a period of time, and (3) they strongly influenced Jewish lifestyle and culture which is still evident in Judaism today.

The origin of the name "Babylon" is uncertain but the Akkadian word "*Bab-ilim*" meaning the "Gate of God" could be the origin for the city's name. The plural of the word, "*Bab-ilani*", became "*Babulon*" in Greek from which we get the modern word, Babylon. The city of Babylon is known to have existed in the third millennium B.C., but it was not until the reign of Hammurabi (ca. 1790-1752 B.C.) that it became the cultural and political center of Mesopotamia. Like Assyria, Babylonia went through periods of expansion and growth as well as periods when they were suppressed, the latter mainly by the Assyrians. In terms of Biblical history, it is the Neo-Babylonian Empire (or "Chaldean" Empire) that had the most direct impact on the Israelite people.

As detailed in Chapter 6, Babylon was largely under the direct rule of the Assyrians from the rise of Tiglath-Pileser III in 745 B.C. to the death of his descendant Ashurbanipal in 627 B.C. Following Ashurbanipal's death, there seems to have been a great deal of confusion regarding the succession to the Assyrian throne, followed by an extended period of internal machinations with various forces vying for control of the empire. A Babylonian general named Nabopolassar saw the growing weakness in Assyria and realized that it was an opportunity for Babylon to throw off the yoke of their Assyrian overlords. He formed an alliance with the Medes and Persians and together, in a series of battles, they defeated the Assyrians culminating in the sacking of Nineveh in 612 B.C. The remainder of the Assyrian army retreated to the west and Nabopolassar, in conjunction with the Medes, defeated them at the battle of Haran. A remnant of the Assyrian army escaped and tried to form an alliance with the Egyptians. In 605 B.C., Nabopolassar sent his son, Nebuchadnezzar, to lead the Babylonian army which gained a crushing and final victory over the Assyrians at the Battle of Carchemish in northern Syria.

Nabopolassar appears to have been very much a self-made man. He is described on some Babylonian monuments as "the son of nobody"; not because he wasn't proud of his father but rather Nabopolassar wanted to emphasize that he came from common stock and rose to create an empire (Table 8). To ensure the stability of the new empire with his allies the Medes, Nabopolassar married his son Nebuchadnezzar to the Median princess, Amytis. Born out of a political necessity, the marriage was one of the true love stories of the ancient world and it is believed that Nebuchadnezzar had the famous "Hanging Gardens of Babylon" built for his Queen to remind her of the lush forests of her homeland in the mountains of Media.

Table 8. Kings of the Neo-Babylonian Empire 626-539 B.C.

King	Years of Reign
Nabopolassar	626-605 B.C.
Nebuchadnezzar II	605-562
Amel-Marduk	562-560
Nergel-Sherezar (Kashaya)	560-556
Labashi-Marduk	556
Nabonidus	556-539
Belshazzar (Regent in Babylon)	556-539

Nebuchadnezzar (whose name means "O Nabu, protect my offspring") inherited almost all of the lands of the Assyrian Empire. To this he added land in Anatolia (modern Turkey) and all of Syria-Palestine as far as the border of Egypt (Figure 89). His Empire was the largest in terms of aerial extent up to that time but interestingly, most of his monuments and inscriptions comment more on his great building projects than on his territorial conquests. Nebuchadnez-zar's great pride (Daniel 4:30) was not without some justification. Babylon rapidly became the greatest city on the face of the earth with a population in excess of 200,000. The city was surrounded by 11 miles of walls, all 100 feet in height – 40 feet of which was buried underground to prevent tunneling. The walls were so wide that it was said a four-horse chariot had room to turn around on the wall without having to back up. Babylon had eight large gates, each named for a particular god. The most famous was the Ishtar Gate, which was covered in blue enamel bricks which served as the backdrop for red and white colored dragons (symbolic of Marduk) and bulls (symbolic of Adad). Leading to the gate was the Great Processional Way, a 65 foot wide walled street that was also adorned with blue enameled bricks covered with gold lions – the symbol of Ishtar. Each of the bricks in the Great Processional Way and in the Ishtar Gate was stamped with Nebuchadnezzar's name and lineage (Figure 90):

"Nabu-kuduri-usur shar Babili

zanin Esgila u Ezida

aplu asharedu

sha Nabu-aplu-usur shar Babili"

Nebuchadnezzar King of Babylon

patron of Esgila and Ezida

eldest son of

Nabopolassar King of Babylon

Babylon was not just the capital of Babylonia; it was the religious and commercial center of the empire as well. There were over 1,100 temples in the city with the greatest being the Temple of Marduk (patron god of Babylon), the Temple of Ishtar, and the Great Ziggurat which was several hundred feet high and constructed with an estimated 15 million mud bricks – each bearing the name of Nebu-

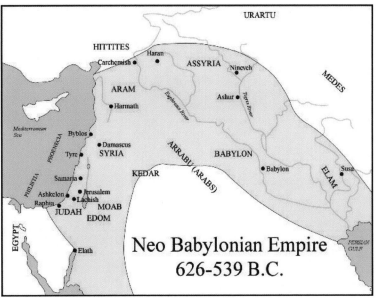

Figure 89. Map of the Neo-Babylonian Empire, 626-539 B.C..
(Map illustrated by Lance K. Trask after Ralph F. Wilson)

Figure 90. Part of a brick from the Great Processional Way in Babylon. Note the cuneiform inscription bearing the name of Nebuchadnezzar. (Wilson W. Crook, III Collection)

Figure 91. Burned cuneiform tablet from Babylon dealing with repayment of debts. (Wilson W. Crook, III Collection)

chadnezzar. It was said that the inside walls of the Temple of Marduk were completely lined with gold such that when the sun came through window slits on the walls, the entire room reflected the sun into a blinding golden light. The remains of Nebuchadnezzar's great palace, containing more than 250 rooms, have also been found. The walls in the main King's chamber were covered with baked enamel bricks depicting scenes of palm trees and oases.

Babylon was also a city full of shops. Each day, the narrow winding streets of the city would be lined with awnings protecting the tables of vendors and their wares. Each day in the evening, all the tables and awnings would all be packed up and taken into the houses only to be set up again the next morning. Besides the necessities of life, the shops of Babylon sold wares from all over the empire. Babylon was the largest center of business in the ancient world and contained numerous banking establishments, insurance companies, money exchange centers and precious jewelry dealers. Thousands of clay cuneiform tablets have been recovered from Babylon which document the ins and outs of daily business life including sales receipts, promissory notes of payment, bank loans, repayment of debts, and insurance for jewelry (Figure 91).

Nabopolasar and Nebuchadnezzar largely modeled the Babylonian army and its tactics after the Assyrians. The army was composed of both heavy and light infantry with strong cavalry forces protecting the wings. Large, four-horse chariots were present which still functioned as formation breaking attack vehicles. The Babylonians also used large siege engines which would be transported in pieces to the besieged city, reassembled, and pushed against the city walls. The wooden frame of the engines was protected by a covering of animal hides which was constantly doused in water to prevent flaming arrows from setting the structure on fire. The top of the engine had a protected platform from which Babylonian archers would fire down at the city defenders. The main weapon of these machines was a large battering ram which was concealed within the structure and would proceed to pound the walls, eventually leading to a breach that enabled the besieging troops to enter the city. Before an attack, engineers would first survey the city and determine the weakest points which would be where the siege engines were placed. The main weapon of the Babylonian army remained the bow and arrow and the Babylonians cast many types of arrow points, some of which contained vicious barbs that could not be pulled out but either had to be pushed through or cut out leaving horrid wounds (Figure 92). Most soldiers were lightly armored, wearing bronze helmets and carrying metal-coated wooden shields. The heavy infantry, as with the Assyrians, wore plated bronze mail armor and carried spears and swords. Officers also carried short daggers as a symbol of their rank (Figure 93).

The Babylonians adopted a similar process to the Assyrians of deportation of peoples from

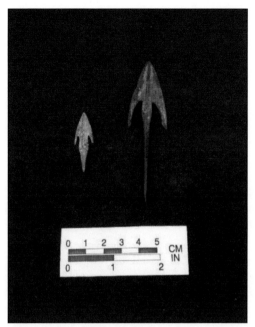

Figure 92. Babylonian bronze arrowheads with prominent razor sharp barbs.
(Wilson W. Crook, III Collection)

Figure 93. Babylonian bronze officer dagger.
(Wilson W. Crook, III Collection)

conquered lands, but their execution of the exile was vastly different. That does not mean to say that the Babylonians were always less cruel than the Assyrians; they could be just as harsh if the situation called for it. After all, they did defeat the Assyrians and destroy their empire. Nebuchadnezzar had a policy where he would take selected young men from conquered lands, men who came from prominent families, and place then "in training" in the Babylonian court. They would be raised and educated as Babylonians loyal to the King, and then at a later date, returned to their homelands where they would help Nebuchadnezzar rule the territories as Babylonian vassals. The story of the prophet Daniel and his companions is a demonstration of this policy. Moreover, the rest of the people who were deported would not just be resettled into the Babylonian Empire but would be allowed, even encouraged, to participate in Babylonian society including owning businesses and even slaves of their own. In fact, as evidenced by the long Babylonian (and later Persian) history of many Jews, life within the Babylonian Empire could be very prosperous.

Like most sedentary civilizations, the Babylonian diet was cereal grain based. Barley was the primary grain crop as wheat was not as hardy in the environment of the Tigris-Euphrates River Valley. Bread was baked in the form of flat loaves similar to elsewhere in the Ancient Middle East. Vegetables were abundant, especially lentils, but also included carrots, cucumbers, onions, lettuce, gourds, pumpkins and heart-of-palm. Fruits could be grown in some regions; apricots, dates, figs, grapes, pomegranates, peaches, plums, olives and even apples are recorded in Babylonian records. Nuts were also a common part of the diet, mainly almonds and pistachios. Milk was rare and not frequently consumed; butter, curds and cheese – mostly from goat milk – were consumed. Wine was made from both grapes and palm trees (from fermented sap) and a bitter tasting beer was made from barley. The latter, still made today, is very dark and thick and continues to ferment in the consumer's stomach making him drunker and drunker as time goes on. Meat was not abundant but the people did occasionally eat roasted fowl (ducks, geese, partridge, quail and doves) and animal meat (mutton, goat, pork, and rarely, antelope and beef). If they lived on the Euphrates or in the delta, fish and oysters would be consumed. Locusts would also be dried, ground up, and mixed with honey. As many meals were rather bland (bread and vegetables), spices were a major commodity. Babylonian tablets tell of meals being prepared using coriander, fennel, garlic, mustard, rue, saffron and thyme. Other condiments included honey, palm sugar and sesame seed oil. Recently a tablet has been found at Larsa in southern Babylon which contains a list of 25 recipes for soups and stews. The following is one for pigeon stew:

>*"Split the pigeon in half. Prepare the water. Add salt and fat to taste. Add bread*
>*crumbs, onion, samidu, leeks and garlic (first soak the herbs in milk). When it is*
>*cooked it is ready to serve."*

Only the herb "samidu" is unknown.

The Babylonians were a deeply religious people, with a large pantheon of gods and goddesses that numbered into the thousands (Table 9). The Babylonians worshiped an eclectic mixture of traditional Mesopotamian (mainly Sumerian) gods blended with those of the Semitic peoples to the west. The principal deities consisted of Apsu and Tiamet – the two entities responsible for creation, Anu (Sumerian An) – the god of the heavens, Enlil – king of the land, Ea (Sumerian Enki) – god of wisdom and magic, Sin (Sumerian Nanna) – god of the moon, Shamash (Sumerian Utu) – god of the sun, Adad (Semitic Hadad) – god of lightning and rain, and Ishtar (Sumerian Inanna) – goddess of the planet Venus. To Ishtar were added the characteristics of the Semitic fertility goddesses and she also became the goddess of love, fertility and war. Originally a minor deity, by the time of the Neo-Babylonian Empire the principal god in the entire pantheon was Marduk – king of the gods and patron god of the city of Babylon and its rulers. All the gods were sexual beings who married, raised families, and were subject to injury, even death. Humankind was created merely to relieve the gods of the burden of physical labor and to perform worship and service to the gods. Due to their belief in so many gods, the Babylonians did not impose their beliefs on new peoples brought into the empire. By and large, people were free to worship as they wished, as long as their beliefs did not interfere with the functioning of Babylonian society.

The elevation of Marduk to the principal Babylonian deity stemmed from an epic creation story known as the *"Enuma Elish"*. Copies of this story consisting of a 1,000 lines on seven tablets were found in Ashurbanipal's great library. In the beginning, according to the epic, before the earth was formed, there were two primordial beings, Apsu, god of the fresh waters, and Tiamet, goddess of the salt waters (oceans). The two gods were married and had a large number of children which became the lesser gods. The noise from the play of the lesser

Table 9. Principal Gods in the Babylonian Pantheon

Name	Sacred Number	Celestial Representation	Sacred Symbol	Patron City
Apsu	0	Fresh Waters	0	0
Tiamet	0	Salt Waters	0	0
Anu	60	Equatorial Stars	Bull	Der
Enlil	50	Pleiades	0	Nippur
Ea	40	Pisces	Goat-Fish	Eridu
Sin	30	Moon	Crescent Moon	Ur
Shamash	20	Sun	Sun Disk	Sippur
Adad	6	Lightning	Bull	Borsippa
Marduk	60	Jupiter	Dragon	Babylon
Ishtar	15	Venus	Lion; Star	Babylon

gods annoyed Apsu and he threatened to kill all of the children. Ea, the god of wisdom and magic, was forewarned of this action and created a potion which put Apsu to sleep, making it possible for Ea to then kill his father Apsu. Tiamet was enraged and vowed to kill the lesser gods, creating 11 terrible monsters to help her do this. All of the lesser gods were fearful until Marduk stepped forward and said he would take on Tiamet and her monsters, but only if the other gods would then acknowledge him as their King. Marduk slew all of the monsters and ripped Tiamet in two, using both portions of her body to create the heavens and the earth. From her blood he created all of mankind and the animals, thus freeing the rest of the gods from manual labor so that they could honor and pay homage to Marduk. The gods acknowledged Marduk as the supreme deity of the universe and bestowed 50 honorific names to him. The *Enuma Elish* depicting Marduk's ascension to the head of the gods was read each year at the time of the New Year Festival ("*Akitu*" Festival) during which a solid gold statue of Marduk would be taken out of his temple and paraded through the streets to the palace of the King. The King would then ceremonially grasp the hand of Marduk, thus ensuring the god's favor for the coming year.

The Babylonians saw the world as a single closed system in which events in one realm (the earth) would be directly reflected in another (the heavens). As such, ritual prostitution, notably in the Temple of the goddess Ishtar, was common. Even the King was expected to participate as were almost all young women at some time prior to marriage. Given their belief in a cause-and-effect relationship between people and events, the Babylonians developed massive pseudo-sciences for observing unusual phenomena and the events that followed. Through divination, the will of the gods could be determined and potentially predicted. A large number of omen-predicting techniques were practiced including observing the behavior of birds, celestial phenomena, the patterns of oil on water, smoke from incense, and the reading of animal entrails, especially the liver (Figure 94). Schools were set up to teach young practitioners how to read these various omens. People also kept in their houses small "household gods". Many of these small figurines were made of bronze and depicted winged deities which would carry the thoughts of the owners to the gods (Figure 95). Babylonians also frequently carried small stone "cylinder seals" which had a lengthwise hole so that they could be worn either around the owner's neck or attached to his belt. The seals were engraved such that in order to see the complete scene depicted, a small stick had to be placed through the hole and the cylinder rolled across a wet piece of clay (Figure 96). Most of these cylinder seals depict a petitioner (the seal's owner?) kneeling or making supplications to one or more of the gods in the Babylonian pantheon.

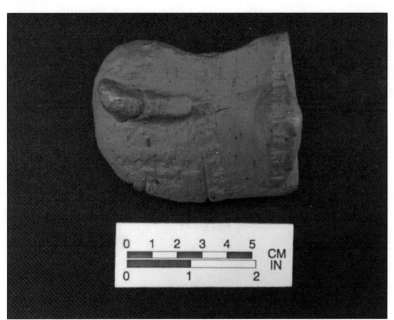

Figure 94. Reproduction of Babylonian liver model. The cuneiform written in four places on the model says the following:
"One King will bend down to another";
"An enemy will attack my country";
"Forgiveness will be granted by a god";
"A servant will rebel against his Lord"
(Wilson W. Crook, III Collection)

Babylonian medicine was a mixture of actual care for the patient coupled with magic and incantations and spells. When a person was ill, the "*Apishu*" or doctor would come to visit. If the person needed extensive treatment, a dead sparrow would be nailed to the patient's door as a sign to all that the *Apishu* was at work. Babylonians had a strong belief in demons, spirits

Figure 96. Babylonian cylinder seal (left) and its rolled out scene which depicts a worshiper before the seated figure of the moon god Sin (note the crescent moon shape over the two figures). (Wilson W. Crook, III Collection)

Figure 95.   Babylonian household winged gods. (Wilson W. Crook, III Collection)

and ghosts, and much of the ills of the world, and of people in particular, were ascribed to the intervention of these malevolent spirits into a person's life. Thus, medical cures were often as much of an exorcism as a medicinal treatment. A number of medical tablets have survived regarding cures; some more typical texts are shown below:

> *"If a patent keeps crying out, 'My skull! My skull!', it is the hand of a god."*

> *"If a man's body is yellow, his face is yellow, and his eyes are yellow, and the flesh is flabby, it is the yellow disease."*

> *"If a man is stricken with a stroke and his whole torso feels paralyzed, it is the work of a stroke; he will die."*

> *"There are 25 drugs for an ointment against the hand of a ghost."*

> *"If a man has drunk too much strong wine, if his head is confused, if he forgets his words and his speech becomes blurred, if his thoughts wander and his eyes are glassy, the cure is to take (11 drugs listed) and mix them with oil and wine at the approach of the*

goddess Gula in the morning before sunrise and before anyone has kissed the patient, let him take the draught. He will recover."

The Babylonians also made significant discoveries and contributions in science, notably in mathematics and astronomy. Hundreds of mathematical tables have been found on cuneiform tablets, many showing a knowledge of algebra and geometry that would not be equaled in Europe for another 2,000 years. One tablet recovered from a Babylonian library is nothing but a long list of solutions for the length of the long side of a triangle which would later be "discovered" by the Greeks and recorded as the "Pythagorean Theorem". In all their mathematical calculations, the Babylonians used a sexagesimal system based on the number 60 (Marduk's sacred number) which has come down to us in the form of the 60-minute hour and the 360-degree circle.

Large scribal schools preserved a great deal of Babylonian (and other Mesopotamian) literature including a large number of proverbs and sayings. Many of these are not dissimilar from Biblical proverbs and show the same sense of moral right and wrong as well as human frailty and sense of fatalism that is present in some of the Biblical writings. Some of the more famous (and humorous) Babylonians proverbs are listed below:

"Do not return evil to your adversary; maintain justice for your enemy, do good things, be kind in all your days; what you say in haste you may regret later."

"The gods alone live forever under the divine sun; but as for mankind, their days are numbered, all their activities will be nothing but wind."

"Making loans is as easy as making love, but repaying them is as hard as bearing a child."

"Who has not supported a wife; his nose has not borne a leash."

"Has she become pregnant without intercourse? Has she become fat without eating?"

"Go up to the ancient ruin heaps and walk around; look at the skulls of the lowly and great. Which belongs to someone who did evil and which to someone who did good?"

The above writing comes from a literature form known as "wisdom literature". In addition to simple one-line proverbs and maxims, there are several lengthy Babylonian poems that deal with topics familiar to all readers. The most famous of these is entitled the "*Ludlul Bel Nemeqi*" or "I will praise the Lord of Wisdom". Also known as "The Poem of the Righteous Sufferer", it deals with the topic of unmerited human suffering. In the poem, the human narrator suffers a series of calamities: he is victimized by the King, afflicted with diseases and rejected as a social outcast. Eventually he finds out that his ills are really not the result of human actions, but instead his fate is being controlled by the god Marduk. In a dream, he discovers that Marduk has eventually been appeased and his fortunes are to be restored. While sometimes referred to as "the Babylonian Job", the story is not a direct correlation to the Biblical story but the similarities are obvious.

The Neo-Babylonian Empire reached its zenith under Nebuchadnezzar II. Following his death in 562 B.C., three successive weak rulers assumed the throne: his son Amel-Marduk (Biblical Evil Merodach – II Kings 25:27), who ruled for an ineffective two years, Nebuchadnezzar's son-in-law, Nergel-Sherezar, who ruled for four years, and the latter's son, Labashi-Marduk, who ruled for less than a year. Amel-Marduk was assassinated by Nergel-Sherezar, a general in the army. The latter was married to Nebuchadnezzar's daughter, Kashiya, who apparently was the real power and brains behind the coup of her brother. Nergel-Sherezar died mysteriously and of his son, Labashi-Marduk, little is known other than he ruled for a very short time. It is customary to place Nabonidus ("Nabu is Praised") into the line of the Neo-Babylonian Kings but he was not of the direct lineage of Nabopolasar. He is believed to have been a general in the Babylonian army and succeeded to the throne after yet another coup. He may have been responsible for one or both of Nergel-Sherezar's and Labashi-Marduk's deaths. It seems that Nabonidus mainly wanted to stabilize the situation in the empire and never really wanted to rule. Shortly after taking the throne, he withdrew "into the desert" to build a temple to the moon god Sin and worship him. He left his eldest son, Belshazzar, as co-regent in Babylon to keep an eye on civil administration.

Belshazzar ("May Bel (Marduk) Protect His Life") was the Hugh Hefner of the Neo-Babylonian Empire. All he wanted to do was party and live the good life in the palace. As his father is known to have been a devoted follower of the moon god Sin, Belshazzar may also have worshiped Sin as his primary god. What is known is that Belshazzar did not maintain the upkeep of the Temple of Marduk and also apparently failed to keep the annual *Akitu* festival tradition. This angered many of the citizens of Babylon who ardently believed Marduk was not only the chief god in the pantheon but also the special protector of Babylon itself. As a result, when Cyrus the Great of Persia came to Babylon in 539 B.C., the people generally welcomed him as a liberator and he captured the city in one day without "firing a shot". Belshazzar was warned of the event at one of his parties by the famous "hand writing on the wall" (Daniel 5). The prediction came true in the form of Cyrus and the Persians, and the 87 year reign of the Neo-Babylonian Empire ended. Babylonia forever ceased to be a separate entity and was absorbed into the new regional power, the Persian Empire.

8. PERSIANS

The story of the Persian Empire is really the story of two peoples: the Medes and the Persians. The Medes and the Persians were two closely related Indo-European peoples that entered the Iranian Plateau sometime after the middle of the second millennium B.C. They are believed to have originated from Central Asia, either to the east or west of the Caspian Sea, and moved into the Zagros Mountain region of western Iran. The capital of the Medes was Ecbatana (modern Hamadan) which lies on a major east-west trade route between Anatolia, Mesopotamia and Iran. The Medes were regarded as some of the best horsemen in the world and Assyrian texts specifically mention Tiglath-Pileser III acquiring 1,615 horses from them in the form of tribute. The Medes seem to have had a highly decentralized society as the records of Sargon II of Assyria mention some 50 Median chieftains. As the Neo-Assyrian Empire began to wane in the latter parts of the 7th Century B.C., the Medes, like the Babylonians, sensed an opportunity to throw off Assyrian control. King Cyaxares (ca. 625-585 B.C.) is credited with uniting the Median tribes and expanding the territory of the Medes to its greatest extant. He was the leader who joined forces with Nabopolassar of Babylon and captured the Assyrian capital of Nineveh in 612 B.C. The last independent King of the Median Kingdom was Astyages (ca. 585-550 B.C.). His daughter, Mandana, married a Persian, Cambyses I, and later gave birth to the famous Cyrus the Great. Cyrus led the Persians in a successful revolt against the Medes, defeating his grandfather Astyages in 550 B.C. Thereafter the Medes were relegated to a subordinate role under the Persians during the next two centuries.

The Persian Empire of 559-331 B.C. was also known as the Achaemenid Empire after an eponymous ancestor, Achaemenes (ca. 700 B.C.) (Table 10). The great grandson of Achaemenes was Cambyses I, whose son was Cyrus II or Cyrus the Great. From the reign of Cyrus the Great to their ultimate defeat at the hands of Alexander of Macedon in 331 B.C., the Persians ruled the largest of all the ancient empires of the world, stretching from India in the east to the Nile in the west; from the Arabian Desert to Central Asia, and even including parts of Greece (Figure 97). Cyrus II began his reign over the Persians in 559 B.C. and defeated the Medes on the plains of Pasargadae in 550 B.C., where he later built his capital. Both the Nabonidus Chronicle and the Greek historian Herodotus state that Cyrus was aided in his

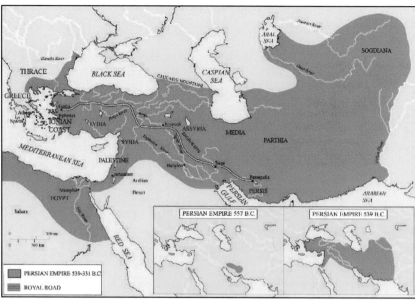

Figure 97. Map of the Persian Empire, 559-331 B.C.
(Map illustrated by Lance K. Trask)

victory through the defection of several key Median chiefs. After consolidating the Persians and the Medes into a single entity (Cyrus was after all, half Persian and half Median), he moved northwestward into Anatolia where he defeated the Lydian King, Croesus, in 546 B.C. The expression "rich as Croesus" implies that the Persians likely acquired significant wealth after their victory over the Lydians. Moreover, with Lydia a Persian province, the door was opened to the entire Ionian coast which was also absorbed into the growing Persian Empire.

The Persians then turned their attention to the weakened Babylonian Empire and, as recounted in the previous chapter, conquered Babylon in a single night with no loss of life. Cyrus entered Babylon on October 12, 539 B.C. and was warmly welcomed by the populace as a liberator over the hated playboy Belshazzar. Cyrus listened to the peoples' complaints and began an enlightened policy whereby he (1) brought food to the people (many had been starved by Belshazzar's "all-for-me" policy), (2) repaired and restored the temples, especially the Temple of Marduk, and (3) issued an edict of human rights and freedom for all of the deported peoples living in Babylonia. Known as the "Cyrus Cylinder" (see Figure 56), a copy of this great document resides in the entry hall of the United Nations Building in New York (the original is in the Persian room at the British Museum in London). A Hebrew copy of the edict can be found in Ezra 1:2-4 and an Aramean copy of the same decree in Ezra 6:3-5.

Table 10. The Achaemenid Dynasty of Persia, 559-331 B.C.

		Achaemenes (ca. 700 B.C.)		
		Teispes		
Araiamnes			Cyrus I	
Hystaspes			Cambyses I	
			Cyrus II (The Great)	559-530 B.C.
			Cambyses II	530-522
			Bardiya (Smerdis)	522
Darius I	522-486			
Xerxes	486-465			
Artaxerxes I	465-425			
Xerxes II	425-424			
Darius II	424-404			
Artaxerxes II	404-359			
Artaxerxes III	359-339			
Arses	339-336			
Darius III	336-331			

In 530 B.C., while nearly 70 years old, Cyrus was campaigning in Scythia (modern Uzbekistan) when he was killed at Syr Darya. His body was transported back to Pasargadae where he was buried in a relatively modest tomb, now a World Heritage Site. His tomb is marked by a simple inscription: "O man, whoever you are and wherever you come from, for I know you will come, I am Cyrus who won the Persians their empire. Do not therefore begrudge me this bit of earth that covers my bones."

Cyrus the Great is one of the few non-Jewish foreign rulers that is highly regarded in the Bible. Cyrus is specifically mentioned by name 23 times and is alluded to in several more passages (Isaiah 39:6-7; 42:1-9; 42:24-25; 43:14). He is called "my servant" by God and is prophetically shown to be God's agent who will save the remnant of the Jews from Babylonian captivity and return them to Israel.

Cyrus was followed on the Persian throne by his eldest son, Cambyses II. Cambyses was known for two things: (1) his conquest of Egypt in 625 B.C., and (2) his exceptional cruelty. By finally capturing Egypt, Cambyses extended the Persian Empire beyond that achieved by either Assyria or Babylonia. Both had marched to the border of Egypt and had even gained some tribute, but neither had actually absorbed Egypt into their empires. With regard to his cruelty, Herodotus recorded one story of Cambyses' treatment of a Persian judge named Sisamnes. Sisamnes apparently held a very high judicial position in the Persian Empire, probably the equivalent of a Supreme Court Justice. Evidence was presented that Sisamnes had privately accepted a large bribe and then delivered an unjust verdict. Cambyses had Sisamnes skinned alive and then upholstered the judge's chair with his skin so that all future holders of that position would realize who was in control of the empire and that graft and corruption were not tolerated.

While Cambyses was away on campaign in 522 B.C., he learned of a coup d'état by his younger brother and rushed back to the capital. On the way, he is reported to have accidently stabbed himself in the leg and died of an infection several weeks later. The story may or may not be true as the succession following Cambyses' death is somewhat muddled. Some historians say that Cambyses killed his younger brother secretly before he began his Egyptian campaign. Other sources indicate that this younger brother, variously named Bardiya or Smerdis, tried to take the throne after Cambyses' death. There is yet another story that Bardiya-Smerdis was indeed dead and an imposter look-alike named Guamata tried to assume the throne. In any event, Bardiya-Smerdis was killed as was Guamata and after a year of intrigue, a general named Darius emerged as the new King of Persia. Darius was not of the direct line from Cyrus the Great but from a collateral line that also descended from Achaemenes (see Table 10). Some scholars believe that Darius invented his genealogy in order to legitimize his ascension to the throne. Regardless of this issue, Darius I would prove to be one of the greatest Kings in the history of the Persian Empire.

As usual after a period of uncertainty over the royal succession, there were revolts around the edges of the empire following the death of Cambyses. Darius spent several years campaigning and putting down the revolts, one of which was in Egypt. While there, he was reported to have built a canal between the Nile and Red Sea, a story most historians believed was apocryphal until several monuments were unearthed in 1972, confirming the story.

Darius reorganized the empire into 22 "Satraps" or provinces, one of which was the sub-province of Judah which lay within the larger province of "Beyond the River". Persia under Darius was indeed colossus itself, with Persian records listing 67 different peoples and nations under his control. Darius moved the capital from Pasargadae to Persepolis, where it would remain for the next two centuries. He standardized all weights and measures to be used throughout the empire and started issuing coins – both silver coins (*"sigloi"*) and gold coins (*"darics"*). Persia thus became the first nation to mint and use standardized coinage which all other nations to this day have adopted. Darius is also credited with establishing a standardized mail system which was essentially the forerunner of the "Pony Express". The Royal Road started in Susa in Persia and extended for 1,700 miles to western Anatolia (see Figure 97). By establishing stations along the route with fresh horses and riders, messages that had taken as long as 90 days to travel across the empire could subsequently be delivered in about a week. The motto of the Persian pony express is almost word for word the motto used today by the U.S. Post Office.

Darius is mentioned in the Bible when, after a 15 year hiatus, work was restarted on the rebuilding of the Temple in Jerusalem. Judah's neighbors complained that rebuilding the Temple was tantamount to rebellion against the Persian King. A search was made of the historic documents in the Persian capital and a copy of Cyrus' edict of religious freedom was found:

> *"King Darius then issued an order, and they searched in the archives stored in the treasury at Babylon. A scroll was found in the citadel at Ecbatana in the province of Media and thus was written on it: 'In the first year of King Cyrus, the King issued a decree concerning the temple of God in Jerusalem. Let the temple be rebuilt as a place to present sacrifices, and let its foundations be laid'." (Ezra 6:1-3)*

Darius was also the first Persian ruler to dream of conquering Greece, which he invaded in 490 B.C. The invasion led to the famous Battle of Marathon where armored Greek hoplites (heavy infantry) defeated a superior force of lightly armored Persians. A Greek soldier, Pheidippides, was dispatched the 26.2 miles to Athens with the message of "Nenikikkamen" ("Rejoice, we conquer"). He then collapsed and died from the strain of the run made in his armor. Darius retreated back into Persia in order to raise a new army but died in Persepolis in 486 B.C. before he could resume his Greek campaign.

Darius was succeeded by his eldest son, Xerxes, who ruled Persia from 486 to 465 B.C. Upon assuming the throne, Xerxes (Biblical Ahasuerus – Ezra 4:6 and the Book of Esther) had to put down revolts first in Egypt and then in Babylon, both of which were suppressed harshly. He was then ready to resume the mission given to him by his father: the invasion and subjugation of Greece. In this cause, he amassed the largest army ever assembled in the ancient world. Herodotus recorded that Xerxes had a force of 1.7 million infantry and cavalry plus 1,200 trireme warships and 3,000 merchant vessels. The enormity of these figures has been challenged for years but reports from Greek scouts that Xerxes' army was "drinking the rivers dry" do support a figure that may have approached a half million men or more. Chief among the army were the "Immortals", a division of elite Persian soldiers that was made up of the finest soldiers in the army. The group was called "the Immortals" because its ranks were always maintained at exactly 10,000 men, with already chosen replacements ready to step into the ranks upon the death of a member of the regiment. Like the Assyrians and the Babylonians, the main weapon of the Persians was the bow. A new style of mass-produced bronze arrowpoints with three barbs was the standard weapon (Figure 98). The Immortals,

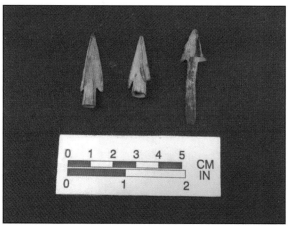

Figure 98. Persian bronze arrowheads from ca. 500 B.C. (Wilson W. Crook, III Collection)

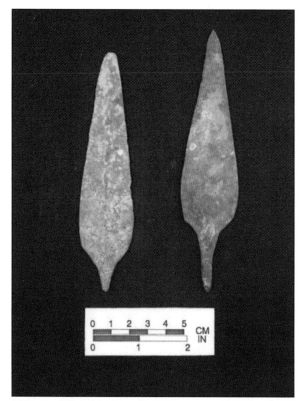

Figure 99. Persian bronze spear points from ca. 500 B.C. (Wilson W. Crook, III Collection)

clad in bright, multi-colored silk uniforms, were armed with stabbing spears (Figure 99) and swords as well as bows. After being held up by the Spartan King Leonidas' gallant "300" at

Thermopylae, Xerxes' army swept down through Greece and burned Athens. But ultimate victory over the Greeks was lost when the Athenian Admiral Themistocles destroyed most of the Persian fleet at the naval battle of Salamis. Without naval support and transport, Xerxes was forced to retire to Asia. Before doing so, the great King had his men line up and whip the ocean with lashes for denying him the ultimate victory over the Greeks.

Herodotus recorded that Xerxes had a very powerful Queen named Amestris, who is believed to be Queen Vashti as recorded in the Book of Esther (assuming certain phonetic modifications, "Amestris" can be made into "Vashti"). Further correlations can be made with the time gaps of the King's absence from the capital mentioned in the Book of Esther to the campaign in Greece between 480-479 B.C. Additionally, among the roster of court officials listed in Persian records, there is a "Mordecai", who is reported to have sat "in the gate" at the capital, an indication of his important status. Mordecai was Ether's guardian and "uncle" (she was his adopted orphaned cousin).

After returning from the aborted Greek campaign, Xerxes spent the remainder of his reign largely focusing inwardly on his empire. He is recorded as having completed the palace structure at Persepolis which was renowned for its multitude of ornately carved columns and beautiful mosaic friezes. In August 465 B.C., Xerxes was assassinated by the head of his palace guard, Artabanus. It is unclear why Artabanus attempted this coup d'état but if he was seeking the throne, the effort failed as after killing Xerxes, Artabanus was swiftly killed by Xerxes' eldest son, Artaxerxes.

Artaxerxes had a long and relatively peaceful reign from 465 to 425 B.C. The primary focus of his reign was inward looking; Artaxerxes appears to have had none of the desire to invade Greece that both his father and grandfather had. It was during the reign of Artaxerxes that first Ezra (ca. 458 B.C.) and later Nehemiah (ca. 445-444 B.C.) returned to Judah to help re-establish worship practice in the Temple as well as rebuild the defensive wall around Jerusalem. The prominence of the Jews within the Persian Empire has been corroborated by papyrus documents found in Egypt as well as records found in Babylon, Ectabana and Persepolis. Many of the Jews who thrived during the Babylonian Exile remained in Persia and had very successful businesses and careers within the Persian Empire. Recently, a large collection of 110 cuneiform tablets has emerged through a London antiquities dealer named David Sofer. The tablets were reportedly clandestinely dug up in Iraq in the 1970's and have recently been smuggled from Iraq to London. The collection of almost pristine documents is known as the "Al Yahuda" (Town of the Jews) Collection and deals with daily life of Jewish people in both Babylon and Persia. The tablets contain mostly business dealings with some spanning four generations of a single family.

During the Persian Empire, a very beautiful style of art was developed, especially related to the decorations and mosaics seen in Persian palaces and major administrative buildings. Persian textiles were known to have been both beautifully colored and extremely soft and sheer, often decorated in ornate patterns of rosettes and other geometric designs. The Persians also made beautifully decorated drinking vessels and jewelry out of gold and silver. The manufacture of these items was aided by the fact that the Persian rulers were able to call upon the skilled craftsmen of much of the known world. Highlights of the best of these masterpieces can be seen today in the Persian Room at the British Museum. The Persians controlled what is today Afghanistan which produced both precious and semi-precious stones in abundance. Of particular note, Persian jewelry and art is frequently highlighted with the use of stunning dark blue lapis lazuli (Figure 100).

Figure 100. Persian necklace made from lapis lazuli stones from ca. 400-500 B.C.
(Wilson W. Crook, III Collection)

The religion of the Persians is difficult to discern precisely as the Persian Kings generally allowed the peoples of the empire to worship whatever deities they chose providing that it did not disrupt the orderly running of the government. As a result, as you would expect with nearly 70 different nationalities absorbed into a single empire, a large number of different gods and goddesses were worshiped from India to Arabia to Egypt and Anatolia. The great founder of the purely Persian religion was Zoroaster (or Zarathustra). Many scholars place Zoroaster in the 6th or 7th Century B.C.; others further back to the last part of the second millennium. Zoroaster preached an ethical dualism in which each person, as he goes through life, must choose between righteousness and lies. Zoroasterism is not a truly monotheistic religion; its fundamental belief is that the world is composed of things that stem from two primordial spirits – a Good Spirit (*"Ahura Mazda"*) and an Evil Spirit (*"Angra Mainyu"*). Those things aligned with the Good Spirit include the sun, light, fire, summer, water, fertile land, health, growth, and domestic animals, especially the dog. Aligned with the Evil Spirit are darkness, night, winter, drought, infertile land, vermin, sickness and death. The key tenets of the belief of Zoroaster are:

- Good thoughts, good words, good deeds (*"Humata"*, *"Hukhta"*, and *"Huvarshta"*)
- There is only one path and that is the path of truth
- Do the right thing in life because it is both the right thing to do and if done, will render beneficial rewards to the good deed doer

It is uncertain if any of the Achaemenid Kings were followers of Zoroasterism. The strongest case for a Zoroastrian belief in ancient Persia can be found in Darius I's inscription at Behistun which mentions the god *Ahura Mazda*. However, numerous other gods are also mentioned in the inscription so it is unclear if the King believed in the practices of Zoroaster or was just recognizing a number of major beliefs present in the empire.

After the death of Artaxerxes in 425 B.C., the Persian Empire continued through another six Kings, none of whom were considered particularly strong rulers. The last King, Darius III, assumed the throne in 336 B.C. Two years later, the Macedonian army and its allies invaded Persia led by their young King, Alexander the Great. In three years, despite being vastly outnumbered, Alexander defeated Darius first at the Granicus River in Anatolia, then at Issus, and finally at the battle of Gaugamela. Darius fled from the battlefield and tried to escape to the northernmost parts of his empire. Finally, as the Greeks were closing in on him, he was assassinated by his cousin, Bessus, the local governor. Alexander had Bessus killed and then saw that Darius was buried with the honor befitting a King, ending the Persian (Achaemenid) Empire.

9. GREEKS

While some Biblical researchers argue that a few books of the Bible, notably the Book of Daniel, were written as late as the mid-2nd Century B.C., the majority of scholars believe that the Old Testament was largely completed before the end of the Persian Period (by ca. 400 B.C.). As such, the Greek Period, which began with Alexander's conquest of Persia in 331 B.C. and ended with the conquering of Palestine by the Romans in 66-63 B.C., does not have a significant impact on the Bible because we have no Biblical literature from this period. However, the forced Hellenization by the descendants of Alexander's Empire did significantly influence the strong pro-Jewish nationalism of Palestine in the First Century A.D. Moreover, it was this policy of forced Hellenization imposed upon the Jews that created the political forces present in First Century A.D. Roman Palestine (Sadducees, Pharisee, Essenes and the Zealots) that played such a significant role in Jesus' life.

After conquering Persia, Alexander lived for only another eight years before succumbing to a disease while in Babylon in 323 B.C. (most scholars believe the description of Alexander's death indicates he died of malaria but there are persistent theories that he could have been poisoned). As he lay dying his generals asked him to whom he wanted to leave his empire; to which Alexander was famously reported to have said, "To the strongest". Whether the story is apocryphal or true, the empire was divided among his leading generals into what was known as "the Diadochi". Originally, Ptolemy was given both Egypt and Palestine while Seleucus Nicator, the commander of Alexander's Companion Cavalry, was granted most of Asia. Peace between the generals lasted for only a few years and then war broke out, principally between Seleucus and Ptolemy. After years of fighting, Seleucus and his descendants took control of Palestine, including Judah, and established what we know today as the Seleucid Dynasty (Table 11). At its apex, the territory controlled by the Seleucid rulers covered almost all of Asia, encompassing the modern countries of Afghanistan, Iran, Iraq, Israel, Jordan, Kuwait, Kyrgyzstan, Lebanon, Pakistan, Palestine, Saudi Arabia, Syria, Tajikistan, Turkey, Turkmenistan and Uzbekistan (Figure 101). Seleucus Nicantor initially made his capital in the city of Seleucia (305-240 B.C.) but later rulers moved it to Antioch in Syria (240-63 B.C.).

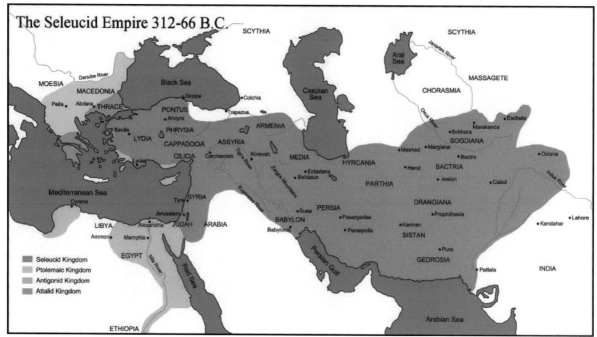

Figure 101. Map of the Seleucid Empire, 312-63 B.C.
(Map illustrated by Lance K. Trask after www.knowingthebible.net)

As can be seen in Table 11, the reigns of the early Kings of the Seleucid Empire were long and prosperous, but with time and constant war with neighboring kingdoms and internal struggles for power, the empire declined and there were frequent double claimants to the throne. In 301 B.C., the Seleucid Empire covered 1,158,306 square miles. This was reduced to 1,003,866 square miles by 240 B.C. After the reign of Antiochus IV, the empire rapidly imploded, shrinking to just 308,882 square miles by 175 B.C., and just a mere 38,610 square miles by 100 B.C. The last 100 years of the Seleucids were marked by constant civil war and decline. Ultimately the eastern part of the empire was lost to the Parthians (Persians) and the western part to Rome.

However, at its height, the Seleucid Empire was a major center of Hellenistic culture. Even though the empire was a melting pot of Persians, Greeks, Armenians, Arabs, Syrians, Jews and dozens of other peoples, the Seleucid rulers imposed a strict policy of ethnic unity. A large number of Greek cities were built throughout the empire and settled by ethnic Greeks colonists. The Greek pantheon of gods, Greek language, Greek education and manner of schooling, were all forced upon the native peoples. This policy ultimately led to a series of revolts, of which the most significant in terms of the Bible was the Maccabean Revolt in Judah of 167-160 B.C.

Table 11. Kings of the Seleucid Empire, 312-63 B.C.

King	Reign
Seleucus Nicator	312-281 B.C.
Antiochus Soter	291-261 (Co-regent with his father for 10 years)
Antiochus II Theos	261-241
Seleucus II Callinicus	246-225
Seleucus III Ceranus	225-223
Antiochus III	223-187
Seleucus IV Philopater	187-175
Antiochus IV Epiphanes	175-163
Antiochus V Eupator	163-161
Demetrius I Soter	161-150
Alexander I Balas	150-145
Demetrius II Nicator	145-138
Antiochus VI Dionysus	145-140
Diodotus Tryphon	140-138
Antiochus VII Sidetes	138-129
Demetrius II Nicator (Second Reign)	29-125
Alexander II Zabinas	129-123
Cleopatra Thera	126-121
Seleucus V Philometer	126-125
Antiochus VIII Grypus	125-96
Antiochus IX Cyzicenus	114-96
Seleucus VI Epiphanes	96-95
Antiochus X	95-92
Demetrius III Eucaerus	95-87
Antiochus XI Epiphanes	95-82
Philip I Philadelphus	95-84
Antiochus XII Dionysus	87-84
Seleucus VIII Kybiosaktes	83-69
Antiochus XIII Asiaticus	69-64
Philip II Philoromaeus	65-63

The Seleucid ruler at the time, Antiochus IV "Epiphanes" did not like the way the Jewish people stubbornly resisted Hellenization (Figure 102). Confrontation between the Jews and the Seleucids came to a head when Antiochus IV issued a decree forbidding the Jews to practice any of their religious rituals including worship in the Temple. To reinforce his edict, he had pigs brought into the Temple in a purposeful effort to publicly defile it. Antiochus then turned the entire Temple Mount area into a Greek gymnasium for training in wrestling and other Olympic sports. At the time, Greek athletes trained and participated in athletic events in the

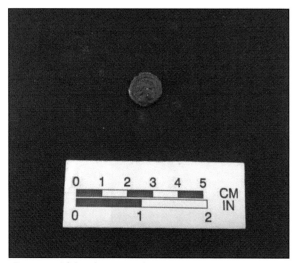

Figure 102. Serrated coin bearing the image of Antiochus IV Epiphanes. (Wilson W. Crook, III Collection)

nude, which Antiochus knew would also offend the Jewish population as yet another defilement of the Temple.

The Jews refused to obey the edicts of Antiochus IV, continuing their worship of God and denouncing the worship of other gods. When one Hellenized Jew tried to make a sacrifice to the Greek gods, he was killed by an ardent Jewish priest named Mattathias ben Johanan who then shouted "Let everyone who has zeal for the law and who stands by the covenant follow me." Mattathias and his

followers fled from Jerusalem into the Judean wilderness and begin to raise a rebel army. After his death in 165 B.C., the cause was taken over by his son, Judah. Primarily because of his knowledge of the terrain, Judah scored a number of major victories over the Seleucids. His string of victories earned him the sobriquet of "Maccabee" which means "the hammer". When Jerusalem was finally recaptured by the Maccabees, the Temple was cleansed of all the pagan Greek images and rededicated to God. The Menorah was located but only a single small vial of purified oil could be found (the vial was known to be sanctified oil as the container still had its sealed cap). The tiny amount of oil was estimated to be only enough to keep the Menorah lit for a single day which did not provide enough time to procure and sanctify additional supplies. In what has been recounted as a major miracle of God, the small amount of oil burned for a total of eight days, allowing new supplies to be brought in and Temple worship restored. This miracle is still celebrated each year by Jews in the Festival of Lights, or Hanukah ("Chanukah").

Judah Maccabee (or sometimes Judas Maccabeus) was successful as long as he could fight a guerilla campaign largely on his terms. However, when finally forced into a major conventional battle with a vastly superior Seleucid army at Elasa near Jerusalem in 160 B.C.,

Judah and many of his followers were killed. Instead of snuffing out the rebellion, Judah's death spurred the entire Jewish nation to join the revolt and by 140 B.C., the Seleucids had not only been pushed out of Judah and back into Syria, but the Jews were able to establish the first independent Jewish state since before the Babylonian Exile. Known as the Hasmonean Kingdom, Jewish rule over Palestine continued from 140 B.C. until the region was conquered by the Romans in 66-63 B.C. The Romans allowed the continuation of the Hasmonean rulers as vassals under Roman control. However, continued expressions of Jewish sovereignty and independence led to the Romans ending the reign of the Hasmonean Kings and beginning the Herodian rule under Herod the Great and his family in 37 B.C.

During the rise of the Hasmonean Kingdom following the Maccabean revolt, there was an increased sense of Jewish nationalism and religious fervor. It was during this period that new leadership arose amongst the rabbis and scholars teaching in the synagogues. Taking the name "Pharisees" or the "separated ones", these religious scholars began the tradition of re-purifying the people by imposing stricter and stricter laws on every aspect of Jewish life. When Rome began to impose its regulations on Jewish Palestine, many people saw the Pharisees as being too apolitical and thus formed more revolutionary groups such as the Zealots and the Sicarii who would later fight Rome in an attempt to restore all-Jewish rule. Contrary to these groups, many of the Temple Priests and those from the upper class joined together into what would become the Sadducees, who focused on maintaining the Temple and Temple-centric worship, even if they had to compromise with the Hellenists and/or the Romans.

In summary, the Intertestamental Period did not have a significant impact on Biblical literature (the exception being the Apocryphal Books of I & II Maccabees), but it did strongly influence the religious and political thinking in Jewish Palestine which extended from the end of the Seleucid Empire through the First Century A.D. Moreover, much of the Greek world that Paul encountered throughout Greece and especially in Asia Minor was comprised of the "Gentiles" that he would preach to and convert to Christianity. Within the Seleucid Empire this included Paul's followers in cities such as Antioch, Colossae, Ephesus, Galatia and elsewhere. In the end, the Seleucid Empire was over extended and far too large to effectively govern. Despite ardent efforts to Hellenize Asia, there were too many nations and ethnic beliefs to form a single unified people. So while the Greeks did in the end influence a great deal of Asia, they could not control and govern it.

10. ROMANS

There is archeological evidence that the area in and around Rome was inhabited from at least 3,000 B.C., but the vast amount of younger material often obscures earlier sites. The city of Rome appears to have originated as a small village of the Latini tribe somewhere in the 9th Century B.C., although there is some evidence that people were living on the Palatine Hill as early as the 10th Century B.C. The traditional date for the founding of Rome is April 21, 753 B.C., and the surrounding region, known as Latium, has had an uninterrupted occupation since that time. Recent excavations have found that a wall existed around the city before 753 B.C., so its true origins are still unknown. Further complicating Roman history is the popular story of the city's founding by the twins, Romulus and Remus. The legend states that Romulus and Remus, descendants of the Trojan survivor Aeneas, were abandoned as young children and raised by a wolf. As they grew toward manhood, they decided to build a city on the spot where they were raised but the brothers argued and Romulus killed his brother Remus. Romulus then built the city and named it for himself. Attempts have been made to find a linguistic origin for "Rome" without any definitive answer other than the Romulus myth. Some scholars believe the name could derive from a Greek word meaning courage or bravery; it also could be connected to the root word "*rum*" meaning teat – again harkening back to the Romulus legend.

The original occupants of central Italy were various tribes of Italic language speakers from the region that included the Latini, the Sabines, the Umbrians, the Sammites, the Oscans and others. They shared the Italian peninsula with two other peoples: the Etruscans to the north and the Greeks in the south. After about 650 B.C., the Etruscans became the dominant power in Italy and expanded southward into north-central Italy. The Etruscans left a lasting impression on Rome including their temples, the triad of gods, Juno, Minerva and Jupiter, and some of their architecture. However, Rome never fully became an Etruscan city; Rome was then, and has always been, primarily a Latin city.

According to tradition, Rome became a Republic in 509 B.C., but it was many years before it became the great city of popular imagination. There were constant wars between Rome and the other Latin peoples, namely the Sabines, as well as the other peoples living on the Italian Peninsula. Rome gained regional dominance in Latium during the 5th Century B.C., and eventually all of Italy by the Third Century B.C. With the Punic Wars (fought against the Phoenician colony of Carthage), Rome gained dominance over the western Mediterranean. Beginning in the Second Century B.C., the city of Rome went through a significant population expansion as a number of peoples, especially small farmers, were driven from their lands by the advent of massive, slave-operated farms called "*latifundia.*" The victory over the Carthaginians brought the first provinces outside of Italy under Roman control (Sicily, Sardinia); Spain and North Africa soon followed. The Romans then moved east, conquering all of Greece and the Greek colonies in less than 50 years. In the last part of the First Century B.C., Rome conquered Syria, Palestine and Egypt, making the Mediterranean truly a Roman lake. Gaul (modern France), part of Germany, the low countries, and Britain were also added to the growing empire between the First Century B.C. and the First Century A.D. (Figure 103).

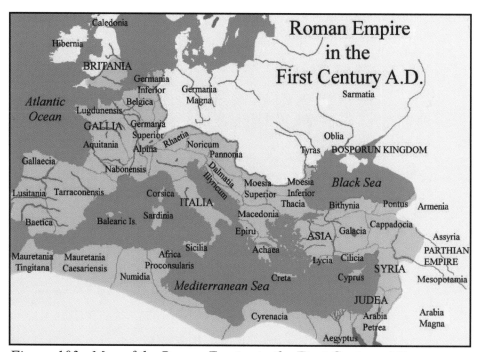

Figure 103. Map of the Roman Empire in the First Century A.D. (Map drawn by Lance K. Trask)

During these years of growth, Rome was governed as a Republic, with a nominal head or a collective of leaders, but the real power rested with the Roman Senate. However, the growth of Roman power and land created new problems and new demands that the old structure of shared power and annually elected magistrates could not solve. In 49 B.C., Julius Caesar, conqueror of Gaul, marched his legions against Rome. In the following years, he vanquished his opponents (principally Pompey the Great, conqueror of Syria and Palestine) and set himself up as dictator of Rome. Many of the members of the Roman Senate did not want to see their power diminished and placed into the hand of a single man, so Caesar was assassinated by his erstwhile colleagues in 44 B.C. The Senate tried to re-establish the Roman Republic but its champions, Marcus Junius Brutus and Gaius Cassius Longinus were defeated by a combined army of Caesar's chief lieutenant, Marcus Antonius (Marc Anthony) and Caesar's nephew, Octavian.

After several years of internal struggle, a loose confederation was established with Octavian ruling in Rome and the western part of the empire and Anthony ruling in the east. Anthony began to consort with the Egyptian Queen Cleopatra (the last member of the Macedonian-Greek dynasty of Ptolemy) and went into semi-retirement. Octavian illicitly obtained a copy of Anthony's will in which he stated that upon his death, all of his possessions were to be given to Cleopatra and his body was to be buried in Egypt. This was not the way a Roman ruler was expected to behave (Romans had a great mistrust of Egypt) and Octavian used it to gather support against his co-ruler. In 31 B.C., the armies of the two men met at Actium in Greece, and after a great naval battle, Octavian emerged victorious. He chased Anthony to Egypt where first Anthony, and then Cleopatra, committed suicide. This left Octavian the sole ruler of the Roman Empire. Octavian went through the motions of handing power back to the Senate, but the Senate, knowing full well where the power resided, handed it all back to Octavian who took the title "Augustus" and became the first Emperor of Rome (Figure 104). For the next century, his descendants would rule the empire as the Julio-Claudian Dynasty (Table 12).

Octavian's father had been a member of the Senate but it was through his grand-mother, Julia, that he gained his ultimate connection to the path of Emperor. Julia was Julius Caesar's sister and when Caesar had no male children of his own (there is a question of whether Cleopatra's son, Caesarion, was Caesar's child or not), he made his grand-nephew, Octavian, his legal heir. Octavian served with Caesar in Spain in 46 A.D. when

Figure 104. Heavily weathered coin of Caesar Augustus (Octavian), 27 B.C. – 14 A.D. (Wilson W. Crook, III Collection)

Table 12. Roman Emperors of the First Century A.D

Emperor	Reign
Augustus	27 B.C.-14 A.D.
Tiberius	14-37 A.D.
Caligula	37-41 A.D.
Claudius	41-54 A.D.
Nero	54-68 A.D.
Galba	68-69 A.D.
Otho	69 A.D.
Vitellius	69 A.D.
Vespasian	69-79 A.D.
Titus	79-81 A.D.
Domitian	81-96 A.D.

he was only 16 years old and was in Illyricum (modern Albania) waiting to join Caesar on a new campaign to Parthia (Persia) when he received the news of Caesar's assassination. The Roman historian Suetonius described Octavian (Augustus):

"He was unusually handsome and exceedingly graceful in all periods of his life, though he cared nothing for personal adornment. He was so far from being particular about the dressing of his hair, that he would have several barbers working in a hurry at the same time, and as far as for his beard he now had it clipped and now shaved, while at the same time he would either be reading or writing something."

Augustus was keen to be seen as ushering in a new era for Rome so he spent much of his early career as Emperor repairing temples and building new public structures including the famous Pantheon. One building he did not construct was a palace for himself; instead he continued to live in a modest but spacious house on the Palatine Hill. He is remembered in the Bible as the Emperor that issued the great census that resulted in Joseph and Mary having to travel from Galilee to Bethlehem where Jesus was born (Luke 2:1). Augustus was not a great soldier but that does not mean that he did not care about the military successes of his army. In 9 A.D., Quintilius Varus, commander of the Legions on the German frontier along the Rhine

River, was ambushed in a trap set by the Germans in the Teutoburg Forest. All three Legions (XVII, XVIII, and XIX) were completely destroyed and their eagle standards, touched by Augustus himself, were captured. Augustus was so stunned by this loss that it may have ultimately led to his death. It is recorded that for months afterwards, he went into a virtual state of mourning, neither shaving his beard nor cutting his hair. He was also seen from time to time hitting his head against a door and crying out "Quintilius Varus, give me back my Legions".

In later life, Augustus began to withdraw from public activity, citing old age and health issues. He also became more and more conservative, and frequently chided the members of his court and the Senate for living too lavishly. Augustus also promulgated a number of conservative laws which attempted to curb Roman vice, notably homosexuality. All of these new edicts were met with opposition by his peers and as soon as Augustus died in 14 A.D., most of his more conservative social laws were either changed or functionally ignored.

Augustus, like Caesar, had no male heirs. He did have two grandsons of whom he was very fond, so much so that he adopted them as his sons and intended for them to be his heirs. However, both died before Augustus and he was forced to adopt his step-son, Tiberius. Augustus' reign was longer and more successful than he or anyone else could have anticipated (effectively from 44 B.C. to 14 A.D.). Since Romans for almost two generations had not known any other leader, having someone from his lineage as his successor proved to be an easy and smooth process and Tiberius became Emperor in 14 A.D.

The Emperor Tiberius (14-37 A.D.) remains a somewhat enigmatic figure as some historians portray him as a blood thirsty and cruel tyrant while others point to a life of sexual depravity and degeneracy. It must be remembered that because of Augustus' long life, Tiberius did not assume the throne until he was 54 years of age; he retired from public life at the age of 67 and died at the age of 77. In his early life, Tiberius had been a soldier of some note having served against the Parthians in Syria, then in Gaul, and finally on the German frontier. By 6 B.C., he had had enough of military life and effectively retired, only to be brought out of retirement when Augustus designated him as his political heir. There are some indications that Tiberius never wanted to be Emperor but was gradually persuaded to come out of retirement for the good of Rome.

Much of Tiberius' active term as Emperor was colored by a man named Sejanus, who was head of the Emperor's personal body guard, the Praetorian Guard. Sejanus was an extremely ambitious individual who is believed to have committed several murders of potential heirs to the throne in order to set himself up as a possible successor to Tiberius. Sejanus was also known to be strongly anti-Semitic. It is unknown for certain, but a number of scholars believe that Pontius Pilate, a known friend of Sejanus, received his appointment as Procurator to Judea due to his mentor's closeness to the Emperor. If true, then Pontius Pilate may also have been influenced politically by Sejanus which could then explain Pilate's constant attempts to aggravate the Jewish community during his 10 year term as Procurator of Judea.

Tiberius, continuing to retire from public life, placed more and more power under the control of Sejanus. In 31 A.D., Tiberius appointed Sejanus to the Senate. However, almost as soon as he had appointed him to the Senate, Tiberius seems to have had second thoughts about granting Sejanus so much control in his absence. He may have been forewarned of a plot to stage a coup d'état as shortly after appointing Sejanus to the Senate, Tiberius had him arrested and killed.

Tiberius was never the popular ruler that his predecessor Augustus had been. He was seen both by the Senate as well as the populace as stiff and arrogant. Tiberius became increasingly unpopular over his refusal to host lavish games for the people's entertainment. His complete dislike for public life culminated in his retirement to the island of Capri. It is during his retreat to Capri that the Bible mentions the beginning of John the Baptist's ministry, "in the 15th year of the reign of Caesar Tiberius" (Luke 3:1-2). At the Imperial Residence on Capri, all excesses were allowed. Many stories of extreme cruelty and depravity have been written about the aging Emperor, most of which were written by political enemies so their truthfulness is questionable. Tiberius' villa was adjacent to a nearly 1,000 foot cliff from which he supposedly had those people who he was tired of or displeased him thrown to their deaths in what became known as the "Tiberius Leap" or *Salto di Tiberio*. Tiberius is said to have enjoyed the company of young adolescent boys whom he liked to call "his minnows". Tiberius was very careful to control rumors of what went on in Capri and when he believed someone might talk about things the Emperor did not want disclosed, over the cliff and into the sea they went. One of those "minnows" who was invited to Capri was his grandnephew, Caligula. Caligula came to Capri in 31 A.D., and many thought that the young man would never outlive his stay. But Caligula had a knack for acting and Tiberius grew to enjoy his company, even to the extent of formally adopting him as his grandson. Tiberius became seriously ill in 37 A.D., and died at the age of

77 while still at Capri. Historians to this day are uncertain if Tiberius finally died of natural causes or if he was smothered by a pillow held by Caligula. In either event, Caligula assumed the throne as the third Emperor of the Julio-Claudian Dynasty at age 24.

Gaius Julius Caesar Germanicus was descended from Julius Caesar through Tiberius. His father, Germanicus, was a famous and successful general and it is said that he took young Gaius at age 2 on a military campaign to Germany. The soldiers were so amused at the general's son dressed in his tiny military uniform that they nicknamed him "Caligula" ("little boots"), a diminutive form of the word for Roman army shoes, *Caliga*. The nickname stuck and he was known as Caligula for the remainder of his life.

Caligula was a noble and moderate ruler for the first six months of his reign. He returned to Rome from Capri and was seen at the games and other public events, which endeared him to the masses. Caligula was perceived by the public to be a return to the days of Augustus in direct opposition to Tiberius' disdain for public spectacle. In the latter part of his first year as Emperor, Caligula became seriously ill, almost dying. He recovered but the brush with death seems to have severely changed his personality. He appears to have suffered from both epilepsy as well as extreme insomnia, seldom sleeping more than three hours a night. Caligula's personality changed dramatically to a person bent on cruelty, sadism and sexual promiscuity. He raped women in public; had his enemies beheaded in front of him while he ate dinner; he slept with the wives of prominent Roman men and then discussed his conquests in public. He is reported to have had an incestuous relationship with all three of his sisters, especially his favorite sister, Drusilla. When she died in 38 A.D., Caligula ordered her immediate deification and went into mourning for a period in Sicily.

Caligula was famous for his love of his favorite racehorse Incitatus. The horse was kept in a marble stall with purple blankets and a special harness festooned with precious gems. He built two immense ships to serve as lavish floating palaces on Lake Nemi. The lake was drained in the 1930's by Benito Mussolini and the remains of the ships and all their fabulous artifacts were recovered. So lavish was his lifestyle that he completely went through Tiberius' immense legacy in only two years. In order to raise money, Caligula instituted taxes on marriage, divorce, lawsuits, prostitution and the like. He began to live like and demanded to be treated as a living god. In the eastern part of the empire he was readily deified. He even demanded that an immense statue of himself be placed in the Temple in Jerusalem, but he died before the order could be carried out.

Caligula is not mentioned in the Bible but one of his associates and friends is. Caligula was great friends with Herod Agrippa I and when he became Emperor, he had Herod Antipas banished to Gaul and placed Agrippa on the throne of Judea (Herod Agrippa I was the grandson of Herod the Great). This re-creation of a King of Judea temporarily stopped the system of Roman Procurators, which was re-established with Herod Agrippa's death in 44 A.D. (see Table 6).

In the latter part of Caligula's reign, relations with the Senate began to become extremely strained. Finally, several members of the Senate acted and in 41 A.D., Caligula was assassinated in much the same manner as his ancestor, Julius Caesar. It appears that the Senate believed with Caligula out of the way and no obvious successor, that they could restore the Roman Republic. They were surprised when the day after the assassination, the Praetorian Guard publicly named Caligula's uncle, Claudius, Emperor.

Claudius was the most unlikely choice for Emperor. To avoid the wrath of his crazed nephew, Claudius played the fool at court. Suetonius described Claudius in the following manner:

"He was tall but not slender, with an attractive face, becoming white hair, and a full neck. But when he walked, his weak knees gave way under him and he had many disagreeable traits. He would foam at the mouth and trickle at the nose; he stammered besides and his head was very shaky at all times."

He amused Caligula and thus Caligula let him live. When the Senatorial conspirators struck Caligula down, the Praetorian Guard went on a rampage searching for and killing the conspirators and anyone else they could find who was suspected to have been part of the plot. One soldier, in searching the royal palace, saw a pair of feet sticking out from behind a curtain, drew back the curtain, recognized Claudius, and fell down and proclaimed him Emperor.

Claudius was 50 years old when he became Emperor in 41 A.D. He had distinguished parents but despite his high birth, he lived in relative obscurity. His jerky movements, speech impediment and tendency to dribble made him an embarrassment to his family and he was kept out of public eye (his symptoms seem to suggest he may have suffered from cerebral palsy). His mental faculties were not impaired and Claudius spent his life studying Roman and Etruscan history, even writing several books on the subject (none have survived). He also took refuge in other pursuits, mainly gambling and drinking. Claudius may in fact, have been an alcoholic.

Claudius' reign has been criticized for allowing the major women in his life to dominate him. Messalina was Claudius' third wife, yet the first to bear him a son (Britannicus). Messalina saw her son as the logical heir to the throne and arranged to have all potential rivals and unwanted family members killed. Messalina was not only notorious for her killing of rivals to the throne but also for her adulteries. Her lovers ranged from leading Senators to actors. Either Claudius did not know about her escapades or he turned a blind eye. Pliny the Elder stated that Messalina even worked in a Roman brothel under the name "She-Wolf". She is famously said to have entered into a 24 hour contest with all the other famous prostitutes in Rome, at the end of which she claimed victory with a score of 25 partners. While Claudius was away at Ostia, Messalina forced a high-ranking consul designate, Gaius Silius, to divorce his wife and marry Messalina in front of witnesses. It is unclear what Messalina hoped to accomplish by this affront to the Emperor, but Claudius on his return to Rome had both Silius and Messalina arrested and executed.

Claudius had no intention of ever marrying again but was eventually persuaded to marry Caligula's surviving sister, Agrippina. Claudius married Agrippina in 49 A.D., with special dispensation from the Senate as she was his niece. Agrippina proved to be as scheming as Messalina; her main objective was to ensure that her son from a previous marriage would be placed ahead of Britannicus (the son of Claudius and Messalina). In 50 A.D., she had Claudius formally adopt Lucius Domitius Ahenobarbus as his son, who then took the adopted name of "Nero". Nero was soon promoted ahead of Britannicus and made the heir apparent and in 53 A.D., Agrippina also arranged for Nero to marry Claudius' daughter Octavia. Claudius by this time was already gravely ill but Agrippina could not afford to wait for him to die of natural causes. She enlisted the help of an expert poisoner and Claudius was dispatched to his ancestors on the night of October 12-13, 54 A.D., leaving his stepson Nero to succeed him.

Claudius is mentioned briefly in the Bible, the most famous being in Acts 18:2 where he is said to have expelled the Jews from Rome. This is believed to have occurred around 49 A.D., and is also referred to by Roman historians:

"Since the Jews constantly made disturbances at the instigation of Chrestus, he [the Emperor Claudius] expelled them from Rome." (Suetonius)

It is interesting to note that, at least at this time, the Romans made no distinction between the Jews and the early Christians as "Chrestus" clearly refers to Christ. Other than this one expulsion, Claudius is not known to have been a persecutor of the Christians as were Nero and Domitian later.

Nero is the one Roman Emperor that everyone, regardless of knowledge of history, has heard of. In film he is always portrayed as a monster, living a luxurious lifestyle while his subjects are treated poorly and his enemies are tortured and killed in gruesome ways. The historical Nero is a bit more complex than that. Nero was 16 years old when Claudius died.

Figure 105. Coin of Nero Claudius Caesar Augustus Germanicus (Nero), 54-68 A.D. (Wilson W. Crook, III Collection)

Despite his relatively young age, he was almost universally supported by the Praetorian Guard, the army and the Senate. During the first five years of his reign, Nero seemed to justify that support. In the early part of his reign he made a speech before the Senate in which he promised to grant the Senate a greater role in the government. He made a huge donation to the support of the Praetorian Guard and he was generally well regarded by the people (Figure 105).

Nero came to the throne because his mother Agrippina was the sister of Caligula and the last wife of the Emperor Claudius. Yet there was still the problem of Britannicus, Claudius' real and not adopted son. Nero saw Britannicus as a very real rival so on the night of February 11, 55 A.D., less than four months after his father died, Britannicus was poisoned. When he collapsed at the dinner table, Nero claimed that Britannicus was having a seizure and had him carried to his bedroom where he expired without any interference from a doctor. The body was secretly carried out the next day and hastily buried.

The next problem was his mother Agrippina, who sought to rule through her son. In 59 A.D., Nero invited her to dine with him at a coastal estate in Baiae. For the return trip, he put her aboard a specially designed boat. Part way through the voyage, the lead-filled canopy over her chair collapsed and she was saved only by the height of the furniture's arms. Next, the boat was capsized on purpose but somehow Agrippina was able to swim to shore and make it to one of her villas. Finally, soldiers were sent to dispatch her.

While working on how to eliminate his mother, Nero fell in love with a woman of great beauty named Poppaea Sabina. She was married to Marcus Otho, one of his closest friends, but that did not hinder Nero from making her his lover. The problem was that Nero was still married to Claudius' daughter Octavia. Only in 62 A.D. did he feel secure enough from the Senate that he was able to divorce Octavia and marry Poppaea. She bore him a daughter that died several months after birth. After she became pregnant again, Nero kicked her in the stomach in a fit of temper and both Poppaea and the baby died.

Nero was known as a great patron of the arts. He became quite skilled at playing the harp and enjoyed playing and singing in various venues in Italy as well as in Greece. While performances from a minstrel or an actor were enjoyed by the Patrician class, the profession itself was considered very lowly and not something that a person of quality in Roman life, let alone the Emperor, should engage in. Nero was oblivious to the Senators' scorn but his reputation among many Romans was damaged. In 64 A.D., a great fire broke out which ravaged Rome and further damaged the Emperor's reputation, this time with the average citizen. The fire broke out in the region of the Circus Maximus and spread through 10 of the city's 14 regions. Despite the fact that Nero, who was away at the time, rushed back to his capital and did everything he could to organize relief measures, he was not only blamed for the disaster but many Romans believed he had set the fire. This belief stemmed from the fact that shortly afterwards, Nero appropriated 300 acres of the best land in the center of Rome and built a lavish palace known as the *Domus Aurea* ("Golden House"). The house also had a colossal 120 foot high statue of the Emperor. Contemporaries regarded the waste of space and lavish spending on the Golden House as a crime. To try and deflect attention away from himself, Nero blamed the fire on the new emerging sect of Christians:

"Nero substituted as culprits, and punished with the utmost refinements of cruelty, a class of men, loathed for their vices, whom the crowd styled as Christians. Vast numbers were convicted, not so much on the count of arson as for hatred of the human race. And derision accompanied their end; they were covered with wild beasts' skins and torn to death by dogs; or they were fastened on crosses, and when daylight failed were burned to serve as lamps by night."
Tacitus Annals XV.44

Nero is alluded to in the Bible (Acts 25:11; Philippians 1:12; 4:22) but never actually mentioned by name. He is believed to have been the Emperor who judged and condemned Paul, and later Peter, to death. Paul was executed by way of beheading as he was a Roman citizen and could not be crucified as Peter was.

Nero's lavish spending largely bankrupted the State so he increasingly raised taxes on virtually everything, which did not endear him further to the public. A revolt broke out in Spain in 68 A.D., which gathered support among the Senate and also the Praetorian Guard. Nero tried to escape to the sea but receiving no help from his guards, he retreated back to his palace. He was found hiding in one of the back rooms when the soldiers came to arrest him. Nero cried out, "What an artist the world is losing" and then stabbed himself in the neck and died; he was just 30 years old.

The death of Nero left a huge vacuum of power in the empire as there was no heir. The Julio-Claudian Dynasty was finally over after 95 years of rule. The army put forth candidates from every part of the empire: from the west in Spain was General Galba; from the north in Germania the army supported Vitellius; Marcus Otho, close friend of Nero, saw himself as a contender and was supported by the armies in Italy; and finally General Vespasian had the support of the armies in the eastern part of the empire.

Galba reached Rome in mid-68 A.D. and was proclaimed Emperor by the Senate. He was already 70 years old and was seen by most as just a stop-gap selection to forestall any additional revolts around the empire. Galba refused to pay any tribute to the army for supporting him, saying that he was used to imposing levies on troops, not buying them. Thus, when the forces of Otho marched on Rome in early 69 A.D., Galba was stabbed to death by one of his own soldiers and Otho became the new Emperor. Many members of the Roman Senate did not trust Otho because of his close friendship with Nero so, when Vitellius and the armies from the north arrived in Rome, Otho found he had no real support. He quietly retired to his room and committed suicide. Vitellius was then proclaimed Emperor, the third such proclamation in less than a year.

While all this unrest was unfolding in Rome, the armies in the east proclaimed that their general, Vespasian, should be Emperor. At first, Vespasian balked at the idea but was quickly convinced that he was indeed in position to save Rome from disaster. His army fought their way into Rome on December 20, 69 A.D. His troops found Vitellius in his home, dragged him to the Forum where he was tortured and killed, and threw his body into the Tiber River. Vespasian was proclaimed Emperor which signaled the start of a new line of Emperors known as the Flavian Dynasty after Vespasian's family name.

Vespasian was a completely new kind of Emperor, middle class (not Patrician), and a man with experience in almost every part of the empire (Figure 106). He had served as a

military tribune in Thrace (modern Bulgaria) and later in Crete and Cyrene (North Africa). He had commanded the 2nd Legion ("Augusta") in the conquest of Britain in 43-47 A.D. He then served as Governor of North Africa. Nero had placed him in charge of all the armies participating in the Jewish War (66-70 A.D.) and he was in the process of initiating the siege of Jerusalem when he was called to march on Rome. Vespasian left his eldest son, Titus, in charge of the army when he left for Rome.

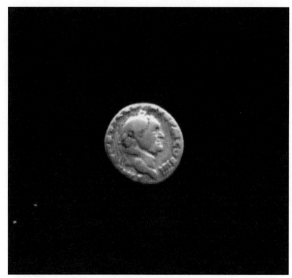

Figure 106. Coin of Caesar Vespasianus Augustus (Vespasian), 69-79 A.D. (Wilson W. Crook, III Collection)

Vespasian was considered by most scholars to be one of, if not the best Emperor of First Century A.D. Rome. His conscientious attention to the welfare of the general populace of both Rome and the provinces won him widespread support. The Roman historian Tacitus wrote that "He, unlike all his predecessors, was the only Emperor that was changed for the better by his office". Vespasian did not build a palace for himself, but rather lived in a house full of gardens on the northern side of the city. He also did not travel far from Rome during his 10 years as Emperor and was always available to address any pressing problems of the empire. According to Suetonius, Vespasian had a strict routine which he maintained every day. He would arise before dawn and spend the first half of the day meeting with Senators and officials and reading reports on the activities of the empire. He would then have a drive through the city with his wife, and after her death, with one of his concubines. This was followed by a nap and then a visit to the baths. He ended the day with dinner usually with friends and/or officials, where the business of the empire would be further discussed.

Vespasian found the treasury of the empire severely depleted after the abuses of Nero. He declared that the sum of 40 thousand million sesterces was needed to regain financial stability (Roman officials always quoted large sums in thousands of millions). To restock the Government coffers, Vespasian imposed a wide range of taxes, including increases on traditional taxes and the institution of new taxes. One of his most infamous taxes was the imposition of a levy on the use of public latrines. When his son Titus objected that such a levy was beneath the dignity of the Emperor, Vespasian was reported to have held up a handful of golden coins and said, "See, my son, if they have any smell". Vespasian was also not above selling lower ranking public offices.

Titus concluded the Jewish War in 70 A.D. with the complete sacking of Jerusalem including the destruction of Herod's Temple. With this victory came a huge amount of wealth which Vespasian used to build his greatest contribution to Rome, the Vespasian Amphitheater, better known as the Colosseum (so-named as it was built on the site near Nero's colossal statue to himself). Archeologists exploring the outer entrance ways of the Colosseum have found a series of holes which appear to have corresponded to bronze letters that once were present over the portals. As examples of Roman bronze letters are known, the location of the holes can be assigned to specific letters. Reconstructing the message indicates that the famous Roman Colosseum was not only built by the treasures gained from the Temple in Jerusalem, but some of the building itself was done by Jewish slave labor.

Vespasian died in 79 A.D. after a sudden and brief illness. The succession had long since been established as Titus was mentioned no fewer than 14 times in Roman records as the heir apparent. Titus, who ruled for only two years from 79-81 A.D., is a bit of a historical enigma. He served in the army as a young man, first in Britain and Germany, and then as commander of a Legion ("Apollinaris") under his father in the Jewish War. He assumed command of the eastern army when his father moved on Rome, and concluded the Jewish War with the successful siege and destruction of Jerusalem in 70 A.D. While he was seen as his father's constant helper and protector, it was his passion for the Jewish Queen Berenice that brought him the most scorn. Berenice was the sister, lover and queen to Herod Agrippa II (Acts 25:13, 23; 26:30). Apparently Titus fell in love with her during the Jewish War but eastern monarchs were so disliked by the Romans that he did not invite her to Rome until 75 A.D. She lived openly with the Emperor-to-be, but such was her unpopularity that he had to send her back to Judea.

Titus continued his father's policy of compassion for the subjects of the empire. He is recorded to have said to dinner guests one evening that he had not done anything for anyone that day and thus he considered it to have been a "lost day". This attitude of compassion for the populace was best demonstrated when the twin cities of Pompeii and Herculaneum were destroyed by the eruption of Mount Vesuvius in 79 A.D. Titus poured disaster relief into the area and visited the region twice to make sure that the people affected by the disaster were being treated well.

Titus' end came suddenly and completely unexpectedly. While journeying from Rome to the family's hill country estate, he came down with severe fever and chills (probably malaria). Within a few days, Titus was dead at the age of 42. His dying words were "I have made but one mistake". Nobody knows what he meant by these enigmatic words but it may have had to do with his younger brother, Domitian. There has been endless speculation that Domitian had something to do with Titus' death. After Titus became ill but before he died, Domitian sped back to Rome in order to assume the throne. Titus and Domitian had never had a warm relationship and there is no indication that Domitian was ever in line for the succession. However, Titus died childless and the Praetorian Guard proclaimed Domitian Emperor the day after Titus' death.

Domitian saw the role of Emperor as one of an autocratic monarch with absolute power. He was not as handsome as Titus and he went bald in early middle age; portraits of the Emperor however, always show him with flowing locks and curled hair. Despite his personal vanity, he appears to have been an able administrator and he did not neglect the needs of the empire. He attempted to raise the standards of public morality, passing laws forbidding the castration of any male and meting out punishment of any Senator or public official who was caught practicing homosexuality. Domitian was not the soldier his brother or his father had been, but that did not stop him from embarking on a campaign in Germany and awarding himself the title "Germanicus" after a minor victory. He also won victories over the Dacians in what is now modern day Romania.

Domitian was not a happy individual and he suffered from a severe sense of inadequacy. He was also a fearful man, always afraid that someone in the empire was going to kill him. His paranoia began to take hold of his entire life and he had his palace festooned with polished marble and mirrors so he could see if anyone was plotting against him. He turned against the Senate, having many of its members arrested, tortured and put to death for supposed treason. His reign of terror actually served to work against him as members of his family and the royal household became so fearful for their lives that they collaborated to kill the Emperor. The royal chamberlain struck first and then was joined by all the members of the family who hacked him to death. Domitian had no male heirs so the Senate viewed his death as an opportunity to regain control and placed one of its older members, Nerva, on the throne. Thus the Flavian Dynasty ended after a relatively short period of 27 years (69-96 A.D.).

While Hollywood typically portrays Nero as the great antagonist of the Christians, it was actually Domitian who was the greatest persecutor of the early Christian faith. The Emperor Domitian perceived Christianity as a direct threat to the empire and had many Christians crucified, imprisoned or exiled. The best known exile of this period was the Apostle John, who was sent to the island of Patmos to work in the mines (Revelation 1). God, however, not only spared the apostle's life, but used John's exile to give him His final revelation which comes down to us in the last book of the New Testament, Revelation.

Unlike most of the previous empires of the Ancient Middle East, we have a good idea of what the Roman rulers actually looked like because beginning with the Julio-Claudian Dynasty, all the Roman Emperors placed their likenesses on coins which were abundantly minted. The base denomination of ancient Rome was the *As* (pronounced more like "asze"). These were common copper coins and were generally only carried and used by more common citizens. The values of all of the other denominations were based on the value of this one coin (Table 13). In the early days of the empire, smaller coins such as the *Semis* and *Quadrans* were used but they were largely phased out over time. Even the *As* became largely replaced by the larger *Dupondius* because brass lasted longer in circulation than copper (see Figure 105). In making fiscal reports on the welfare of the empire, the Emperors usually quoted monetary figures in terms of *Sesterces*, a brass coin worth 4 *Asses*. The most common silver coin minted was the *Denarius* (plural *Denarii*) which was worth 16 *Asses*. Over time, the *Denarius* came to stand for the value of a day's labor and was the standard unit with which soldiers in the army were paid. Gold coins, such as the *Aureas*, were minted but not frequently used by common citizens. Smaller value coins depicting a local Governor or even his wife were allowed to be minted and used in Roman Provinces as long as the mintage was approved by the Emperor. Good examples of this type of coin are the small, copper coins found in Judea showing the local Procurator, such as Pontius Pilate.

Table 13. Roman and Jewish Coins of the First Century A.D.

Denomination	Metal	Weight	Size	Value
Aureus	Gold	7.85 gm	20 mm	25 Denarii
Quinarius	Gold	4.00 gm	15 mm	12.5 Denarii
Denarius	Silver	3.80 gm	19 mm	16 Asses
Quinarius	Silver	2.00 gm	15 mm	8 Asses
Sestersius	Brass	25.00 gm	25-35 mm	4 Asses
Dupondius	Brass	12.00 gm	28 mm	2 Asses
As	Copper	11.00 gm	24-28 mm	Base Unit
Semis	Brass	3.00-4.00 gm	18 mm	½ Ass
Quadrans	Copper	3.00 gm	15 mm	¼ Ass
		Jewish Measures		
Talent	Any	34.02 kg	75 lbs.	3,000 Shekels
Maneh	Any	0.57 kg	1.25 lbs.	50 Shekels
Shekel	Silver	3.8 gm	0.134 oz.	Base Unit
Bekah	Copper	1.9 gm	0.067 oz.	½ Shekel
Lepton (Mite)	Copper	0.05 gm	0.0017 oz.	1/38 Shekel

In addition to the head of the Roman Emperor (usually turned sideways in profile), Roman coins had a number of other symbols and abbreviations on them. The most commonly used are listed below:

- AVG – Augustus (revered or worthy of veneration)
- C, CAE, CAES – Caesar
- COS – Consol
- DIVOS – Divine (*Divi Filus* or Son of the Divine One)
- IMP – *Imperator* or Emperor
- PP – *Pater Patriae* or Father of the Country
- PIVS – Pious and Dutiful
- PM – *Pontifex Maximus* (title of head of Roman religion)
- SC – *Senatus Consulto* (by decree of the Senate)

Jewish coins differed from Roman coins in that they did not depict any human figures on them in order not to violate the commandment forbidding graven images. The basic Jewish coin was the Shekel, a silver coin roughly equivalent in weight and value to the *Denarius*. The Temple minted a special half-shekel coin which had to be purchased from the Temple treasury in order to pay a person's annual donation to the Temple. The Sadducees, who controlled the Temple treasury, cheated people on the exchange rate with foreign coins in order to make more money. The other coin typically used in Judea was the small *Lepton* or "mite". At a value of $1/38^{th}$ of a Shekel, the Lepton was one of the smallest denomination coins ever minted. It is familiar to us today because of the famous story told by Jesus of the widow and her synagogue donation of two mites, which was all she had (Luke 21:1-4; Mark 12:41-44).

Any treatise of the Roman Empire in the First Century A.D. is not complete without a discussion of the Roman military. The Roman army was divided into Legions, which although considerably smaller than modern divisions, served basically the same purpose. A Roman Legion contained roughly 6,000 men including cavalry and auxiliary troops (the auxiliary troops typically provided the artillery and siege engines for the Legion). A Legion contained 10 "Cohorts" – each Cohort made up of five "Centuries" plus a single, special Cohort of double strength. The Legion was commanded by a "*Legatus Legionus*" or Legion Commander – roughly equivalent to the modern rank of General. A *Tribunas Laticlavius* (Broad Band Tribune) was appointed by the Emperor to each Legion. This was usually a young man of Senatorial rank who was to be given some military experience before assuming his political role in the government. During battle, he was not actually second in command due to his inexperience; however, if the Legion Commander were to be killed he would assume command of the

Legion. Third in command was the *Praefectus Castrorum* (Camp Prefect), generally a senior officer with 25+ years of experience who was in charge of the Legion's training regimen. Next were five *Tribuni Augusticlacii* (Narrow Band Tribunes) who were young officers that primarily served as the staff officers of the Legion. In terms of modern military equivalences, the five Narrow Band Tribunes held essentially the rank of Major; the Camp Prefect and the Senatorial Tribune were Lieutenant Colonels. A commander of two or more Legions was known as the *Legatus Augusti pro Praetore* (Imperial Legate) and was appointed as army commander by the Emperor for a term of usually 3-4 years.

At the heart of the Legion were the Centuries (essentially modern Companies) which were commanded by a Centurion. The lead Centurion of the Legion was the *Primus Pilas* (First Spear) who commanded the First Century of the First Cohort. The rank of Centurion is difficult to equate to our modern military; he was generally from the ranks and thus technically not an officer (more like a Warrant Officer) but in terms of command responsibility, he had the rank of a First Lieutenant while the senior Centurion, the *Primus Pilas*, was more like a Captain. The Roman army operated largely as a meritocracy and any solider, even one who was not an ethnic Roman, could rise to the rank of Centurion through bravery on the battlefield.

Each Century had a second in command, the *Optio*, who functioned as a Second Lieutenant and would take over command of the Century if the Centurion was killed. The Century was divided into 10 groups of 8 men (*Contubernium*) and each group was commanded by a *Decanus* – essentially a sergeant. Each *Contubernium* shared a tent and lived and fought as a unit. Legions also had standard bearers (*Signifers*) as well as trumpeters (*Cornicen*). A Legionnaire signed up for 20 years of military service and was only allowed to muster out early in the event of a crippling injury. Soldiers were paid 225 denarii a year (a daily wage was considered to be a single denarii but soldiers also got free room and board). Regular Centurions would make 30 times that of a Legionnaire and the Primus Pilus for the Legion up to 60 times base pay. The army was a hard life, but one that promised advancement and better pay if a soldier was brave and survived. In addition, at the end of a soldier's service, the government would typically grant a soldier (and his family) a significant plot of land somewhere across the empire. By settling ex-soldiers along its frontiers, Rome also guaranteed itself a local well-trained militia force if trouble ever broke out.

The Roman army was the ONLY army of the entire ancient world that trained every day, 365 days a year. Soldiers were trained constantly in proficiency of weapons as well as in basic tactics from the level of the *Contubernium* to the Century up to the Legion. Roman soldiers were also the best equipped army in the world with each soldier given a protective metal helmet, metal body armor, a sword, a shield, and two spears known as *"pila"*. The *pilum* was a unique Roman weapon designed as a throwing javelin instead of a spear. The wooden shaft was made of hardwood, usually about four and one-half feet in length. This shaft was connected to an iron rod, which was 0.28 inches in diameter and an additional 24 inches in length, making the overall weapon about six and one-half feet in length. The metal shaft ended in a broad pyramidal point instead of a slender cutting point like most ancient spears (Figure 107). Both *pila* were thrown as the enemy approached, and while they could

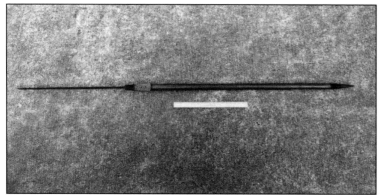

Figure 107. Reproduction of Roman Pilum; wooden ruler is 15 inches in length. (Wilson W. Crook, III Collection)

certainly kill, that was not their principal intent. The pila were designed to penetrate the enemy's shields with the pyramidal tip preventing them from being easily removed. The long wooden shaft would make holding the shield cumbersome, forcing the enemy to drop his main defensive protection. Once disarmed of his shield, he would then face a heavily armored Roman infantry largely defenseless.

A Roman soldier's main means of defense was his large, rectangular curved shield (*"scutum"*) which had an iron boss (*"umbo"*) in the middle. Roman shields were constructed of three layers of wood glued together with leather overlaid on top. Total weight was about 22 pounds but the shield design made them surprisingly maneuverable. The shield would not only be used for defense but the boss could be a powerful offensive weapon as well. Roman soldiers fought in close ranks where the shields could interlock and form a protective barrier. The curved nature of the shield allowed a soldier to pull his shield in and then thrust with his sword. The traditional Roman battle sword was known as the *"gladius"* (Figure 108). The *gladius* was about 30-33 inches in length with a two-foot, double-edged, thick blade. While a *gladius* could be used as a slashing weapon, it was designed to be used in short punching strokes. In ancient warfare, slashes could incapacitate a warrior but he would often recover. A punching stab wound to the abdomen, chest or groin,

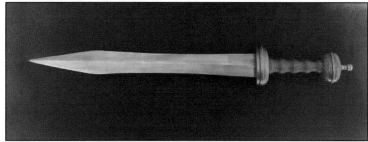

Figure 108. Reproduction of Roman Gladius. (Wilson W. Crook, III Collection)

especially in the days of little to no internal medicine, was nearly always fatal. Locked shield to shield, a Roman formation would march forward, stabbing their typically lightly armored opponents. Stepping over the downed bodies, men in the second and third ranks would stab the fallen enemy to ensure they were dead. A front line soldier would be expected to fight for about five minutes and then, at the Centurion's signal, would move between the files to the rear of the formation to rest. Depending on the depth of the file, a soldier would be expected to fight for only a few minutes each hour. To illustrate how effective Roman tactics were, in the Battle of Watling Street in 61 A.D., a force of 10,000 Roman Legionnaires (roughly one and a half Legions) killed 80,000 armed Britons under the warrior Queen Boudicca for a loss of only 400 Roman soldiers.

Auxiliary troops included teams that manned large catapults ("*ballista*") and smaller machines throwing ballistic darts ("scorpions"). The auxiliary troops also provided archers as well as slingers (Figures 109-110). Many of these troops were foreign mercenaries who were

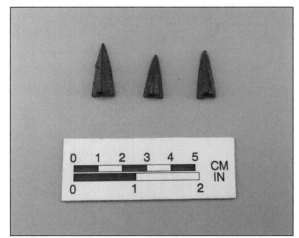

*Figure 109. Roman bronze socketed arrow points.
(Wilson W. Crook, III Collection)*

Figure 110. Roman lead sling stones from the Battle of Munda, Spain, 45 B.C. (Wilson W. Crook, III Collection)

skilled at the use of a particular weapon system. The men from the Balearic Islands were fabled for their ability to use slings and were highly recruited by the Roman army. The Romans cast elongate sling stones out of lead which, when properly thrown, could penetrate virtually any armor.

Roman soldiers were equipped with a solid metal helmet ("*Galea*") which consisted of not only a head covering but also a broad metal band covering the neck and two large cheek plates. Typical Legionnaires had no feathers on their helmets, however Centurions wore a transversely mounted crest of horsehair, usually dyed red, so they could be readily seen by all the ranks in their Century. Roman commanders typically wore more upright plumes of feathers or hair, frequently died green or some other bright color.

Each Legionnaire was equipped with a segmented chest armor plate called a "*Lorica Segmentata*". Strips of metal made from case-hardened iron were sewn together over leather backing in overlapping patterns. Extra plating was added to the shoulders. The individuality of the plates allowed for complete freedom of movement while providing complete protection. The entire body armor weighed about 14-15 pounds. A Legionnaire wore a tunic underneath his armor to absorb sweat and provide comfort for the body. A cloak would be carried for protection in bad or cold weather. Around the waist, each soldier had a special belt called a "*balteus*". In addition to the leather band around the waist, the *balteus* had a number of metal-studded leather strips which hung down in the front to protect the soldier's groin and genital region. Lastly, each soldier was equipped with a pair of hobnail boots known as "*caligae*". The boots were more of an open toed sandal-like shoe which tied around the ankle with the hobnails providing foot protection and serving to make the boots last longer. *Caligae* were typically worn without socks but woolen socks could be added if the weather was particularly cold.

The appearance of Roman soldiers outfitted in the above garb was something very familiar to every Roman citizen. In the First Century A.D., there were 28 active Legions with two in Italy (the Praetorian Guard), two stationed in Britain, five along the Rhine in Germany, eight along the Danube from Austria to Thrace, one in North Africa, one in Egypt, five in Syria and Palestine, and four along the Parthian border. Therefore, when Paul used his military metaphors to describe the armor of God, it would have been readily apparent to the average citizen of the First Century A.D. that he was describing in detail a typical Roman soldier:

"Finally my brethren, be strong in the Lord and in the power of his might. Put on the whole armor of God, that you may be able to stand against the wiles of the devil. For we do not wrestle against flesh and blood, but against principalities, against powers, against the rulers of the darkness of this age, against spiritual wickedness in the heavenly places. Therefore take up the whole armor of God, that you may be able to withstand in the evil day, and having done all, to stand. Stand therefore, having put on the belt of truth, having put on the breastplate of righteousness, and having shod your feet with the preparation of the gospel of peace; above all, taking the shield of faith with which you will be able to quench all the fiery arrows of the wicked one. And take the helmet of salvation, and the sword of the Spirit, which is the word of God". Ephesians 6:10-17

The city of Rome was unquestionably the center of the known world during the First Century A.D. Historians variously estimate the total population at between 800,000 and 1,200,000, of which as much as 50-60 percent were slaves. Roman society was almost entirely dependent on slaves, and contrary to the common portrayal in movies, slaves were highly prized and generally well-treated. This was especially true of household slaves who not only helped with all the chores around the house but took care of the owner's children as well. Educated Greek slaves were typically employed as tutors for the children not yet of school age. This does not mean that some slaves were not ill-treated. Captured enemy soldiers, criminals or those deemed a danger to the empire would be sent to work in the mines. Life there was brutal and usually short. Slaves either wore a collar or a tag of ownership. These could be removed if the owner decided to free a slave but a freed slave needed to have a document of manumission to prove to the authorities that he was indeed a freed man.

Romans lived either in a house ("*domus*") or an apartment complex ("*insula*"). Typical Roman houses were styled after Etruscan homes and built as a series of inward facing rooms around a central courtyard or *atrium* – the latter having either a fountain or a garden. Houses typically had several bedrooms ("*cubicula*") which were often quite small and only used for sleeping; a "*tablinium*" (library) where family records were kept as well as portraits of ancestors

(ancestors were revered); a *"triclinia"* or dining room as well as a kitchen and a lavatory. Houses usually had only a single door which faced the main street. Windows were rare and houses seldom had more than a few, also facing the main street. Well-to-do Romans may also have owned a villa in the countryside or near the ocean. Such villas were designed for rest and

pleasure and frequently contained a bath or a swimming pool. Many Romans decorated the walls of their homes with painted murals or mosaics. Country villas and resort towns, such as Pompeii, were especially rich in such decoration (Figure 111). Many Roman house murals contained scenes of either people or gods engaging in sexual activity. The Romans saw sex as one of the pleasures of life and thus it was not considered as pornography. Houses, and especially country villas, used a great deal of terracotta tiles and bricks, both for roofing as well as flooring and walkways. As a result, such bricks and tiles were mass produced and could be found all across the empire. Like all open-air factories, things don't always go as planned and animals would occasionally come into the factory while the terracotta tiles were waiting to be fired. Figure 112 shows a preserved part of a tile with a clear dog footprint in the clay which was subsequently fired and used without change!

*Figure 111. Decorated plaster wall fragment from Pompeii, 79 A.D.
(Wilson W. Crook, III Collection)*

*Figure 112. Roman terracotta tile brick with preserved dog footprint.
(Wilson W. Crook, III Collection)*

Roman clothing was typically simple; men wore a tunic which was like a long t-shirt that was tightened at the waist by a belt. Both men and women wore an undergarment called an *indutus* which could either be a loincloth or a leather bikini-like garment. Tunics were always short sleeved; long-sleeved garments, especially for men, were considered effeminate. A *toga* would generally be worn over the tunic, especially when outside the house. *Togas* were made from a single piece of cloth, typically about 18 feet in length and 7 feet in width which could be wrapped and folded around the body in several styles. *Togas* were very much a status symbol and their color and decoration were meant to distinguish social classes. *Togas* were also expensive and required frequent cleaning, adding to their cost. In cold or inclement weather, a cape or cloak could be worn as an outer garment.

Women also wore tunics around the house, but when going outside, women, especially those who were married, wore a one-piece full length dress called a "*stola.*" The *stola* would be gathered at the waist by a wide belt. The *stola*, like the *toga*, was a symbol of wealth and thus social class could be determined by the fabric and colors used. Women wore a shawl or "*palla*" if the weather was cold.

Beards were not popular and the men either kept them well-trimmed or were clean shaven. As such, there were a lot of barbers in Rome. Women spent a great deal of time arranging their hair in layers and in curls. As a result, wigs were also very fashionable among women and blonde German wigs or jet-black wigs from India were the fashion rage in the First Century A.D.

Shops were everywhere in Rome; people could buy literally everything in a Roman market from food to pottery to clothing. Since there was no refrigeration, food was purchased almost daily. The average Roman diet was largely based on bread. As a consequence, bakeries were the single most common shop in Rome and the streets would be filled with the smell of fresh baked bread every morning. Romans typically ate only one large meal a day, at mid-day ("*cena*"). Breakfast was typically bread, perhaps accompanied by some cheese or honey. The mid-day meal would consist of a stew or soup with bread and vegetables. Bread would be sweetened or flavored with honey or cheese and eaten along with sausage, chicken, fish or oysters. Vegetables such as cabbage, beans, lentils, onions, lettuce, garlic and parsnips were commonly available. Meat was not common except for the very wealthy. If people lived near the coast, fish and shellfish could be added to the diet. To provide meat for the general population, the Romans introduced the commercial raising and eating of chicken. Chickens do not take up much space and they can be grown from egg to full-size fryer in less than 40 days. Chickens often accompanied the army and many Roman murals and mosaics depict chickens or roosters. Dinner was usually a light meal unless the family was giving a dinner party. Dinners with guests were special events and the hosts typically went all out to impress their guests with their wealth. Special delicacies including foods from all over the empire would be served, which not only emphasized the host's wealth and status but reinforced that Rome was the one great power in the world. Special meals could include such delicacies as stuffed dormice, an abundance of oysters, eels or caviar, and birds or meats that were stuffed in multiple layers (think "Turducken"). Romans loved wine but drank it diluted and heated and spiced; drinking undiluted raw wine was considered barbaric. Only nursing babies drank milk. Drinking animal milk was also considered barbaric so milk was used primarily for making cheese and various

Figure 113. Roman Terra Sigillata or Samian Ware plate. (Wilson W. Crook, III Collection)

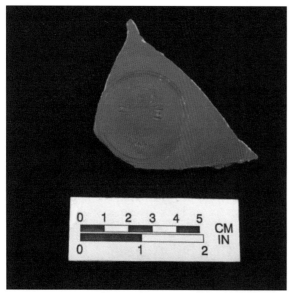

Figure 114. Broken sherd of Roman Samian Ware plate with imprinted Chi-Rho symbol, Fourth Century A.D. (Wilson W. Crook, III Collection)

medicines. The Romans cut their food with a knife but generally ate almost all of the meals with their hands.

Just as important as the food the guests were served was the tableware on which the food was served and eaten. Prior to the First Century A.D., common people ate their meals on very plain, buff to terracotta-colored tableware. A much fancier form of tableware, known as *Terra Sigillata* or Samian Ware, was being made but was generally above the price that the average Roman citizen could afford. The Emperor Augustus decreed that *Terra Sigillata* should be mass produced in order to make the finer ware affordable to all citizens. Production centers in Italy (Arretium) and Gaul began to produce *Terra Sigillata* ware in huge quantities which were shipped all over the empire. They were characterized by a glossy red-orange slip and a high degree of burnishment (polish). Common *Terra Sigillata* can be found in almost every Roman site from the First Century

A.D., from Palestine and Syria to North Africa to all across Europe (Figure 113). More lavish versions contained molded reliefs of animals, gods or goddesses along the rim. By the Fourth Century A.D. when Christianity was declared the state religion of Rome by Constantine the Great, many Samian Ware plates were stamped with a "Chi-Rho" symbol, the first two letters in Greek for Christ ("CRistos") (Figure 114). Other common Roman ceramic vessels included large, elongate storage vessels known as *amphorae* (singular, *amphora*). A Roman *amphora* typically held just under 26 liters of liquid, most commonly wine or olive oil and sometimes pickled fish. The Romans believed that an *amphora* was no longer useful if it had contained olive oil or fish packed in olive oil because the oil and its smell permeated all the pores of the vessel. Therefore they were not recycled but merely thrown onto a large rubbish pile. In Rome today there is a hill called "Monte Testaccio" which covers nearly a square kilometer and is 115 feet in height. The mound is purely artificial and is composed of nothing but broken and discarded Roman pottery vessels, mainly *amphorae* (the hill has an estimated 25 million pottery sherds). Roman sites from the First Century A.D. frequently contain several million pottery sherds and of these, 50-80 percent will come from *amphorae*. Other common ceramic vessels

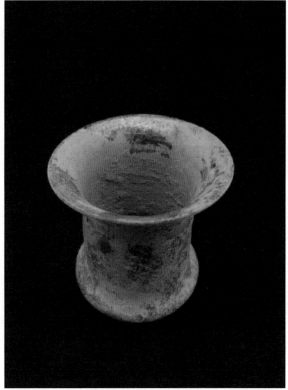

included thick storage jars ("*dolla*" or "*pithos*"), buff to terracotta-colored cooking pots, and thick vessels called "*mortaria*" which were used for grinding and processing foods.

While many average citizens still drank from cups made of pottery, the fastest growing fad was the use of glassware, fueled by innovations in the production of glass. Glass manufacture had been known as far back as the 8th Century B.C., but the Romans developed a new process using sodium carbonate which allowed the glass to be blown, opening up an almost unlimited variety of shapes and forms. The most common glass

Figure 115. Roman glass drinking cup, First Century A.D. (Wilson W. Crook, III Collection)

vessels were drinking cups (Figure 115) and small bottles to hold special oils or perfumes.

Roman citizens, especially those living in the capital, enjoyed spectacular entertainment. Games in the Colosseum (Flavian Amphitheater) or other arenas as well as chariot races in the Circus Maximus were always popular attractions. Many productions in the arena would restage famous battles or mythological adventures (Hercules was very popular) and the contests were often between gladiators and various animals. Some arenas could even be filled with a few feet of water in order to stage naval battles for the peoples' entertainment. Contrary to most modern depictions, gladiators did not always fight to the death. The owners and trainers of the gladiators knew the people wanted to see blood, but frequent killing of gladiators was an expensive proposition as it took many months of training and experience to make a good fighter for the arena. Recently, a gladiator cemetery has been discovered near Ephesus in Asia Minor. Detailed examination of the bones has shown that the gladiators were much larger and fatter that the ripped, muscled fighters depicted in the movies. The bones show that gladiators ate a huge carbohydrate-based diet which added both muscle and fat. When cut by a sword or other weapon, fat bleeds profusely but the wound does little damage to the underlying muscle tissue. Thus the crowds would get their show of blood without necessarily causing the death of the gladiator. A diet rich in carbohydrates tends to leach calcium from bones and gladiators needed bone strength to wear and use their armor and weapons (some gladiator helmets alone weighed up to 8 pounds). There are some ancient texts which refer to gladiators taking a drink of "vinegar and ashes" after a match. Wood ash is very high in calcium and would have served as a calcium supplement for the gladiators' carbohydrate-rich diet.

The most common form of entertainment that Roman citizens enjoyed was the bath. Baths were typically segregated between the classes but the Emperors provided many public baths that the average citizen could enjoy. A Roman bath was a drawn-out process involving up to seven steps. First, oil would be rubbed into the skin. This would be followed by some exercise (Roman baths were not just baths but combination baths, gymnasiums or exercise clubs, and swimming pools). After exercising, the bathers would retire to a hot room, essentially equivalent to a modern sauna. Men would discuss politics or the problems of the day while women would discuss their families in their own hot baths. Next came a swim in a thermally heated pool, during which time men in particular would drink wine and play board games. Games of chance involving dice were particularly popular throughout all classes of Roman

Figure 116. Examples of Roman dice from the First Century A.D. (Wilson W. Crook, III Collection)

society, up to and including the Emperor (Figure 116). Sometime during the hot bath, slaves would take specially designed bronze scrapers ("*strigil*") and scrape the bathers' skins to remove the sweat and oil. The sweat of gladiators would often be collected and saved in glass vials for later resale. Many Roman women believed that gladiator sweat was a powerful aphrodisiac and perfume and it was highly prized, especially if it came from a champion gladiator. Lastly came a quick dip in a cold pool followed by a massage. Romans typically arose early in the day and worked until mid-day or early afternoon. Most of the afternoon was reserved for baths and relaxation to be followed by a family meal and then bed.

Education in the ancient world was generally something that was reserved for the well-to-do. The Romans believed that all free citizens should receive at least a basic education as this would help the empire run more efficiently in terms of people being able to read Imperial decrees and legal decisions as well as run their own businesses and conduct trade. In the First Century A.D., Roman education was divided into three phases – Primary School, Secondary School, and Oratory School. Prior to attending school, children would be taught basic education at home, either by the father or by an educated Greek slave. Primary School was taught by a *Literator* or *Magister Ludi* and consisted of learning to read (alphabet, simple letters, phrases, texts, inscriptions) and write, the latter using erasable wax tablets and a metal stylus (Figure 117). Basic mathematics using an abacus or pebbles was also taught. Primary Schools had low fees and were open to all students – male and female; mixed social classes were common. Lessons were taught

Figure 117. Reproduction of typical Roman writing tablet and stylus from the First Century A.D. (Wilson W. Crook, III Collection)

by rote learning with the specific lesson for the day displayed on scrolls. Children would copy the lessons using wax tablets, and then once checked, erase their work with the flat back end of the stylus (see Figure 117). Discipline was strict with punishment administered by the *Magister Ludi* using a rod. Roman children started school at age seven and Primary School would continue until approximately age 12 (Sixth Grade). School started at 7 AM with a short recess for lunch, children bringing their own meals from home in a backpack. Classes resumed after lunch and continued until 3 PM. Simple homework consisting of writing practice and/or math problems was typically assigned and checked the next day.

Secondary School was taught by a *Grammaticus*, a man who typically had a higher educational level than a *Magister Ludi*. The focus of Secondary School included Latin and Greek, with an emphasis on grammar, poetry, beginning rhetoric and writing using parchment and ink. Secondary Schools, roughly the equivalent of our modern day Middle and High School, were typically reserved for the sons of men who wanted them to go into civic duties or politics.

Oratory School was essentially the Roman college or university education, and as such, was reserved for only the sons of the highest ranking men in Roman society. Oratory School was taught by a Rhetor, himself the product of the highest education available. The main focus was on oration and rhetoric (logic) – the two aspects needed for a successful life in Roman politics.

The fact that most people could both read and write is borne out by several recent archeological discoveries. In Pompeii, there is a famous fresco found in a small shop which depicts the owners, a man and his wife. The woman is holding a stylus and writing tablet while the man is holding a papyrus scroll. Clearly they wished the patrons to see immediately that they both could read and write. In Vindolanda, a fort along Hadrian's Wall in northern England, a large number of tablets have been found with extensive letters between both men and women. A new discovery in London of nearly 400 such tablets may provide additional evidence regarding literacy in the Roman world. Lastly, a letter was found in Egypt from a soldier named Aurelius Polion writing to his family:

"I pray that you are in good health night and day, and I always make offerings before all the gods on your behalf. I do not cease writing to you, but you do not

have me in mind. I do my part writing to you always and do not cease bearing you in mind and having you in my heart. But you never wrote to me concerning your health and how you are doing. I am worried about you because although you received letters from me often, you never wrote back to me so that I may know how you are."

"I sent six letters to you. The moment you have me in your mind, I shall obtain leave from the consular (commander), and I shall come to you so that you may know that I am your brother. For I demanded nothing from you for the army, but I fault you because although I write to you, none of you has consideration. I am your brother."

This was a lower ranking soldier, not even from Rome, who was stationed on the frontier in Pannonia (western Hungary-eastern Austria) and not only could he write, but he expressed himself quite well and desperately wanted a letter from home so he could read and re-read it. Clearly this shows that a large percentage of the Roman Empire had a considerable degree of at least elementary education and used it on a regular basis.

The Roman educational system has influenced many similar systems around the world ever since, especially that in Europe. Although times are changing, advanced college education is still largely only available for the children of high ranking men in most countries of the world. The fact that anyone can go to college in the U.S. is still a novel concept for most of the world.

The Romans, like most ancient peoples, worshiped a large pantheon of gods and goddesses. Many of these deities were taken from the Greeks and "Romanized". The Romans also adopted a number of foreign gods and allowed worship of these deities alongside their traditional gods and goddesses; Isis from Egypt is a notable example of this practice.

Generally the Romans practiced religious tolerance as long as people were loyal to the empire and paid their taxes. Judaism, while considered strange to the Romans due to its monotheism and moralistic laws, was generally tolerated across the empire. The expulsion of the Jews from Rome in 49 A.D. was due to the "continued radical worship of Chrestos". The Romans feared Christianity because of its preaching of the kingdom greater than Rome (Kingdom of Heaven) and that all people were equal and free under God. This was considered a direct threat to the institution of slavery and thus a direct threat to Rome's economy which was built upon slavery.

By the First Century A.D., most Roman males of the Patrician / Senatorial class did not really believe in any of the gods. As such, religious practices were largely "just for show" for the masses. Most working class Romans may have believed in a god that oversaw or protected his particular profession. This is akin to, and may actually be the origin of the modern practice of having a "Patron Saint". Women were the most ardent believers in the gods, especially in goddesses that protected fertility, motherhood, children and the home. The cults of Artemis (Diana) and Venus (Aphrodite) were very popular throughout the empire, particularly in Greece and Asia Minor. There were also large cults to Bacchus (Dionysus) as well as to Voluptas (pleasure); cults to the Emperor also became common throughout the First Century A.D., especially in Asia. A listing of most of the major Roman gods and goddesses is shown in Table 14 and a number of the lesser gods and goddesses in Table 15.

Table 14. Major Roman Gods and Goddesses

Roman Name	Greek Name	Roman Description
Jupiter / Jove	Zeus	King of the Gods; Lord of the Sky
Juno	Hera	Protector of Marriage
Apollo	Apollo	God of the Sun, Truth, Music and Hearing
Mercury	Hermes	Messenger of the Gods; God of Commerce and Marketing
Venus	Aphrodite	Goddess of Love and Beauty
Diana	Artemis	Goddess of the Hunt; Fertility
Mars	Aries	God of War
Bellona	Enyo	Goddess of War
Neptune	Poseidon	God of the Sea
Vulcan	Hephaestus	God of Fire and Forge (Iron)
Vesta	Hestia	Goddess of Hearth and Home
Minerva	Athena	Goddess of Wisdom, Education and Science
Pluto	Hades	Ruler of the Underworld; God of Precious Metals
Libitina	–	Goddess of the Underworld (minor)

Table 15. Lesser Roman Gods and Goddesses.

Roman Name	Greek Name	Roman Description
Cupid	Eros	God of Love
Priapus	–	Cause of Fertility
Luciana	Eileithyia	Goddess of Childbirth
Voluptas	–	Goddess of Pleasure
Bacchus	Dionysus	God of Vine, Wine and Merriment
Sol	Helios	God of the Sun
Luna	Selene	Goddess of the Moon
Trivia	Hecate	Goddess of the Dark Side of the Moon; Magic
Aurora	Eos	Goddess of the Dawn
Fortuna	Tyche	Goddess of Fortune
Janus	–	God of Good Beginnings and Bad Endings (Two Faced)
Juventus	–	God of Youth
Persipina	Persephone	Goddess of Spring
Discordia	Eris	Goddess of Discord
Somnus	Hypnos	God of Sleep
Aesculapius	Asklepios	God of Health and Medicine
Terminus	–	God of Land Boundaries
Ceres	Demeter	Goddess of Grain, Earth and Harvest
Saturn	–	Protector of Sowers and Seeds
Sylvanus	–	Protector of Plowmen and Woodcutters
Pomona	–	Protector of Orchards and Gardens
Flora	–	Goddess of Flowers
Fauna	Maia	Goddess of Fields and Wildlife
Pales	–	Strengthener of Cattle
Inuus	Pan	God of Flocks and Sheep
Aquilo	Boreas	God of the North Wind
Auster	Notus	God of the South Wind
Eurus	Eurus	God of the East Wind
Favonius	Zephyr	God of the West Wind

The Romans had a fair system of justice in place including a number of legal rights for both the accused and the accuser. That does not mean that there weren't corrupt officials in the judicial system but by and large, the Roman legal system worked well. Upper class citizens got a jury trial with up to 80 sitting jurors. People would hire lawyers who were skilled orators who tried to persuade the jury of the merits of their case. Frequently, up-and-coming politicians would work as trial lawyers as a means to practice their oratory skills. There was no deliberation after the end of a trial; the jury would vote and the majority decision ruled. Roman prisons were not designed for long-term incarceration; they were typically holding cells to be used for the time between the trial and sentencing. For the lower classes, penalties for minor offenses such as theft could be a monetary fine or a sentence of being beaten with lashes or rods, while major crimes were punishable by death. For major crimes, the wealthy could choose self-

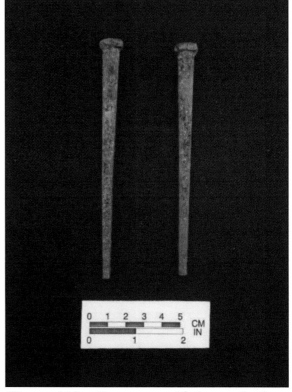

Figure 118.   Roman crucifixion nails from Jerusalem, First Century A.D. (Wilson W. Crook, III Collection)

imposed exile as their punishment. By law, Roman citizens could not be put to death using crucifixion. Beheading was the most common form of execution, which is the way that tradition states that the Apostle Paul was executed. However, people could also be killed by being set on fire, dying in combat in the arena or choosing to work in the mines. Some criminals, such as those working life sentences in the mines, could later be sold to die in the arena. Crucifixion was reserved for use on non-Roman citizens of the empire and was not just a manner of execution but was specifically designed to inflict the maximum amount of torture on the human body before death in order to demonstrate Roman power and bring terror to the population. Specific long square nails were used to pin the individual to the cross (Figure 118). Only after the victim had suffered for several hours would his legs be broken and he be allowed to collapse and thus suffocate to death. This is why, when the soldiers found that Christ was already dead, they thrust the spear into his heart cavity to make sure that he wasn't shamming and was truly dead (John 19:34).

Rome's greatest contribution to the ancient world was arguably their amazing engineering skill, notably producing the Roman system of roads, water systems and city structures. Roman roads were built using a unique, consistent construction style that was so effective that almost every major highway today from Britain to Continental Europe to Turkey to the Middle East follows an ancient Roman road; and in many places where there are no modern highways, the 2,000 year old Roman road can still be seen and used today! When building a road, the Romans cleared a path 23 feet in width and three feet in depth. First, large foundation stones interlaced with sand covered the lower foot. On top of this, a foot of fine-grain gravel and pebbles was laid. Lastly, flat paving stones were laid on the surface but in a gradual arc such that the road had a crown in the middle and all water would drain to the sides. Along each side, drainage ditches were dug to catch and carry any runoff. The roads were designed so that there could be two way traffic involving wagons, carts or chariots without the necessity for one party to pull over and wait for another to pass.

People sometimes wonder why God would allow the Romans to conquer and dominate the Holy Land during the time of Christ. It must be noted that the Roman road system and the relative safety of the system through strict Roman control and protection (the "Pax Romana") allowed the Gospel to spread across the entire Mediterranean world in just a few years. The ability to travel safely and quickly was one of the ways Roman civilization was used to fulfill God's plan.

The Romans were also masters of water engineering, able to bring fresh water great distances to cities in order to fill fountains, public water systems ("*nymphaeums*") and their baths. The transportation of water was usually conducted through an "*aqueduct*". If water was to be brought some distance, Roman engineers would take great care in surveying the entire landscape over which the water would be transported in order to select a route that contained an acceptable gradient for the entire distance. If the water flowed at too steep an angle, it would damage the aqueduct over time through scouring. If the flow was too shallow, the water would stagnate and no longer be fresh. Roman aqueducts typically tapped springs in hilly regions to ensure a sufficient fall in elevation over the distance of the flow. Catch basins would be constructed below a number of springs in order to provide a constant flow of water to the system. Most Roman water conduits flowed fairly close to the ground, but at times great arched pathways had to be built to transverse a ridge or a valley. Along the path of the aqueduct, the system would be pierced periodically by a series of vertical manhole shafts in order to facilitate occasional maintenance. Upon arrival at the city's outskirts, the water reached a large distribution tank known as the main "*castellum.*" From there, smaller branch conduits would run to various places in the city where they would enter into a lower secondary *castella.* These branched out yet again, often with lead pipes supplying water under pressure to their final end-use destination such as fountains, nymphaeums or baths. The remains of Roman aqueduct systems can be found throughout Europe and the Middle East today and some are still working, bringing fresh water to the local inhabitants.

Finally, the Romans placed a system of city design and layout over the empire which was repeated over and over. If a city was well-established with classic architecture, such as Athens, Alexandria or Jerusalem, the Romans largely left it alone. However, in rebuilding cities that had been destroyed either by war or natural disaster, the Romans would follow a simple tried-and-true formula. The Biblical cities in Greece (Philippi, Thessalonica, Corinth), Asia Minor (Ephesus, Pergamum, Sardis, Colossae, among others), and Syria-Palestine (Damascus, Jerash and the other cities of the Decapolis) all followed the same basic model layout. A major road or roads would lead into the city through a significant gate structure (Figure 119). Sometimes the gate was relatively modest; in other cities, especially those that had Imperial favor, the entrance arch could be monumentally impressive such as Hadrian's arch at Jerash

Figure 119. Roman arch leading to inner city at Jerash, Jordan.

Figure 120. Hadrian's arch at main gateway to Jerash, Jordan.

(Figure 120). If the city was located near a main seaport, the Romans would typically provide a major public bath near the main gate to encourage visitors to "clean up" before entering the more crowded main part of the city. Passing through the gate, a visitor would typically walk

Figure 121. Main North-South colonnaded street at Jerash, Jordan.

along a long, straight street which would be lined with columns (Figure 121). The columns would frequently support an awning or some type of cover to provide shade for the citizens. Shops would line these streets providing almost every commercial item needed from food to clothing to pottery (Figure 122). Cities were laid out in major North-South and East-West grids, with the principal street varying depending on the location of major traffic (closeness to the sea, location on major regional transit way, etc.). Side streets were common and also lined with shops but were typically much smaller than the main thoroughfare (Figure 123). The main street led to, and frequently ended at, the central *forum* or *agora* (literally "assembly" or "meet-

Figure 122. Author standing beside the ruins of shops lining the main North-South colonnaded street at Jerash, Jordan.

Figure 123. Minor side street perpendicular to the main North-South street at Jerash.

ing place"). The forum was also usually lined with shops but also served as an assembly area where public proclamations could be given and sometimes justice dispensed (Figure 124). In many Roman cities of the First Century A.D., the shops lining the forum would be two story

structures with the lower story cut *Figure 124. Main Forum (Agora) at Jerash, Jordan.* into the bedrock in order to provide a cool room for the storage of meat, wine, and other foodstuffs.

Near the main market would be a *"nymphaeum"*, or the location for the city's main public water supply. This was a fountain-like structure where the public was free to bring and fill their water storage vessels (Figure 125). Such structures would either be located near the center of the city, or if the city was large enough, there could be two or more such structures.

Near the city center would be the main location of entertainment for the populace – the amphitheater (Figure 126). Roman amphitheaters were modeled after their Greek predecessors and often built into the side of a hill to help with construction. A large central stage backed by a wall would face the semi-circular audience seating. Roman theaters were typically set up in three sections: people of the highest social rank would occupy the lowest tier of seats, those of middle and lower class would sit in the middle tier, and women and children would occupy the upper levels. Amphitheaters would be designed based on the size of the city but most that have survived from the First Century A.D. were built to

Figure 125. Large public nymphaeum in the center of Jerash.

Figure 126. Main Roman Amphitheater at Jerash.

accommodate anywhere from 10,000 to as many as 30,000 40,000 people. Some of the larger amphitheaters could also be used to stage gladiatorial combat but these events were also held in elongate oval racecourses known as "circuses".

Two amphitheaters in one city, such as in Jerash in Jordan, were rare. If two were present, the second one was usually considerably smaller. Other smaller amphitheater-like structures were called "*odeons*". Unlike large amphitheaters, *odeons* were typically covered and provided a more intimate seating of several hundred to a few thousand. Theatrical performances were the main productions in amphitheaters whereas the *odeons* were used for poetry recitals and singing events. In Corinth, the amphitheater and the *odeon* are situated back-to-back with a small place for shops in between. Excavation of this middle area has revealed the presence of thousands of animal bones, mainly pork ribs and chicken parts. Obviously placed to feed patrons of the two theaters, these shops are believed to be some of the first "fast food" restaurants in the world.

Lastly, Roman cities across the empire were also the home of a number of temples. Large temples to traditional Greek gods, such as Zeus or Apollo, would frequently be located near the center of the city; lesser gods would tend to have smaller temples or shrines located more toward the outskirts. During the First Century A.D., there was a strong cult following of the goddess Diana, especially in places such as Ephesus and Jerash. A large and impressive temple to the goddess would be built, typically away from the main part of the city and frequently on top of a natural high spot overlooking the city (Figure 127). Prostitution associated with temple worship would be located near the temple itself, although almost every major Roman city had numerous brothels located throughout the city. In Ephesus, an inscription has been found on the flagstones of the main street showing a foot, a part of the female anatomy, and the words "turn left at crossroads, buy the love of a woman."

Figure 127. Large temple to Diana on a hill overlooking Jerash.

The Romans continued to dominate most of Europe, North Africa, Asia Minor and Palestine for the next several centuries. When Constantine the Great moved his capital from Rome to Byzantium (Istanbul) in 330 A.D., the Roman period ended and the Byzantine period began. The Byzantines would build churches over every major holy site in Christendom, many of which survive to this day.

ACKNOWLEDGEMENTS

I owe the impetus for writing this book to all my classmates in Adult Sunday School, from when I first started teaching at the Salisbury Presbyterian Church in Midlothian, Virginia in the 1980's to the First Presbyterian Church of Kingwood, Texas where I have taught since 1990. My classmates' encouragement and support of my teaching Biblical archeology and history in conjunction with the Scriptures has led to me amassing much of the material presented in this book. I would also like to thank the organizations which gave their permission for me to reproduce some of their photographs herein, in particular my friends at the Associates for Biblical Research (www.BibleArcheology.org). Their continued work at Jericho, Khirbet el-Maqatir and elsewhere is providing more and more evidence that our Bible is history. I would also like to thank Mr. Lance K. Trask, who illustrated all of the excellent maps contained in this volume as well as a few of the figures. Lastly, I would like to thank my wife, Ginny, for her steadfast love and support throughout my life and my journey as a teacher of the Bible. Ginny painstakingly read, re-read and edited various drafts of the book and greatly improved its content with her comments. She is also responsible for many of the superior photographs included in the book, notably those of the artifacts from my teaching collections.

APPENDIX I.
SUGGESTED BIBLICAL
ARCHEOLOGY READINGS

The list below is by no means meant to be a complete listing of the literally thousands of books one can read on various aspects of the Peoples of the Bible, their history and their archeology. I have selected those books which I consider to be some of the best references on the various subjects covered in this book for those who may wish to delve deeper into a particular area. Most of the below listed references can still be found in book stores and/or on Amazon.com. A great many of these books can also be purchased in the book store of the British Museum in London.

Adan-Bayewitz, David
1993   *Common Pottery in Roman Galilee: A Study in Local Trade*. Bar-Ilan University Press, Ramat-Gan, Israel.

Aldred, Cyril
1987   *The Egyptians*, Third Edition. Thames and Hudson, Ltd. London.

Amiran, Ruth
1969   *Ancient Pottery of the Holy Land*. Masada Press, Ltd. Jerusalem.

Bartlet, John R.
1982   *Jericho*. Cities of the Biblical World Series, William B. Eerdmans Publishing Company. Grand Rapids, Michigan.

Belloni, Stefana
1996   *Jerash: The Heritage of Past Cultures*. Jordan Distribution Agency Ltd., Amman, in association with Casa Editrice Plurigraf. Narni, Italy.

Ben-Tor, Amnon
1992   *The Archeology of Ancient Israel*. Edited by Amnon Ben-Tor. The Open University of Israel and Yale University Press. New Haven and London.

2016   *Hazor, Canaanite Metropolis, Israelite City*. Israel Exploration Society, Jerusalem.

Biran, Avraham
1994   *Biblical Dan*. Israel Exploration Society. Hebrew Union College and the Jewish Institute of Religion. Jerusalem.

Biran, Avraham and J. Naveh
1995   The Tel Dan Inscription: A New Fragment. *Israel Exploration Journal* 45:1-18.

Blum, Howard
1999   *The Gold of Exodus.* Pocket Books, a division of Simon & Schuster. New York.

Boldrini, Fabio and Niccolo Orsi Battaglini
2000   *All of Ancient Rome – Then and Now.* Casa Editrice Bonechi. Florence.

Browning, Iain
1982   *Jerash and the Decapolis.* Jordan Distribution Agency Ltd., Amman, in association
        with Chatto & Windus. London.

Clayton, Peter A.
1994   *Chronicles of the Pharaohs.* Thames and Hudson, Ltd. London.

Cornfield, Gaalyah and David Noel Freedman, Editors
1976   *Archeology and the Bible: Book by Book.* Harper & Row Publishers. San Francisco.

Curtis, John E.
1989   *Ancient Persia.* British Museum Press, British Museum Publications
        Ltd. London.

Curtis, John E. and J. E. Reade
1995   *Art and Empire: Treasures from Assyria in the British Museum.* British Museum
        Press, British Museum Publications Ltd. London.

Davies, Philip R.
1982   *Qumran.* Cities of the Biblical World Series, William B. Eerdmans Publishing Compa-
        ny. Grand Rapids.

Dever, William G.
2003   *Who Were the Early Israelites and Where Did They Come From?* William B. Eerdmans
        Publishing Company. Grand Rapids.

Garfinkel, Yosef, Igor Kreimerman and Peter Zilberg
2016   *Debating Khirbet Qeiyafa: A Fortified City in Judah from the Time of* David.
        Israel Exploration Society, Hebrew University, Jerusalem

Harding, G. Lankester
1967   *The Antiquities of Jordan* (Revised Edition). Jordan Distribution Company by arrange-
        ment with Lutterworth Press. Cambridge.

Hayes, John W.
1997   *Handbook of Mediterranean Roman Pottery.* University of Oklahoma Press,
        Norman.

Healy, Mark
1989a *Joshua, Conqueror of Canaan*. Heroes and Warriors Series, Firebird Books. New York.

1989b *Judas Maccabeas, Rebel of Israel*. Heroes and Warriors Series, Firebird Bird Books. New York.

1989c *King David, Warlord of Israel*. Heroes and Warriors Series, Firebird Books. New York.

1989d *Nebuchadnezzar, Scourge of Zion*. Heroes and Warriors Series, Firebird Books. New York.

Hoerth, Alfred J.
1998 *Archeology & The Old Testament*. Baker Books, Grand Rapids.

Hoerth, Alfred J., Gerald L. Mattingly and Edwin M. Yamanchi, Editors
1994 *Peoples of the Old Testament World*. Lutterworth Press, Cambridge in association with Baker Books, Grand Rapids.

Isserlin, B. S. J.
1998 *The Israelites*. Thames and Hudson, Ltd. London.

Kamm, Antony
1999 *The Israelites*. Routledge Books. London and New York.

King, Philip J. and Lawrence E. Stager
2001 *Life in Biblical Israel*. Westminster John Knox Press. Louisville and London.

Klawans, Zander H.
2012 *Handbook of Ancient Greek and Roman Coins*. Whitman Publishing LLC. Atlanta.

Korb, Scott
2010 *Life in Year One: What the World Was Like in First Century Palestine*. Riverhead Books. New York.

Kramer, Samuel Noah
1963 *The Sumerians: Their History, Culture and Character*. University of Chicago Press. Chicago.

Leick, Gewendolyn
2003 *The Babylonians*. Routledge Books. London and New York.

Loffreda, Stanislao
2001 *Recovering Capharnaum*, Second Edition. Franciscan Printing Press, Jerusalem.

Markoe, Glenn E.
2000   *Phoenicians*. Peoples of the Past Series (Volume 3). University of California Press with special arrangement with the British Museum Press, British Museum Publications Ltd. London.

Mazar, Eilat
2002   *The Complete Guide to the Temple Mount Excavations*. Shoham Academic Research and Publication. Jerusalem.

2007   *Preliminary Report on the City of David Excavations 2005*. Shoham Academic Research and Publication. Jerusalem.

2009   *The Palace of King David: Excavations at the Summit of the City of David, Preliminary Report of Seasons 2005-2007*. Shoham Academic Research and Publication. Jerusalem.

2011   *Discovering the Solomic Wall in Jerusalem*. Shoham Academic Research and Publication. Jerusalem.

McCall, Henrietta
1990   *Mesopotamian Myths*. British Museum Press, British Museum Publications Ltd. London.

McRay, John
2001   *Archeology & The New Testament*, Fourth Edition. Baker Books, Grand Rapids.

Oates, Joan
1986   *Babylon*, Revised Edition. Thames and Hudson, Ltd. London.

Reade, Julian
1983   *Assyrian Sculpture*. British Museum Press, British Museum Publications Ltd. London.

1991   *Mesopotamia*. British Museum Press, British Museum Publications Ltd. London.

Rogerson, John
1999   *Chronicle of the Old Testament Kings*. Thames and Hudson, Ltd. London.

Saggs, H. W. F.
1995   *Babylonians*. Peoples of the Past Series (Volume 1). University of Oklahoma with special arrangement with the British Museum Press, British Museum Publications Ltd. London.

Scarre, Chris
1995   *Chronicles of the Roman Emperors*. Thames and Hudson, Ltd. London.

Shanks, Hershel, Editor
2011   *Ancient Israel from Abraham to the Roman Destruction of the Temple*, Third
       Edition. Biblical Archeology Society. Washington, D.C.

Tubb, Jonathan N.
1998   *Canaanites*. Peoples of the Past Series (Volume 2). British Museum Press, British
       Museum Publications Ltd. London.

Walker, C. B.F.
1987   *Reading the Past: Cuneiform*. British Museum Press, British Museum Publications Ltd.
       London.

Wilson, Ian
1999   *The Bible Is History*. Weidenfield & Nicholson. London.

Wiseman, D. J.
1983   *Nebuchadnezzar and Babylon*. The Schweich Lectures. Published for the British
       Academy by Oxford University Press. Oxford.

Wright, G. Ernest
1962   *Biblical Archeology*, Second Edition. The Westminster Press, Philadelphia and
       Gerald Duckworth and Company, Ltd., London.

1974   *Great People of the Bible and How They Lived*. The Reade's Digest Association,
       Inc. Pleasantville, New York.

APPENDIX II
Holy Land Archeology / Biblical Chronology

Archeological Period	Approximate Date	Major Historical Events	Biblical Events
Neolithic	8,500–4,500 BC	Change from nomadic to more sedentary lifestyle; beginning of modern civilization; first cities (Jericho 8,500 BC); Black Sea flood (~5,600 BC)	Noah (?)
Chalcolithic	4,500-3,300 BC	Beginnings of Sumeria; Pre-Dynastic Egypt; cuneiform writing begins (~3,200 BC)	
Early Bronze Age	3,300-2,900 BC (EB-I)	Early Dynastic Egypt Early Sumer Dynasties	
	2,900-2,700 BC (EB – II)	Old Kingdom Egypt (Great Pyramids built)	
	2,700-2,200 BC (EB – III)	Peak of Sumeria; Assyria begins	
Intermediate Bronze Age	2,200-2,000 BC (EB – IV / IB)	Third Dynasty of Ur; collapse of Sumeria (~1,950-2,000 BC)	Abraham
Middle Bronze Age	2,000-1,750 BC (MB – I)	Middle Kingdom Egypt; Minoan Civilization; Early Babylonian Empire	Age of the Patriarchs Israelites migrate to Egypt
	1,750-1,550 BC (MB – II)	Minoan collapse; Hittite Empire	Israelite slavery in Egypt
Late Bronze Age	1,550-1,400 BC (LB – I)	New Kingdom Egypt	Moses; Exodus ~1,446 BC Conquest of Canaan ~1,406-1,400 BC (Joshua)
	1,400-1,200 BC (LB – II)		Period of the Judges
Iron Age	1,200-1,000 BC (IA – I)	Period of weakness in Egypt and Mesopotamia	Ruth, Samson, Samuel End of Judges; Saul crowned king of Israel
	1,000-539 BC (IA – II)	Neo-Assyrian Empire; Neo-Babylonian Empire (626-539 BC); Rise of Persia (Cyrus the Great 558-530 BC)	United Monarchy – Saul, David, Solomon (1,042-930 BC); First Temple built Divided Kingdom – Israel (930-721 BC), Judah (930-586 BC) Period of Prophets (Isaiah, Jeremiah, Minor Prophets) Fall of Jerusalem (586 BC); First Temple destroyed Babylonian Exile (586-539 BC) Ezekiel, Daniel

APPENDIX II
Holy Land Archeology / Biblical Chronology

Archeological Period	Approximate Date	Major Historical Events	Biblical Events
Persian Period	**539-331 BC**	Fall of Babylon (539); Achaemenid Empire (558-331 BC)	Return to Judah Minor Prophets (Haggai, Zechariah) Second Temple built Nehemiah, Ezra, Esther End of Old Testament Period
Greek Period	**331-66 BC**	Alexander the Great Conquest of Persia (333-323 BC); Alexander's Empire divided - Seleucids rule Palestine until 165 BC Hasmonean (Jewish) rule 165-66 BC Rome conquers Palestine (66-63 BC)	Sects of Sadducees and Pharisees form Essenes settle Qumran (134-104 BC)
Roman Period	**66 BC–330 AD**	Julius Caesar assassinated (44 BC) Roman Civil War (44-31 BC) Augustus (27 BC-14 AD) Tiberius (14-37 AD) Caligula (37-41 AD) Claudius (41-54 AD) Nero (54-68 AD); Rome burns 67 AD Year of Three Emperors (68 AD) Vespasian (69-79 AD) Titus (79-81 AD) Domitian (81-96 AD) Constantine makes Christianity the Roman state religion (313 AD)	Herod the Great (37-4 BC) Palestine broken up after Herod's death (Archelaus, Herod Antipas, Herod Philip) John the Baptist Jesus born; ministry; death Coming of Holy Spirit (Acts 2) Growth of Christianity; Paul and Peter Jewish War (66-70 AD) Jerusalem and Second Temple destroyed (70 AD) Siege of Masada (72-73 AD) John exiled to Patmos; Revelation written End of New Testament Period
Byzantine Period	**330–1453 AD**	Roman capitol moved from Rome to Constantinople (330 AD) Byzantine rulers build Christian churches over all Holy sites	

APPENDIX III.
THE BIBLE IN 50 WORDS

This was sent to me some years ago by a friend and it has always appealed to me as the single simplest example which explains the meaning of the Bible, from Genesis to Revelation, in 25 lines of two words each (50 total words). I am including it here for your entertainment.

God made

Adam bit

Noah arked

Abraham split

Joseph ruled

Jacob fooled

Bush talked

Moses balked

Pharaoh plagued

Peopled walked

Sea divided

Tablets guided

Promise landed

Saul freaked

David peeked

Prophets warned

Jesus born

God walked

Love talked

Anger crucified

Hope died

Love rose

Spirit flamed

Word spread

God remained

ABOUT THE AUTHOR

Wilson W. Crook, III

Wilson W. "Dub" Crook, III retired after a 35 year distinguished career as a Senior Executive with the Exxon Mobil Corporation. Dub has traveled extensively all over the world, starting his archeological adventures as a child accompanying his father, Wilson W. "Bill" Crook, Jr. who was past President and Fellow of the Texas Archeological Society. As a result of his father's lifelong interest in archeology and paleoanthropology, Dub grew up going to and working on archeological and early man sites all around the world. A native of the Dallas area, Dub attended Highland Park High School and Southern Methodist University (SMU) where he majored in Geology (Mineralogy). He is the author of over 160 professional papers in such varied fields as archeology, mineralogy, geology, natural science and Soviet manned space exploration. Dub is a Life Member of the Dallas Archeological Society, a Fellow of the Houston Archeological Society, a member of the Texas Archeo-

logical Society, the Center for the Study of First Americans, a Life Member of the Gault School of Archeological Research, a Research Fellow at the Texas Archeological Research Laboratory in Austin, and a Fellow of the Leakey Foundation. He is also a long time member of First Presbyterian Church of Kingwood and has been teaching Adult Sunday School lessons combining archeology and history with the scriptures for nearly 30 years.